exhibition stands

exhibition
stands

AUTHOR
Arian Mostaedi

PUBLISHERS
Carles Broto & Josep Mª Minguet

CONCEPT & DESIGN
Federico Orozco

EDITORIAL TEAM
Editorial Coordinators: Jacobo Krauel, Thomas Barikosky and Mariana Morales
Text: Contributed by the architects, edited by Amber Ockrassa and Jacobo Krauel
Spanish Translation: Monica Cuende and Francesc Rovira

Cover photograph: © Andreas Keller

© All languages (except spanish language)
Carles Broto i Comerma
Ausias Marc 20, 4-2. 08010 Barcelona, Spain
Tel.: +34-93-301 21 99 · Fax: +34-93-302 67 97
www.linksbooks.net · info@linksbooks.net

ISBN: 84-89861-80-3
D.L.: B-26022-2003

Printed by FILABO, S.A. Barcelona, Spain

No part of this publication may be reproduced, stored in retrieval system or transmitted in any form or means, electronic, mechanical, photocopying, recording or otherwise, without the prior written permission of the owner of the Copyright.

exhibition stands

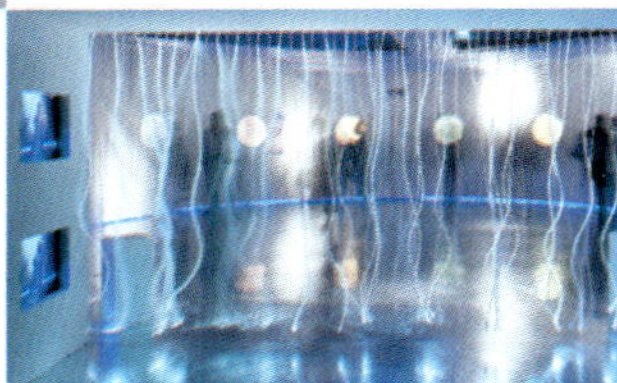

6 Introduction
8 Mercedes-Benz. Frankfurt 2001
12 Ixilum
14 Philips AEG
18 Media Markt
20 Bisazza
24 Art Bit
26 Deutsche Post Immobilien
28 Jazztel
30 Kodak
32 Ecomed
34 Grohe
36 Rolf Benz
40 Siemens mobile
44 Atmosphere
48 Ricoh
52 Bertelsmann
54 General Electric Plastics
58 KPMG
60 Design in Zürich
62 Berker
66 Emap
70 Panasonic
74 Gin Tonic
76 Gaudí
78 Durable
80 Century nidau
82 Mercedes-Benz. Barcelona 1999
86 Gira
90 Heidelberg Druckmaschinen AG
94 Mero
98 YelloMiles GmbH
102 atg. Art Technology Group
104 Océ
106 Appendi-Minimo
108 Windsor
112 Bisazza
116 Gandia Blasco
118 Microsoft
120 Layetana
122 Grundig

124 Azabache Rioja
126 Telefónica
128 BMW
134 Siteco
136 VDP
138 Ellesse
142 La casa en forma
144 Space magazine
146 Audi
150 Florette / VegaMayor
154 Ingersoll-Rand
158 Renault. Barcelona 2001
162 Innoval
168 Bertrandt
172 Baumann
174 Blueprint
176 Mtv
178 Cemex
180 Automotive
182 Casawell
184 LG electronics
186 Welonda
188 Chic
190 Hispalyt
192 Indian Motorcycle
194 Info Pavillion
196 Systemfabrik explore!
200 Damlier Chrysler
204 Edra
206 Wella
208 Prospa
210 Burkhardt Leitner constructiv
214 Live in Spain
216 Looky
218 Knauf
222 Schweizer Textilverband
224 Mercedes-Benz. Detroit 2002
228 VIAG interkom
230 Euroshop 2002
234 Esprit jewel
236 Renault. Brussels 2002

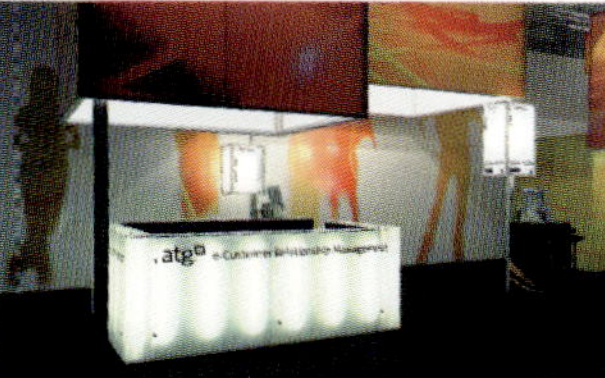
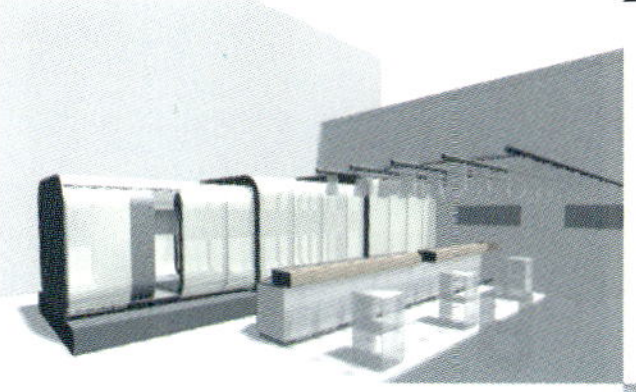

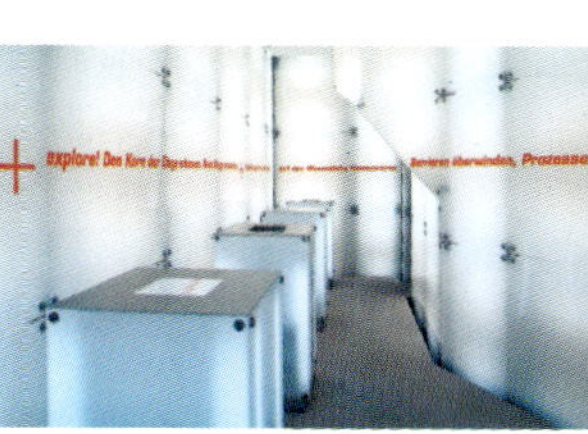

windsor
windsor
PHILIPS
GIRA
HISPALYT

introduction

Any high-ranking company in today's business world owes its success just as much to its image as to the quality of its product. This, coupled with the considerable importance of trade shows in attracting clients, has led many companies to seek the advice of some of the leading names in contemporary architecture and design when planning their trade show stands. Hence, the birth of an entirely new discipline, combining marketing strategies and architectural creativity.

A stand must be, on the one hand, sufficiently innovative and eye-catching to attract visitors and, on the other, in perfect consonance with the product on display. Both factors are equally important; one without the other would result in an ineffective stand design.

The nearly 100 stands in this collection have been selected using this dual criteria. They are examples of some of the finest work being done in architecture today, with outstanding designs displaying creative use of technology and atypical materials; and, from a marketing perspective, they succeed in conveying the company's brand image and in attracting visitors.

From one-room stalls to sprawling multi-storied stands, representing companies as diverse as footwear, automobiles and perfume, this collection covers a spectrum of design schemes: simple and classy, technologically savvy and spectacular, young and brash, sophisticated and sublime. With work from such masters as Fabio Novembre, Richard Hywel Evans, Simone Micheli, Stefan Zwicky and Zaha Hadid, we hope to provide the reader with a thorough and reliable source of inspiration.

Mercedes-Benz

Kauffmann Theilig & Partner
FreieArchitekten BDA

The motorshow Frankfurt 2001

The traditional setting for Mercedes-Benz presentations at the Frankfurt Motor Show is the Frankfurter Festhalle, a nearly century-old concert hall. In the 2001 IAA, and for the first time, the architecture of the hall itself became an integral part of the design concept of the stand.

A two-level stand was inserted, with visitors arriving at a foyer, where they first see the central atrium and the culmination of the show before ascending an escalator for an impeccable view of the exhibition. From here, they work their way down through the unified theme zones on the tiers circumscribing the central space and the various theme zones in the side vaults.

The architectural approach leaves the central space free as a demonstration and display area, which is circumscribed only by the two oval tiers. The space above it –right up to the dome– rests as a void to be filled with sculptures of light, in a changing series of displays setting the space in different moods and colors. The rather moderate architectural intervention of the tiers and the live performance once every hour merge into a comprehensive perceptual experience complementing the overall communications concept.

The two oval tiers form closed rings within the overall architecture of the FestHalle. Seen from a distance, the design elements that encircle them allow the integration of brand theme presentations into the visual presentation of the vehicles themselves. On the four half-tiers, four themes are communicated by means of key visuals, headlines and exhibits. Seen in close-up, the staggered elements come together to form experiential theme areas.

Each of the side rooms to the east and the west of the Hall has its own style in terms of interior design, media and graphic design.

With its atrium-like character, the interior is visible from every point of the exhibition. Visitors reach it by means of a large open stairway. This is where the product and brand communication culminates: individual vehicles form a brand portfolio, illuminated by a film shown on an LED panel that echoes the oval form of the tiers. An axis of showcases displays the brand's ten most important innovations.

Photographs: Andreas Keller / Atelier Markgraph

Second floor

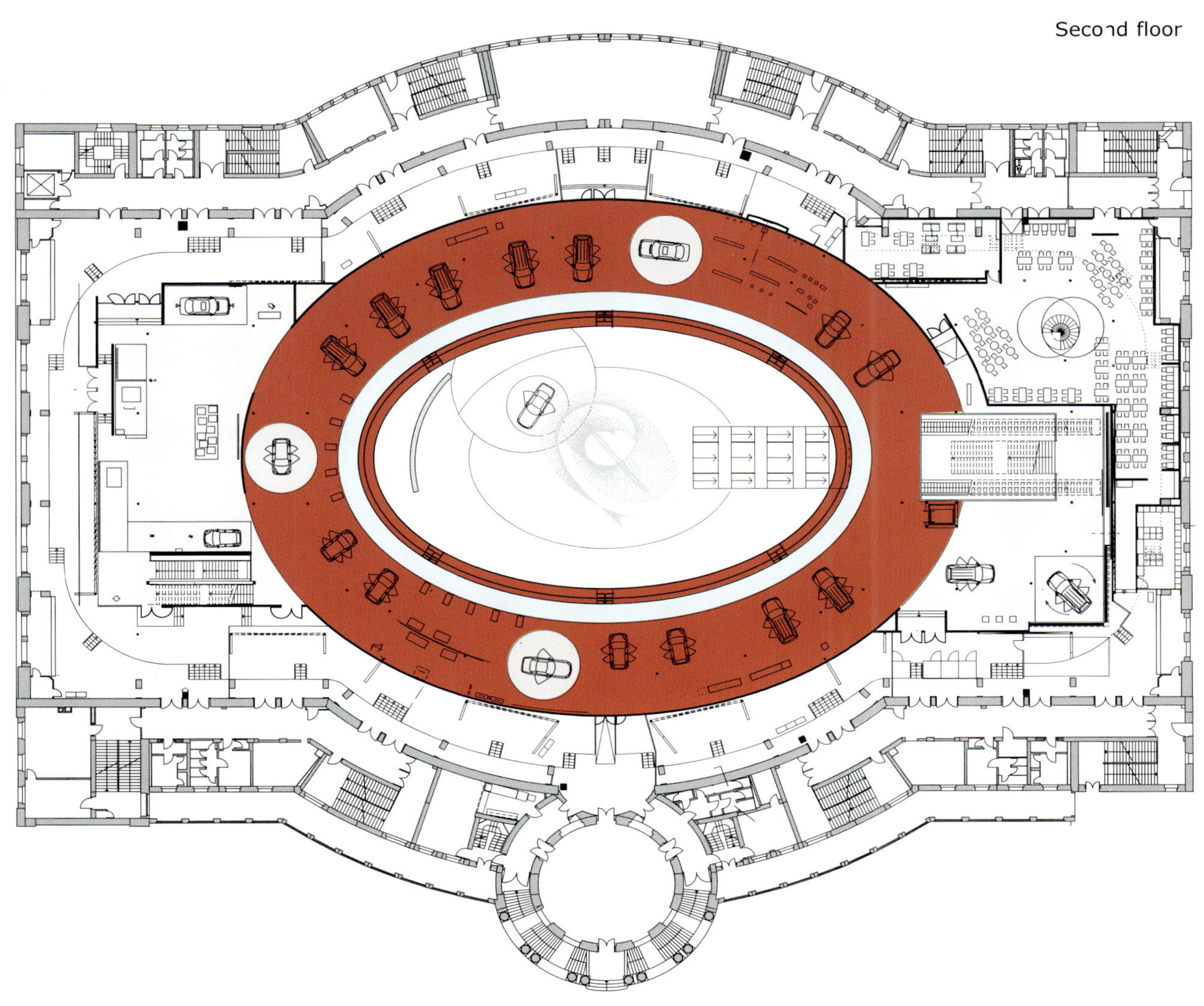

Sehnsucht

PASSION COMES ALIVE
wild

Ixilum

Alan Parkinson + Architects of air

Luminarium, designed by the artist Alan Parkinson, is a walk-in sculpture which immerses visitors in light in color. These unusual structures were inspired by the pure forms of geometry and nature, and by such architectural innovators as Buckminster Fuller and Frei Otto. This monumental air sculpture can cover a ground area of up to 1200 m^2 and rise to a height of over 10m. It is comprised of flexible modules which can be positioned around trees, lamp-posts or statues and which require little time to inflate.

Ixilum is Parkinson's latest luminarium creation; the fruit of 10 years' design development. This particular luminarium is an intricate exploration of light and form that takes its inspiration from Islamic architecture. Its winding tunnels are composed of 82 triaxial domes that create an undulating profile reminiscent of a middle Eastern bazaar.

The structures are built of PVC and made by Architects of Air. The plastic has been hand cut and glued in a former lace factory in Nottingham (UK) and made in easily portable sections that zip together on site. They stretch for over 400m yet fit into a space measuring just 40x40m.

Once inside, there are "pods" where visitors can sit or lie back to absorb the atmosphere. Daylight shining through the colored skin creates fantastic effects within the sculpture. The design is accessible to everyone; for instance, tunnels and airlocks have been designed to provide easy access to people in wheelchairs.

Photographs: Joeri Neudt + Architects of air

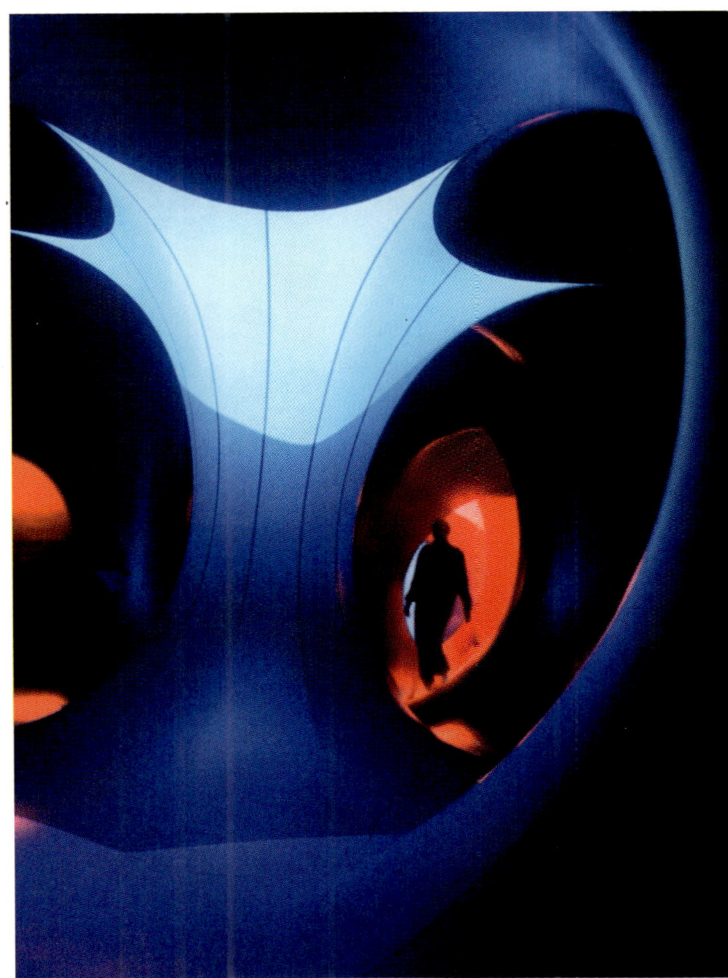

Philips AEG

D'art design gruppe

"More light" is the central theme of this stand, which was designed for the EuroShop 2002 tradeshow. The various products on display are grouped according to a specific context in lighting. In one area, for example, the visitor becomes part of a scene set in a supermarket, where a series of stylized apples are the focal point.
The Philips stand is a fluid space, which nonetheless features three distinct lighting segments, for which three stages were built. The "Ambience Lighting" area is for shopping, "Lighting Solutions" is the more functional segment and, lastly, is the information zone, entitled "Lighting Experience".
In the "Ambience Lighting" zone, the new line of DARUMA products, along with a series of assembly systems, is presented. Its defining elements –divisible square frames– highlight the sculptural presentation of the line.
A bar filled with apples forms the nucleus of the "Lighting Solutions" area, where spotlighting adjusted to varying degrees of brightness changes the coloration of the illuminated objects. As in a typical supermarket scene, strip lighting illuminates a row of, here oversized, canned food.
The primary characteristic of the "Lighting Experience" stage is a modular system of overhead lighting. Each module can be individually adjusted via a remote control system, modifying the color and brightness to achieve different effects.

Photographs: D'art design gruppe

PHILIPS
AEG

FOCUS

MAXOS TL5
maximum open space
TBS 300 / TBS 600
INDOLIGHT / FLATLIGHT

Media Markt

Lorber + Paul Architekten

The latest and most advanced communications technologies were presented at this stand, which exudes an elegant ambience, where analogue and digital technologies are contrasted.

The company's information serves to define and order the space, where the resultant images (places, maps, logos, advertising) are viewed on screens, lighted signs, computer terminals and laptop PCs, all of which is accompanied by CDs and informative pamphlets.

The stand features a modular system of perforated black anthracite panels (or aluminum, as an alternative to steel). This system, which is quick and easy to assemble, can be easily adapted to different settings. The built-in furniture pieces are clad in leather, stainless steel and wood; while the stand's floor surface is covered in a bluish-gray carpet bearing the company's logo.

The lighting fixtures are situated above the information panels, casting indirect light, while not visually interfering with the images on the screens.

Photographs: Paul Ott

N-HOLDING GMBH
Markt

Media Markt
N-HOLDING GMBH

Bisazza

Fabio Novembre

This project, designed by the company's own Art Director, has a central structure comprised of two curves which pull away from the ground and meet overhead to form a large heart silhouette, with a sort of backdrop of two parallel walls behind it. This stage set creates an interesting and amusing visual effect: the heart-shaped holes punched into the back walls mimic and refer back to the main structure.

The big heart of Bisazza at 'Cersaie 2002' has been entirely built using the company's products. White glass agglomerate slabs, an emblematic Bisazza product, cover the background walls and floor. The inner surface of the curved walls of the heart are covered in 20x20 mm mosaic tiles of Vetricolor and Le Gemme enamelwork, in colors ranging from red to a warm brown blend. The aisle is completely clad in pink 20x20 mm enamelled mosaic tiles.

This interplay of curved surfaces calls attention to the versatility of the facing material on display and to its extraordinary decorative potential.

Photographs: Alberto Ferrero

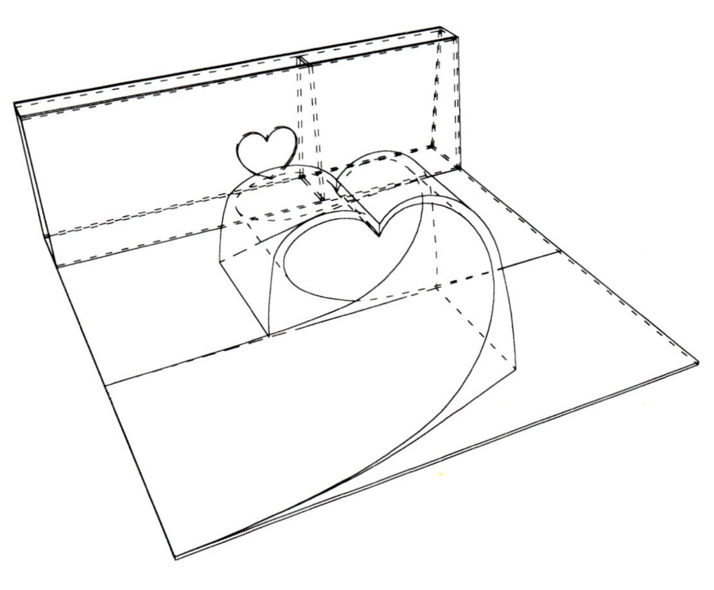

Axonometric projection

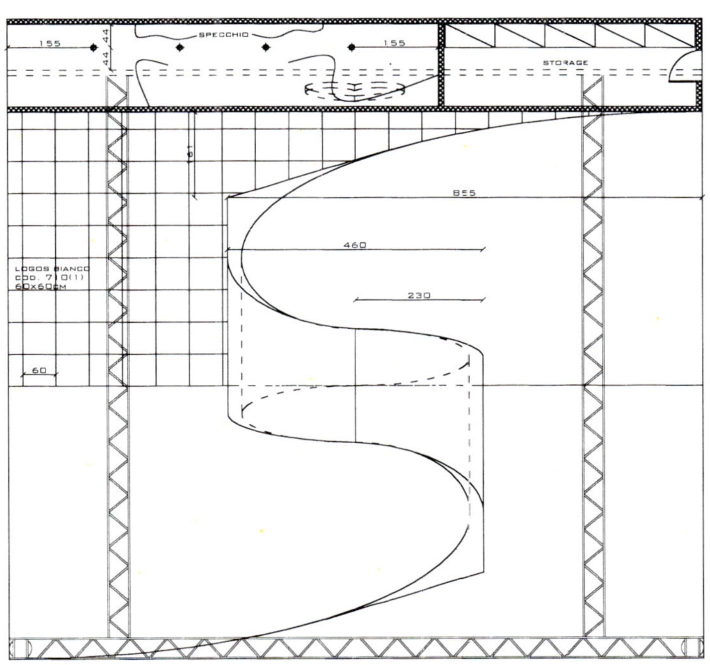

Floor plan

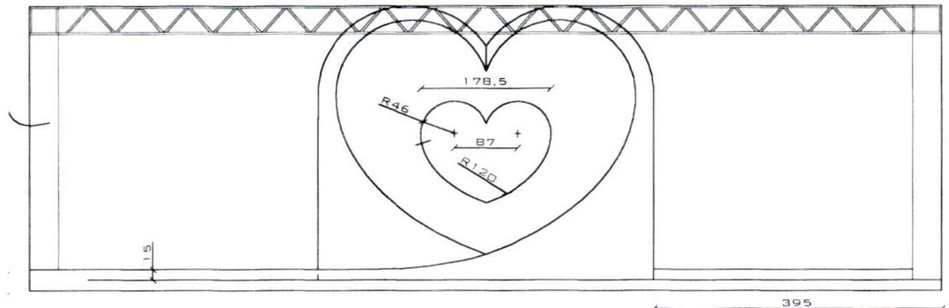

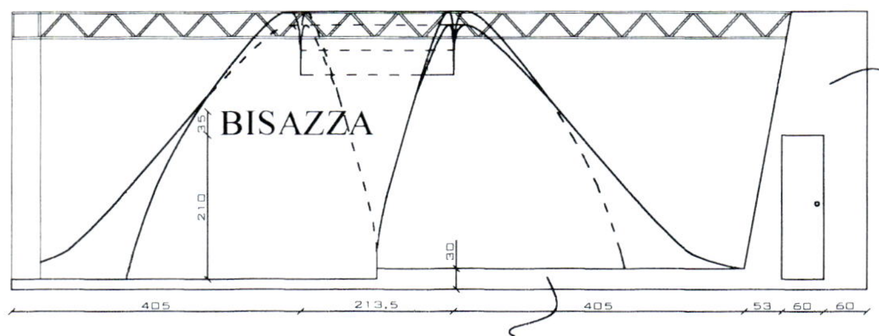

Cross sections

ISAZZA

Art Bit

Whads Accent S.L.

Bit is a trade fair for new technology in digital applications, particularly advances related to the Internet. The fair organizers requested the design of a 300m^2 non-commercial stand, which would display a panorama of current digital art. The ArtBit stand shows different types of both off- and on-line pieces.

Since the interactive pieces are primarily individual, the stand's layout features a series of independent, pod-like modules. Each has room for a single occupant, thus providing the necessary distribution and isolation for viewing the pieces on display.

Each module has a table, where the screen, keyboard and mouse are located, a white support with headsets, a screen containing information on the contents of the module, and a carpet bearing the graphic icon.

The placement of the modules is apparently random, as if in a "forest" in which visitors choose the module that most appeals to them. Each module is accessed by turning the bench or table over its central axis so that, once inside, the visitor is "locked in" and no one else can enter.

Iron tubes and sheet metal, both of which have been left in their raw state, with only a layer of varnish to avoid rusting, are the primary materials.

This "trash" aesthetic, where the materials are untreated, turns the various modules into art pieces in their own right, turning them away from industrial connotations and toward the world of creation.

Photographs: Antonio Galeote

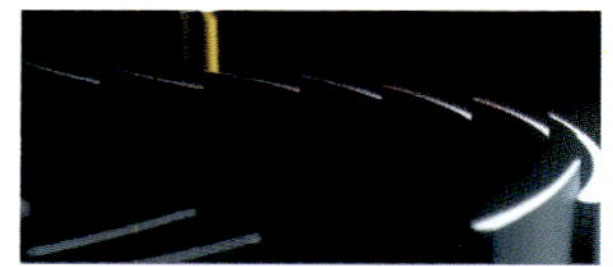

Deutsche Post Immobilien

3e-Werner Sobek Ingenieure

This company opted for a stand displaying a high technological standard for the 'ExpoReal 2000' trade show in Munich. On an area of 120 m2 a number of aerofoil wall-like modules with black rubberized surfaces were arranged in a spiral.

The floor and few furniture fixtures are clad in the same charcoal grey rubber; some of the wall modules have been equipped with colored LEDs (light-emitting diodes), creating a high quality display screen, measuring 9.6 m width and 1.6 m height. On this surface of unprecedented size, more than 600,000 tri-color diodes display brilliant videos and graphics.

In addition to the large LED display screen there are a number of smaller VDUs (visual display units), which pop up from the black cylindrical stands to provide visitors with information concerning individual details and questions. Privacy for personal consultations is provided by custom-designed, three-dimensionally curved furniture.

The stand's primary lighting source comes from zenithal spotlights and a handful of blue neon lights, which create a secluded ambience. Due to the nature of the materials and shapes, the overall appearance of the stand looks like something straight out of the set of a futuristic film.

Photographs: Arthur Agency

Deutsche Post
IMMOBILIEN

Jazztel

Equipo 01

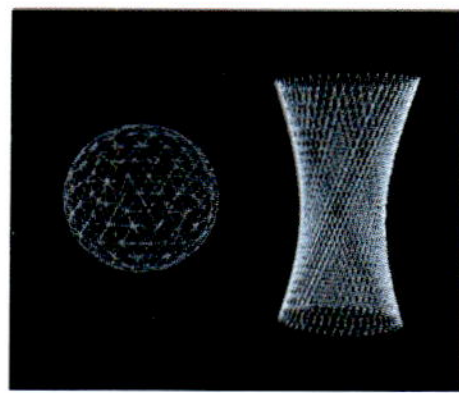

This stand centers on the concept of telecommunications and the Internet as networks for the open flow of information, with neither beginning nor end.

In order to symbolically represent these channels of information, tall pillars of stiffened, expanded metal mesh emerge from the center of large crater-like structures, which were conceived as multi-use seating arrangements. The pillars are equipped with a tenuous spotlight concealed within their base, lending them an incorporeal, luminous appearance.

The considerable load-bearing capacity of these pillars, which are surprisingly resistant for their seeming fragility, meant that they could serve as the only vertical structures, effectively eliminating the rest of the profiles which would have otherwise been necessary. Visitors to the stand can sit around the padded rim of the "craters" and use any of the computers which have been set at the base of each column.

A large screen at the back of the stand displays the logo, lit by flickering beams of light. This light show, along with the mesh pillars, are the stand's most important and visually interesting points.

Photographs: Equipo 01

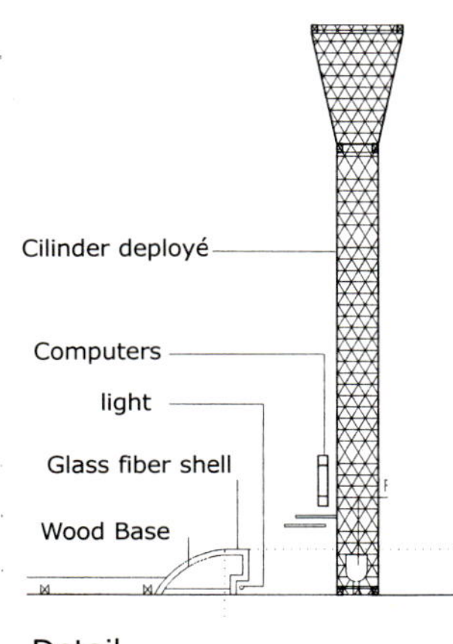

Detail

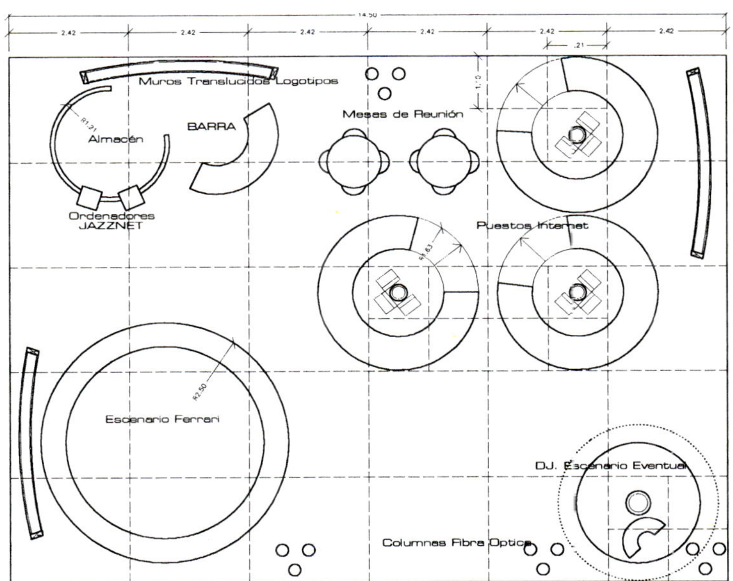

Floor plan

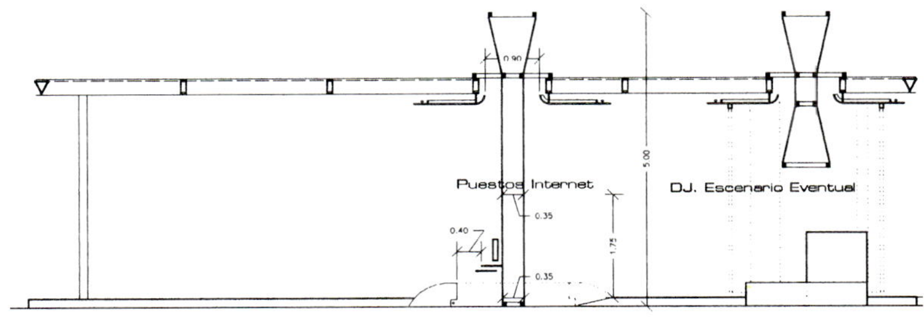

Cross section

Kodak

Atelier Brückner

An enormously heterogenous array of products was integrated into 'The Kodak world of color' and provided the backdrop for the company's corporate philosophy, making the diversity of colors a symbol for the company's unity.

Glowing red, warm yellow, deep blue, wild pink, and delicate white – a wide range of colors and brilliant pictures dominate Kodak's world of color.

The motto 'Kodak pictures, the universal language' is the key behind the design of the stand at Photokina 2000 in Cologne.

Three elements –color, pictures and language– form the core of the design concept.

A colored strip code was elaborated on the basis of the company's colorist motto: an abstract city composed of signs, street, volumes and symbols. The graphic design drew on the resources of the company and formed a logical, convincing and easy to understand orientation system for visitors through the complexity of the company's diverse product range.

Photographs: Atelier Brückner

Kodak@Home

Ecomed

División Efímeros

The Consorcio del Medio Ambiente de Barcelona (the city's "environmental consortium") commissioned this stand for Ecomed 99, where they aimed to provide information on the various fields in which they work in a direct and pleasant setting. The scheme's primary formal weight rests on three foundations: a transverse wall used as a backdrop for information and advertising, a wood and metal walk-through tunnel with information on waste selection exhibited within, and a hanging ceiling which articulates and unifies the different spaces, thereby making up for the lack in perimeter enclosures.

Various cubicles comprising the transverse wall depict the removal of recyclable material, such as paper, glass and plastic. On the other side of the wall is information (in both static and interactive form) on the benefits obtained through the treatment of each material. The public information desk is also located here.

Built from wood and sheet metal, the tunnel's point of reference is the "trommel" device. Its outer face features a combination of closed and open modules so that areas where the tube is laid bare alternate with surfaces bearing informative texts. A large video wall is located at one end of this walk-in tube and displays footage concerning this association's work and reportage. The two areas lying on either side of the tunnel are used for meetings and online consultation.

All of the material –plywood, sheet metal, cardboard and glass– used in the stand is recyclable. Particularly good examples of this are the chairs of corrugated cardboard in the meeting area or the different types of flooring in natural coconut fiber.

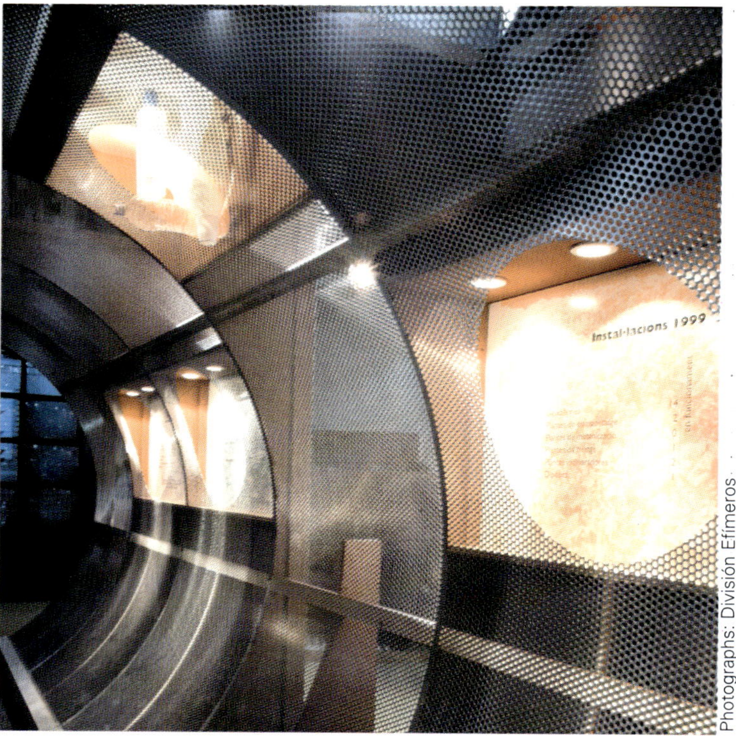

Photographs: División Efímeros

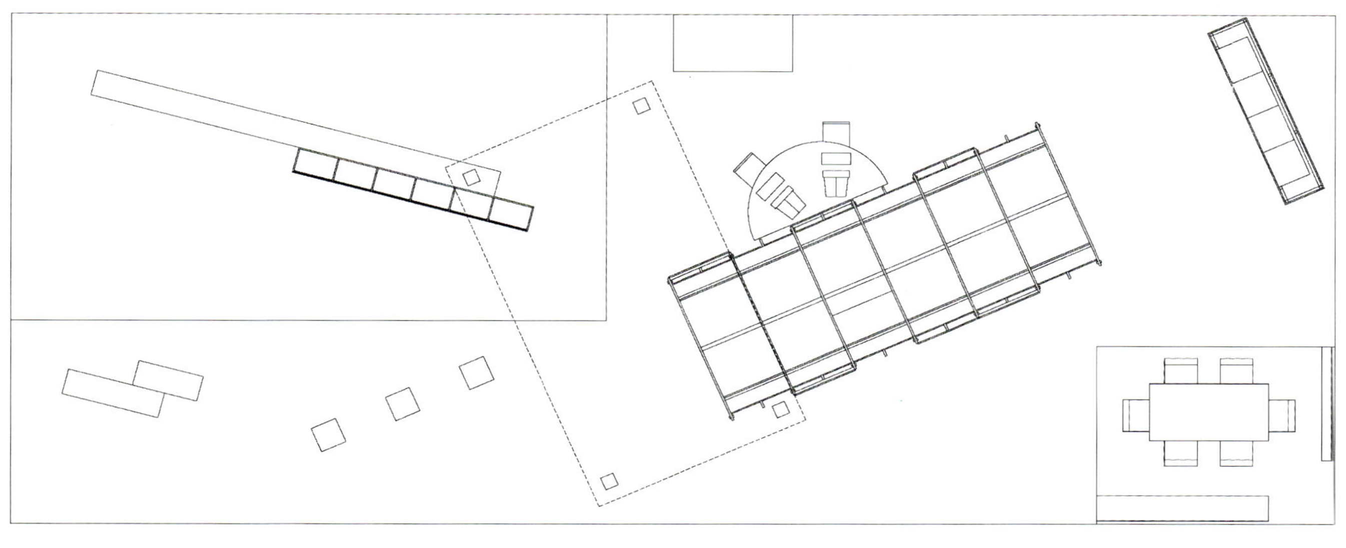

0 1 2 3 4 5 m

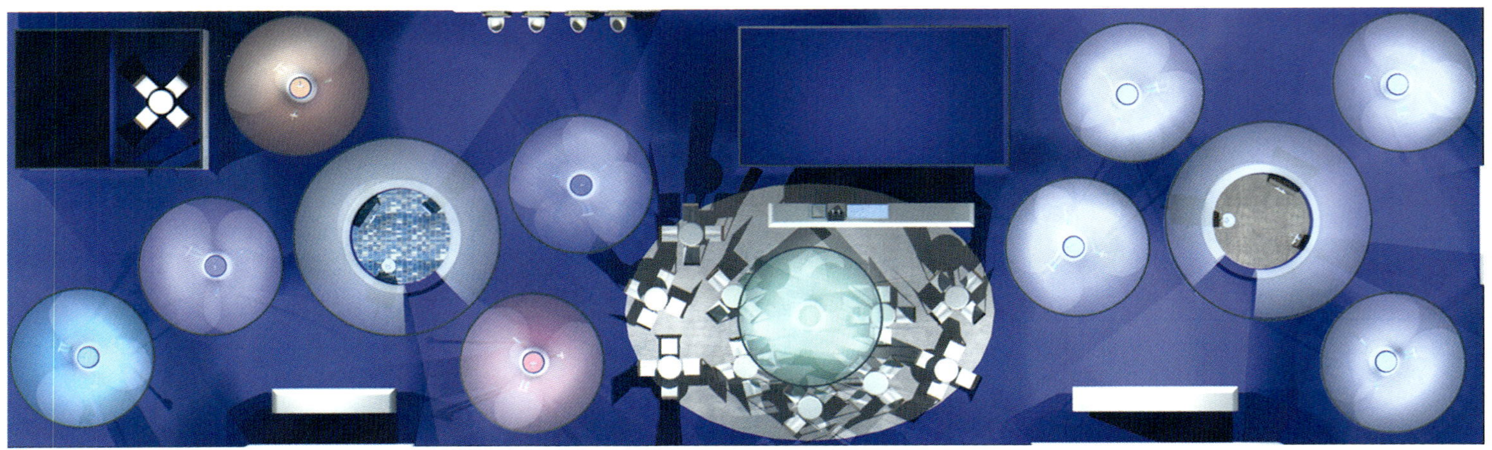

Grohe
Totems

Grohe's image has always been defined by a high technological standard. The diversity of these products demands a well organized and clearly structured product range. This means that, in addition to this high standard of technology, clarity and openness are important issues for this company.

The Grohe motto 'Water is the Source' could be interpreted as a sensation of pureness and freshness. This sensation was taken as a guideline in the development of the final design of the stand. The booth, first built at 'VSK 2002' -an international trade fair for heating, sanitary engineering and air conditioning in the Netherlands- creates a clear and fresh atmosphere in which the visitor comes across the Grohe products in an ultimately seductive way.

Photographs: Markus Mahler

GROHETEC

GROHEart

GROHE
WATER TECHNOLOGY

Rolf Benz

Uniplan International GmbH

At the Internationale Möbelmesse 2001 trade fair in Cologne, in a stand occupying almost 1300m² of floor space, the designers created a sophisticated interplay between architecture and exhibition space. The stand's shape has been patterned after the typical form language of Rolf Benz living room furniture.

Inspired by the style of such avant-garde architects as Mies van der Rohe and Frank Lloyd Wright, the design scheme combines a "house" and a "winter garden" into a water landscape. The unusual design communicated, on the one hand, the durability of the furniture and, on the other, the client's particular claim to be a design classic.

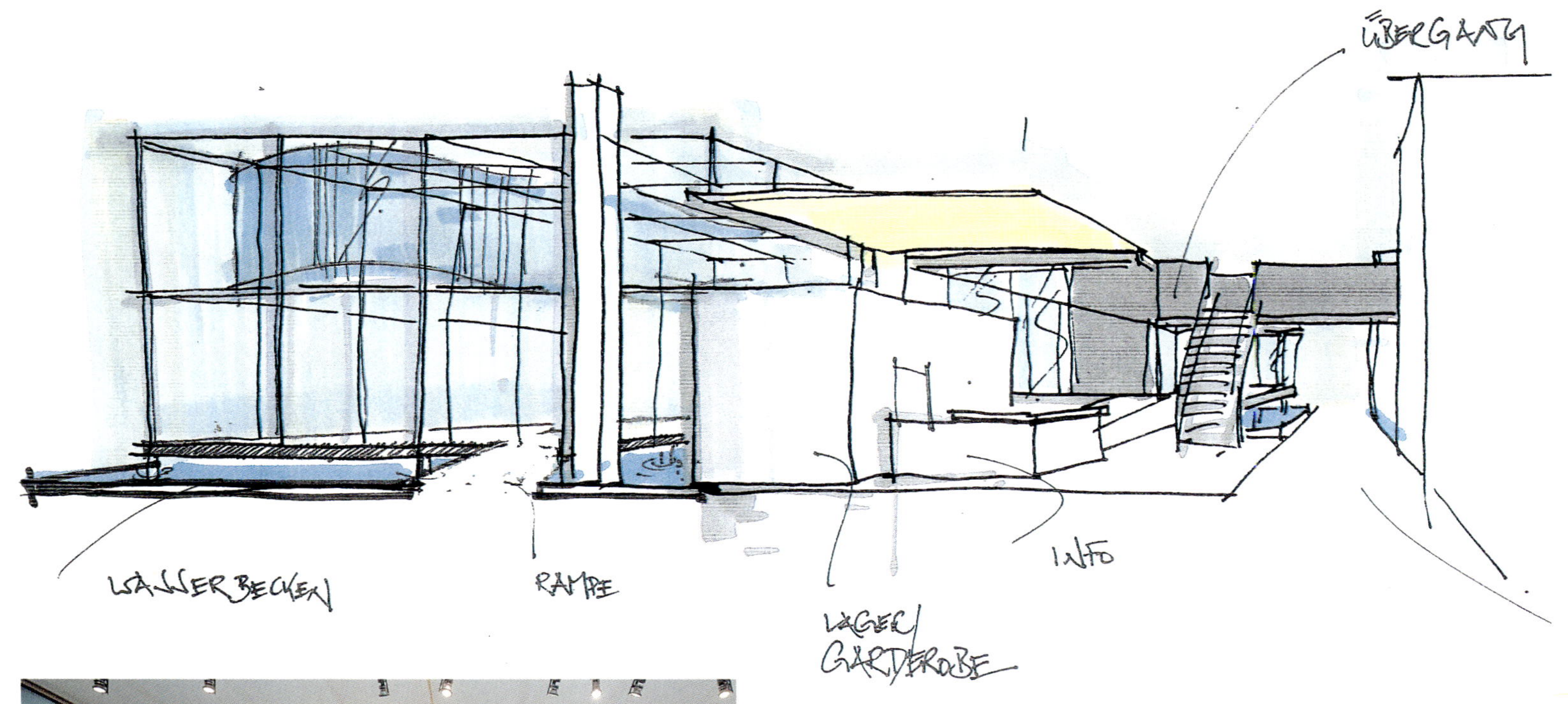

Sketch of floor plan

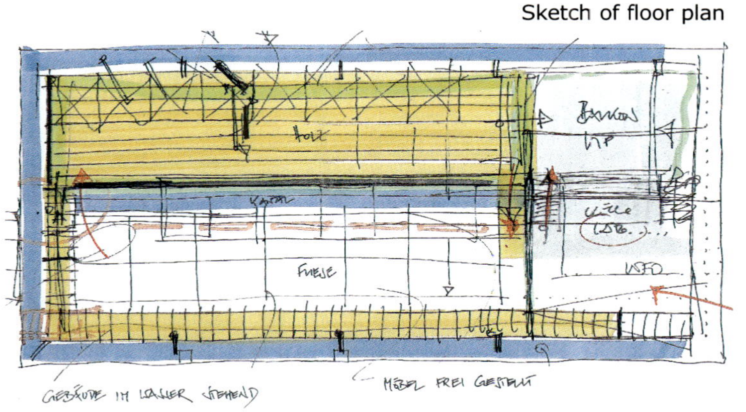

Photographs: H.G. Esch, Chormann

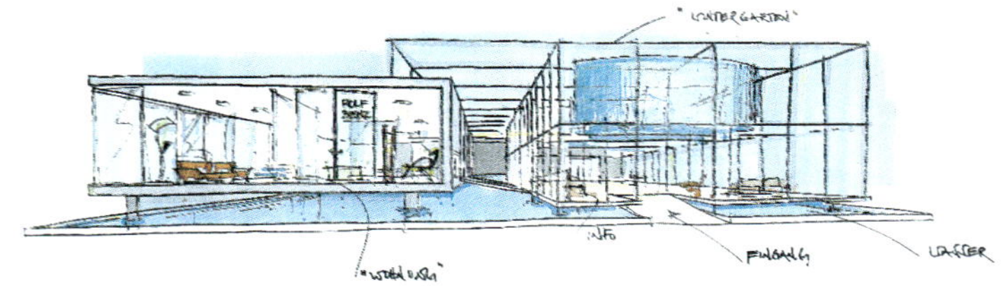
"WINTERGARTEN"
INFO
EINGANG
WASSER

ROLF
BENZ

ROLF
BENZ

Photographs: Wenger & Wittmann

Siemens mobile

Wenger & Wittmann

This stand was designed for inclusion in CeBIT 2002, the Information and Communication Trade Fair in Hanover. It is divided into seven areas to cover the huge diversity of products in the telecommunications business.

The Siemens Mobile presentation was conceived in terms of an innovative and dynamic lifestyle; the end result is an experience of the very latest generation, giving optimum insight into the various business sectors of Information and Communication.

"Be inspired", the slogan used in their print advertising, provided the inspiration behind the design and was subsequently translated into a three-dimensional stand display.

Two large cylindrical segmented volumes, variations of which appear throughout the stand, comprise one of the display's most outstanding features. The soaring, asymmetrical conical design of these two-story volumes demonstrates dynamism and at the same time serves as a linking background element for the illuminated logos. Each volume is topped by a large, orange canopy that doubles as a lighting element, below which is placed the company's illuminated logo.

The print advertising was harmoniously integrated into these volumes, while panels were replaced by illuminated graphic surfaces. Another theme which recurs throughout the stand, from product display cases to wall design, is the use of domed Plexiglass windows, which provide a perfect setting for the exhibits.

For optimal lighting effects, the designers opted for an alternating display of warm and cool colored illumination.

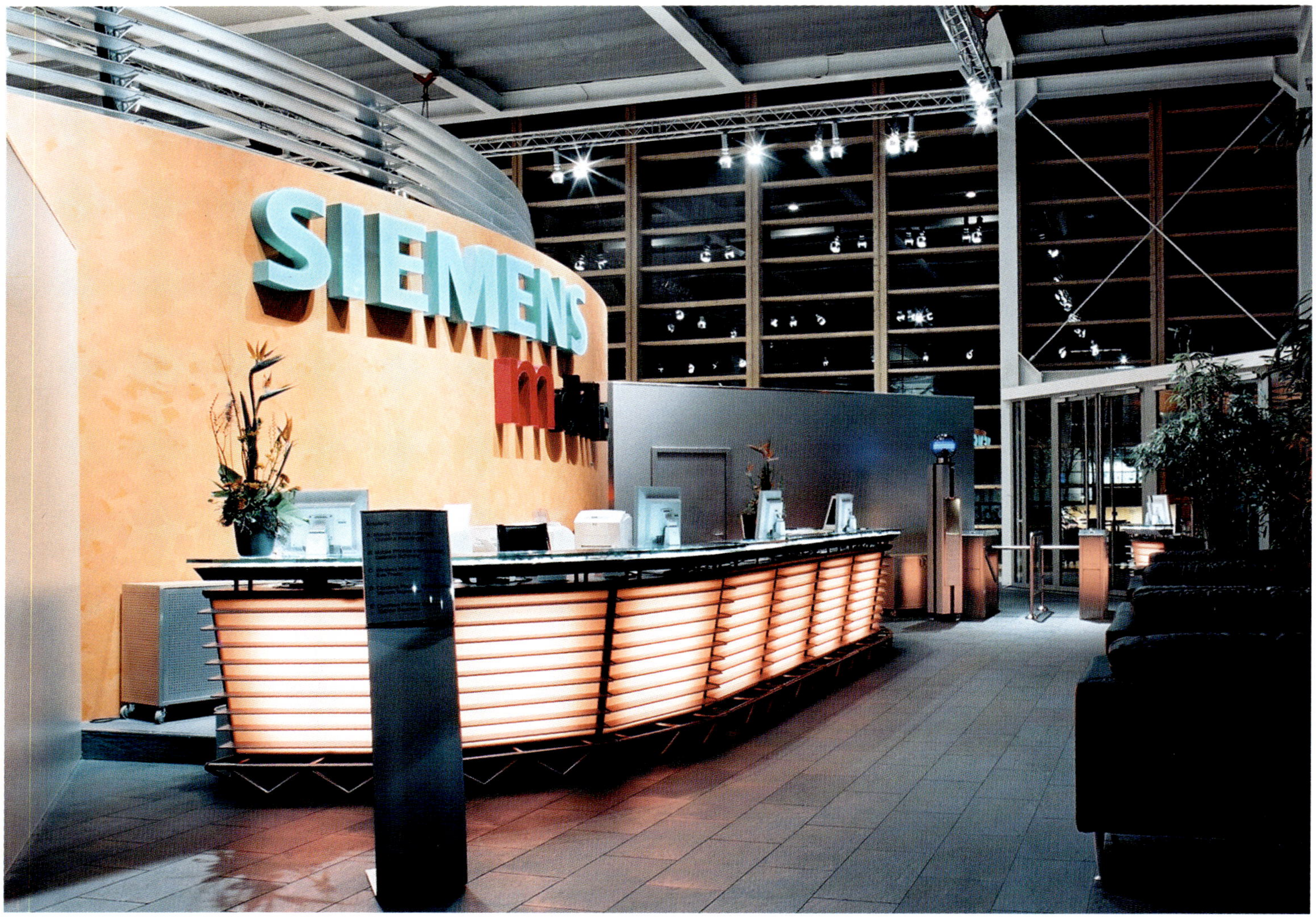

SIEMENS

Floor plan

NOTAUSGANG
GARDEROBE
HANDS
CUSTOMER CARE
HUMAN RESOURCES
08
09
PRESSE
07
05
GPRS
06
UMTS
02
MOBILE PHONES SMART DEVICES
4
INNOVATIONS & VISIONS
3
DOWNLOAD STATION
01
MOBILE PHONES CONSUMER DEVICES
INFORMATION
LAGER
STAND-LEITUNG
PROJEKT-ASSISTENZ
TECHNISCHER SUPPORT
LICHTTECHNIK AV-TECHNIK
WIRELESS MODULES
15
16
10
MODELL HOUSE
11
SIEMENS MOBILE QUIZ-ARENA
MOBILE LIFE @ HOME
14
INFOTAINMENT ACCESSOIRES
GRAFIK
FUTURE HOME
12
13
CORDLESS PRODUCTS

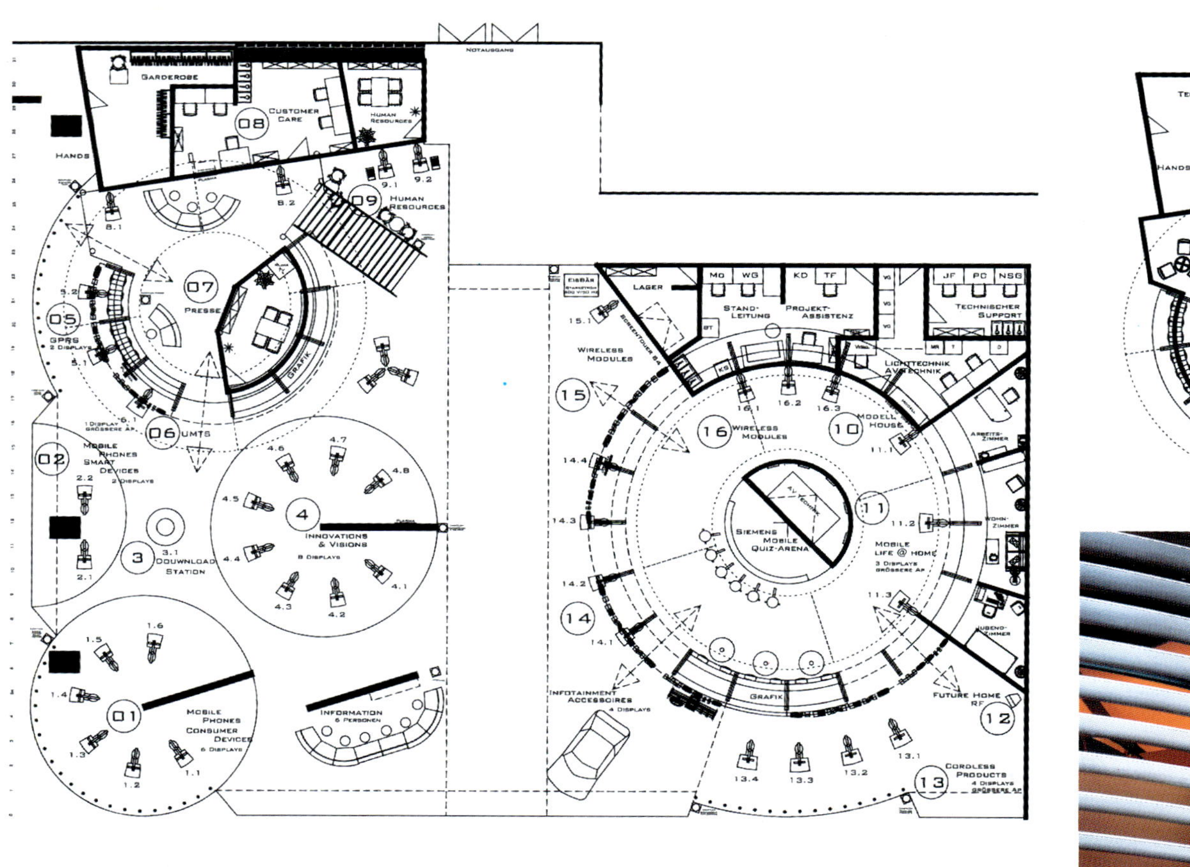

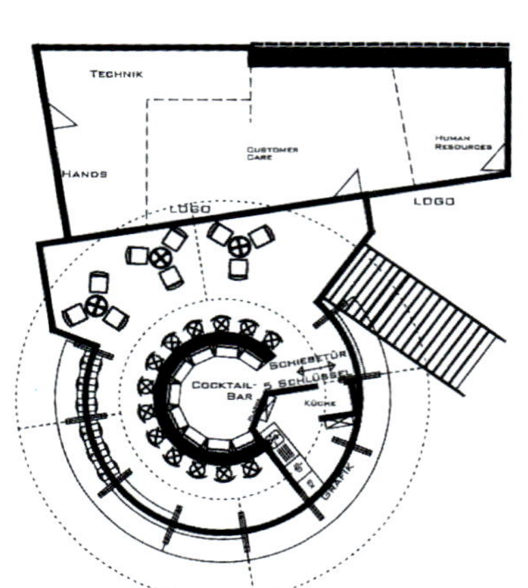

TECHNIK
HANDS
LOGO
COCKTAIL-BAR

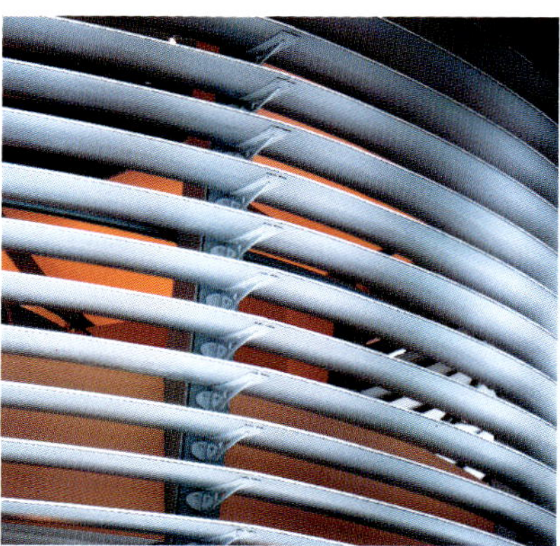

Atmosphere

3 deluxe

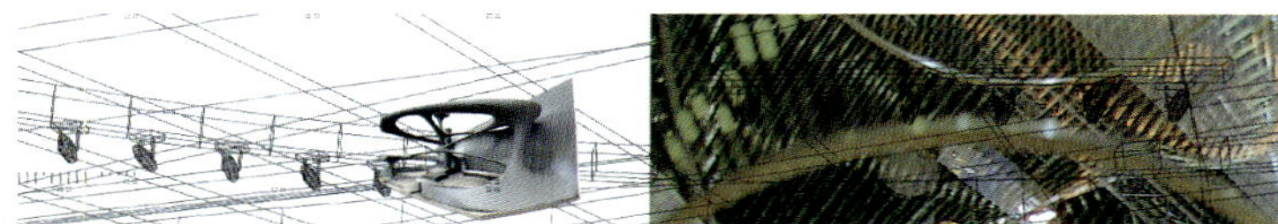

'Atmosphere' is a metaphor for the Autostadt Wolfsburg Corporation. The design concept for the stand focused on addressing the emotional perception of visitors. 'Atmosphere' was a place of arrival and relaxation as well as a communicative hangout at the 'International Motor Show: Passenger Cars 2001' trade fair in Frankfurt.

A semitransparent, white gauze membrane defines the stand as a sphere, encapsulating a micro universe amidst the turbulent fair activity without interrupting visual contact between interior and exterior. Complex branches pull away from the main structure and wind their way throughout the stand. The interior is divided into three areas, which are formally linked by the overarching organic architecture and corresponding choice of colors and materials.

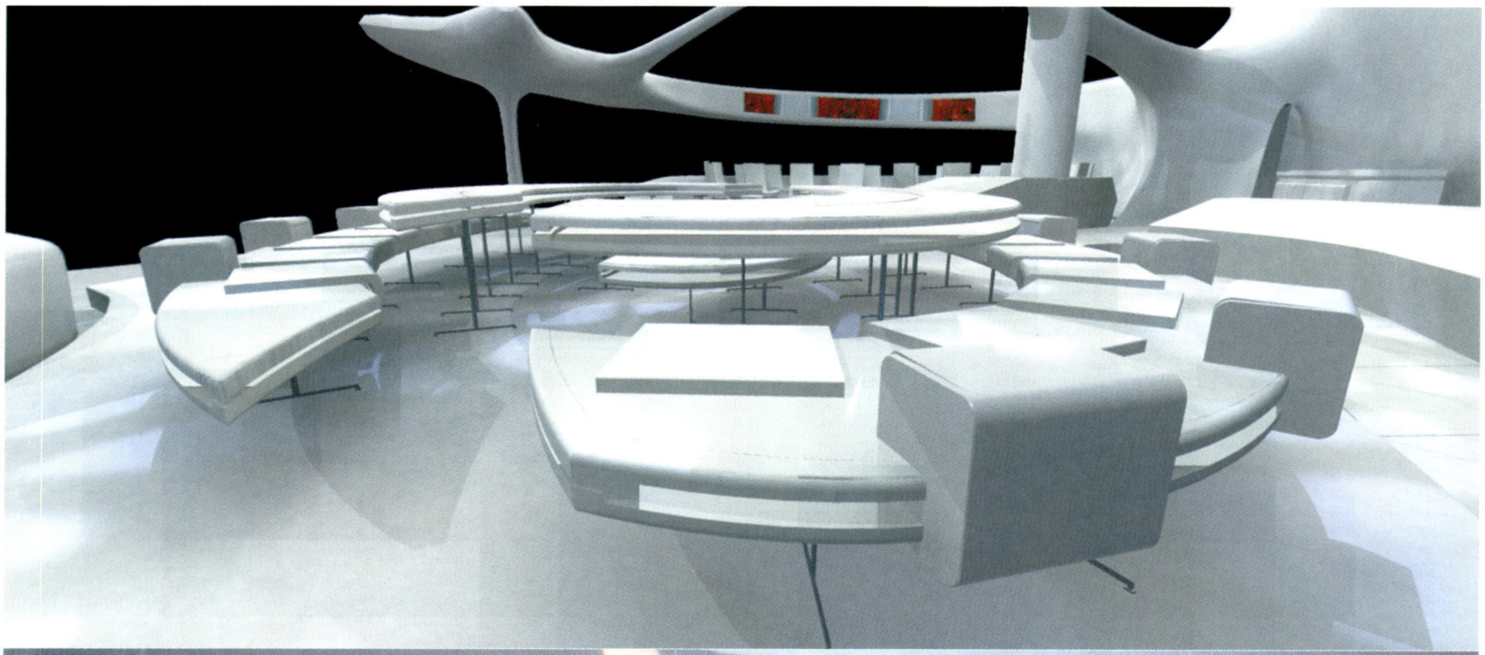

Photographs: 3 deluxe, Emanuel Raab

Guests are welcomed at the entrance by a sculptural service unit made of stainless steel tubes and rotating glass panels, which provide a support for catering.

Two neighboring lounge areas to the left invite visitors to sit and rest a while, meet up with friends and chat. Single seating elements with an integrated rocking mechanism and built-in massage devices further enhance the comforting atmosphere. Two suspended, kinetic nylon objects provide relaxing visual stimuli.

An eight-meter-wide projection displays abstract impressions of the Autostadt. Using special mirroring effects, the film was reproduced in four adjoining images to create a calming effect. A slowly changing light show, subtle fragrance emissions and surround sound audio effects come together to create a pleasant sensorial experience.

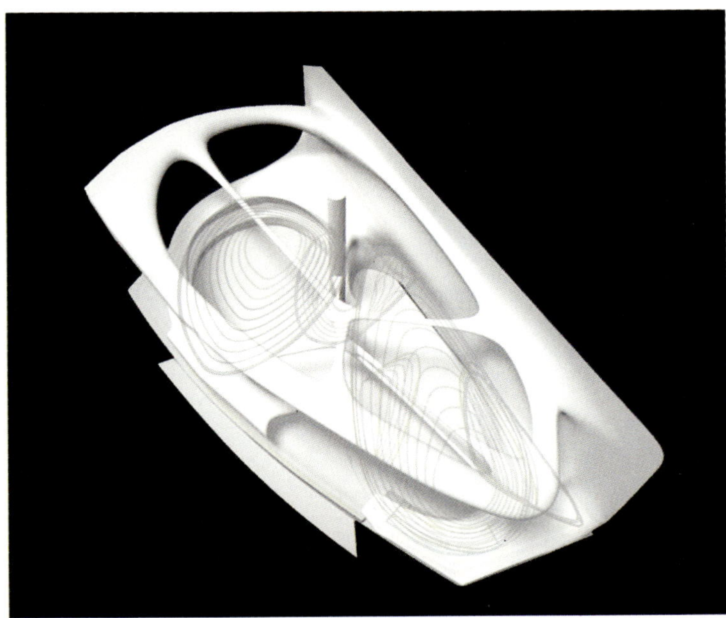

Ricoh

Wimmer design AG

This stand was designed to create an atmosphere of calm and relaxation amidst the busy and chaotic surroundings typically prevailing at such a fair as CeBIT 2001 in Hanover.

Through its more than 1500m² of floor surface, the stand produces a perfect symbiosis of high-tech imagery based on classic elements, in league with natural, recyclable materials, such as wood, steel and glass. The transparency and lightness of the stand creates a free and open feeling for its visitors, which in turn promotes communication and information exchange.

Sophisticated plant and flower decor, an integral part of Ricoh's professional fair presentation, highlights the company's vision of being 'caring, reliable and innovative'. In keeping with this motto, the company provides four advisory units -a visual and integral part of the stand- as an effective resource in enhancing communication between the customer and the company.

Photographs: Heiko Wrensch

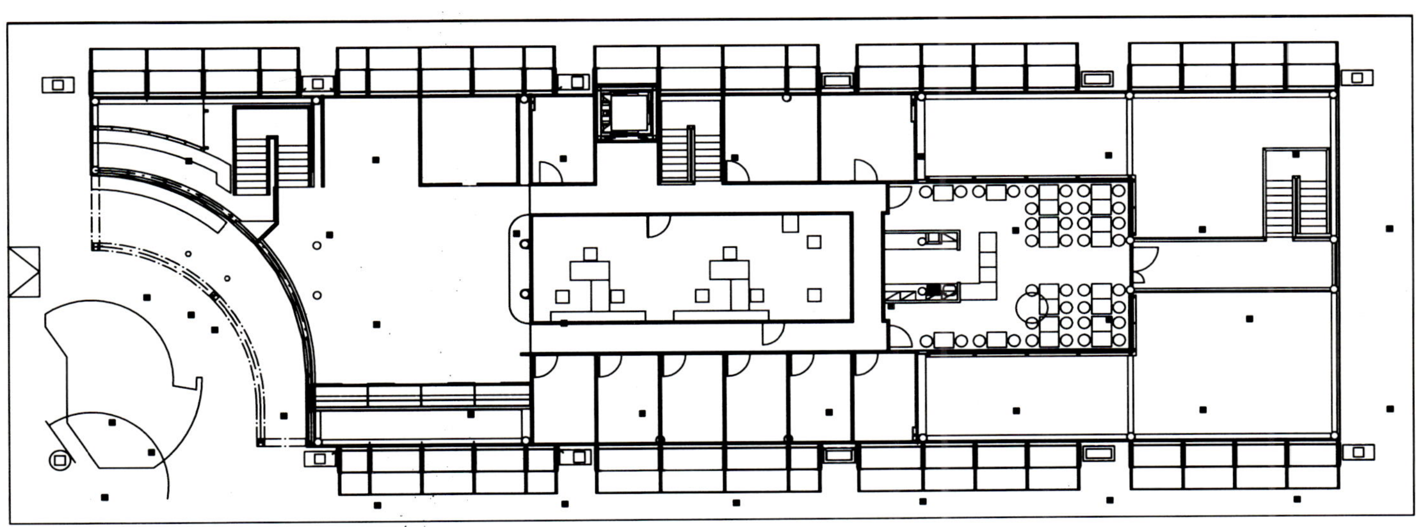

Floor plan

RICOH
RICOH
2h2

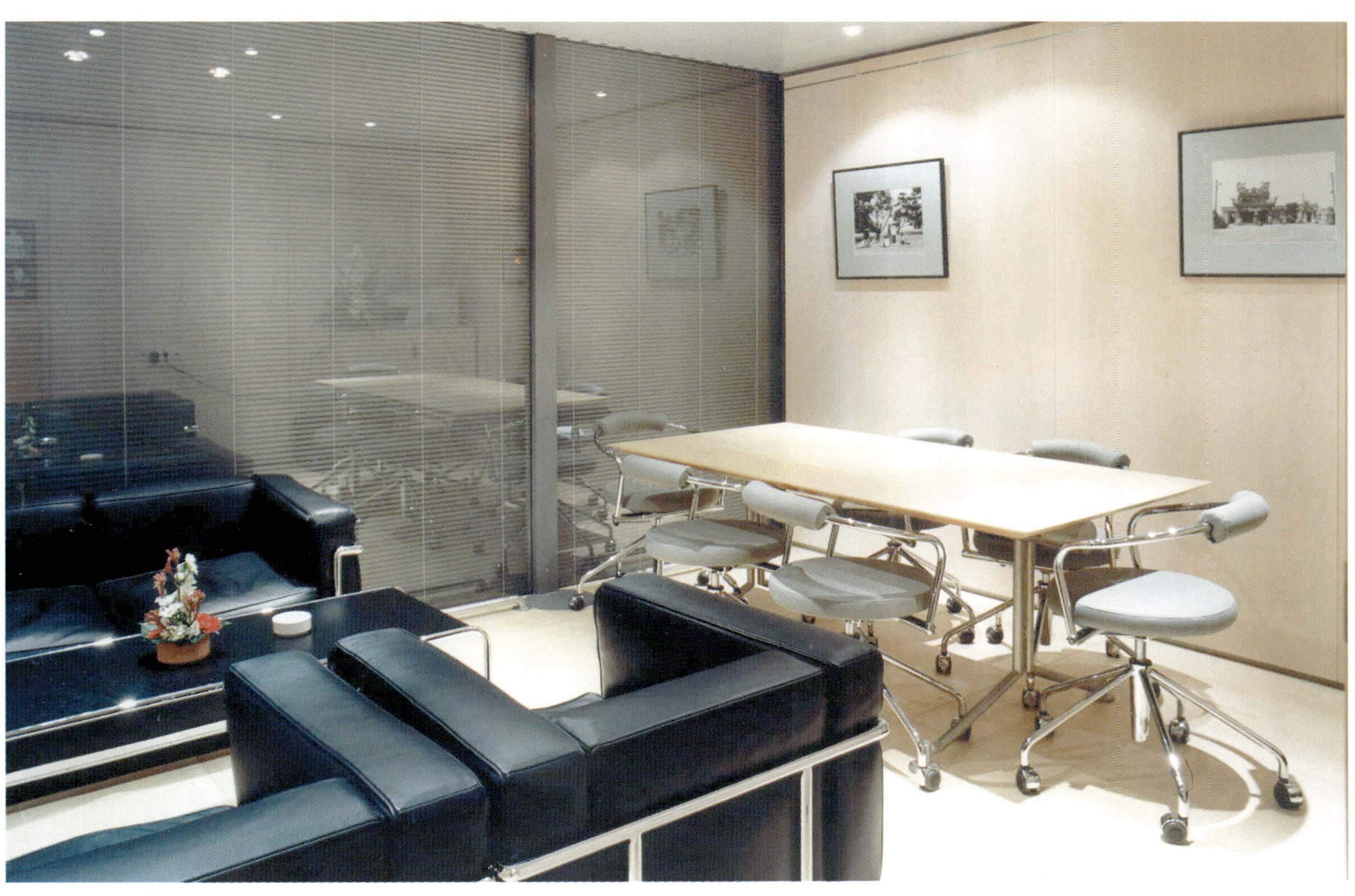

Bertelsmann

tecton GMBH

The focus of Bertelsmann Springer's stand at 'CeBIT 2001' in Hanover was to enable viewers to experience the abstract world of computer information by means of large projections.

These projections show dynamic, modern images combined with an attractive interplay of colors, symbolizing the flow of information. Reflected infinitely via two mirrored walls, the projected images become a part of the architectonic structure of the stand.

The projection surface, which is translucent and thereby allows the images to pass through for viewing on the 'back' side, simultaneously acts as the outer skin of the upper level, where the conference lounge is located. Although the lettering is backwards, reflective material cladding parts of the ceiling, floor and walls send the images back in legible form.

The real dimensions of the space combined with the projections and reflections create a dense, amorphous atmosphere.

In contrast, horizontal shelves on the ground floor running the length of the wall, from the front edge of the stand to the back area, conform the clearly defined visitors' area and magazine displays. Graphics superimposed on glass elements break up and organize the exhibits.

The middle of the stand is spacious and open. Four freestanding operating terminals and plasma screens supported by narrow steel beams have been placed here. The information and subscription counter sits parallel to the wall on the right side. A back-lit, glass section formally divides the two services.

The spatial concept, light, color and the material used all come together to effectively underline the stand's concept.

Photographs: Frank Kleinbach

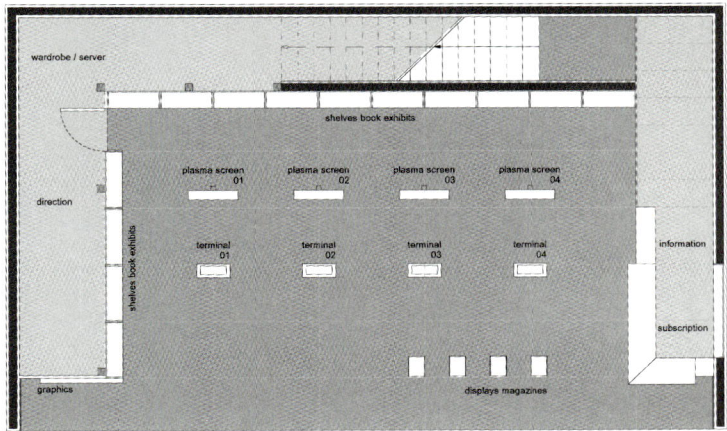

Ground floor plan

First floor plan

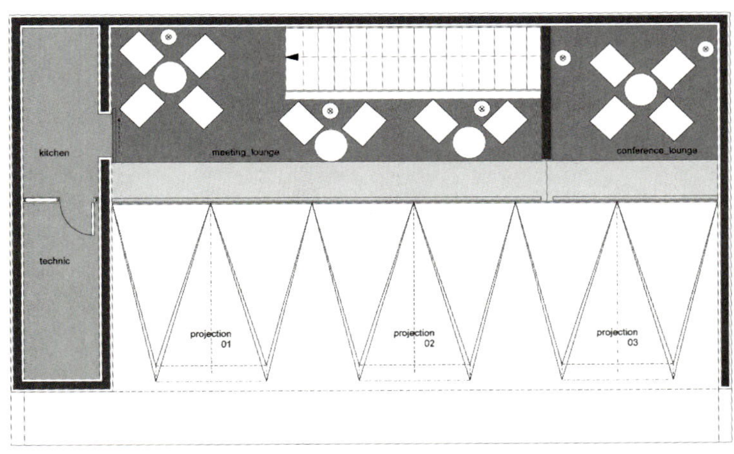

General Electric Plastics

Wenger & Wittmann

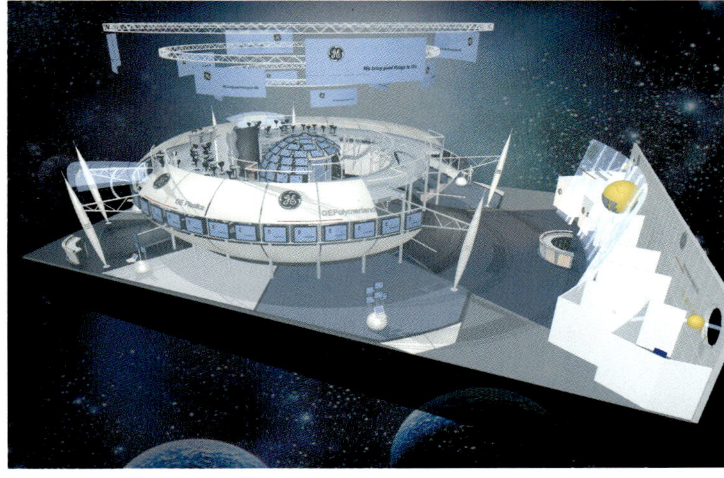

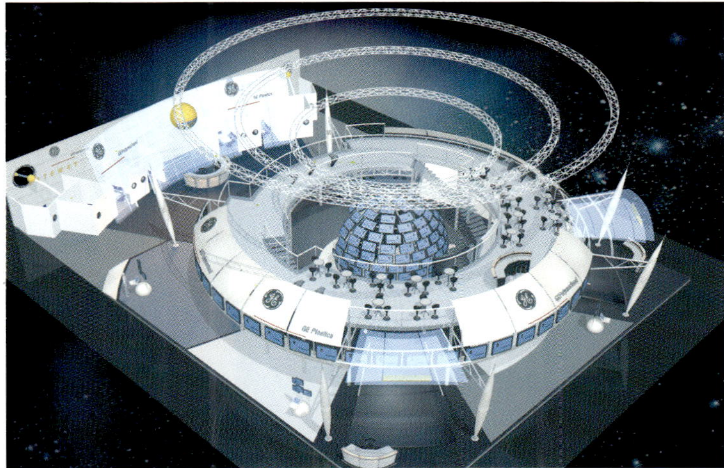

The General Electric Plastics promotion campaign, based on the theme of 'the gateway to the plastics universe', was illustrated entirely in spatial terms in the design concept for its stand at 'K 2001' in Dusseldorf.

The approximately 900-square-meter ground level was planned as functional areas on a basic grid. A discus-shaped plastic cover pulsating in different colors constitutes the center of the GE Plastic universe. The inside surface carries the general presentation of the company, while the moving images outside are indented to communicate the company's individuality.

Three ramps (gateways) marked out by light spindles and projections lead to a raised platform, which acts as an experience walkway highlighting the world of GE's products, which were radially arranged from the center of the stand inside the discus cover. The business areas were presented on the outside, in the open spaces.

A central media sphere of 7.5 m (24.5 feet) in diameter contains over 70 plasma screens, a continuous LED ring with over 90 modules, plus corresponding media satellites and a large network of computers forming the media information centre of 'K 2001'.

With a maximum structural height of 6 m (20'), the steel podium is positioned 5 m (16.5') up, thus giving an eye-level height of around 6.6 m (21.6'). This height provides a view over the roofs of all the other exhibitors.

The whole outer surface pulsates in a succession of soft, atmospheric colors, and back projections, both with remotely controlled elements.

Over 95% of the material in the stand can be reused, which makes it an ecologically sensible, long-term way to plan. The discus shape was conceived in terms of modules so that parts of it can be reused on very small surfaces or the discus can be put to use at ground level as a VIP lounge, for example.

To facilitate transportation and handling, the modular parts have been tailored to Europallet dimensions.

Lexan EXL

to life.
GE Plastics

GE Plastics

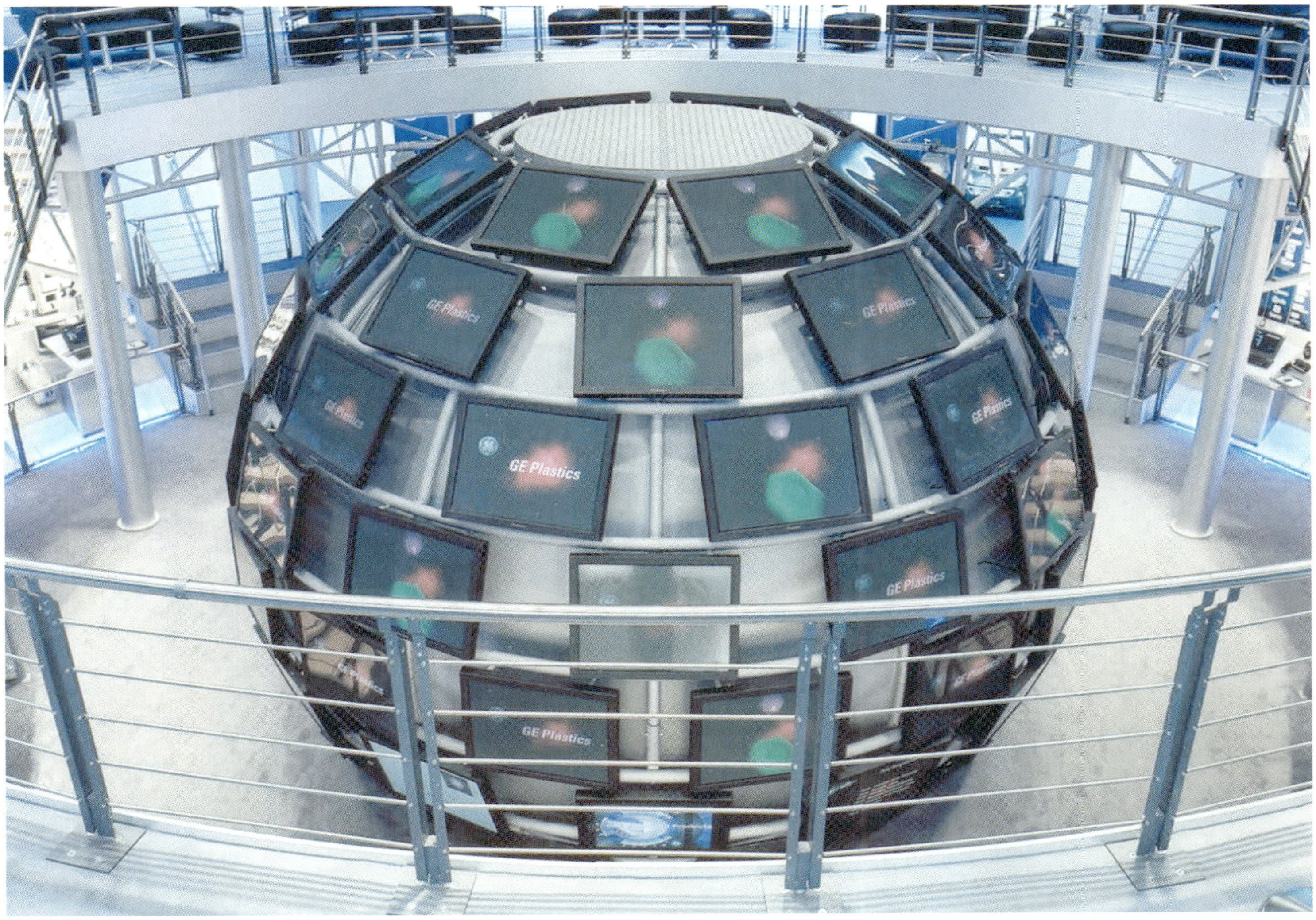

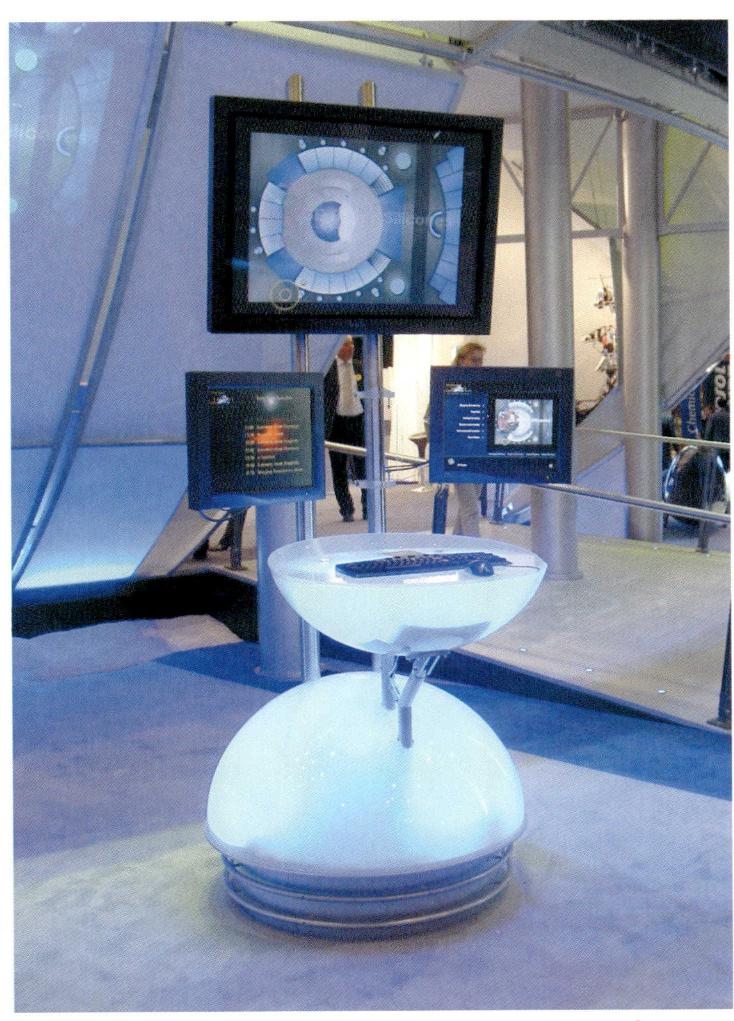

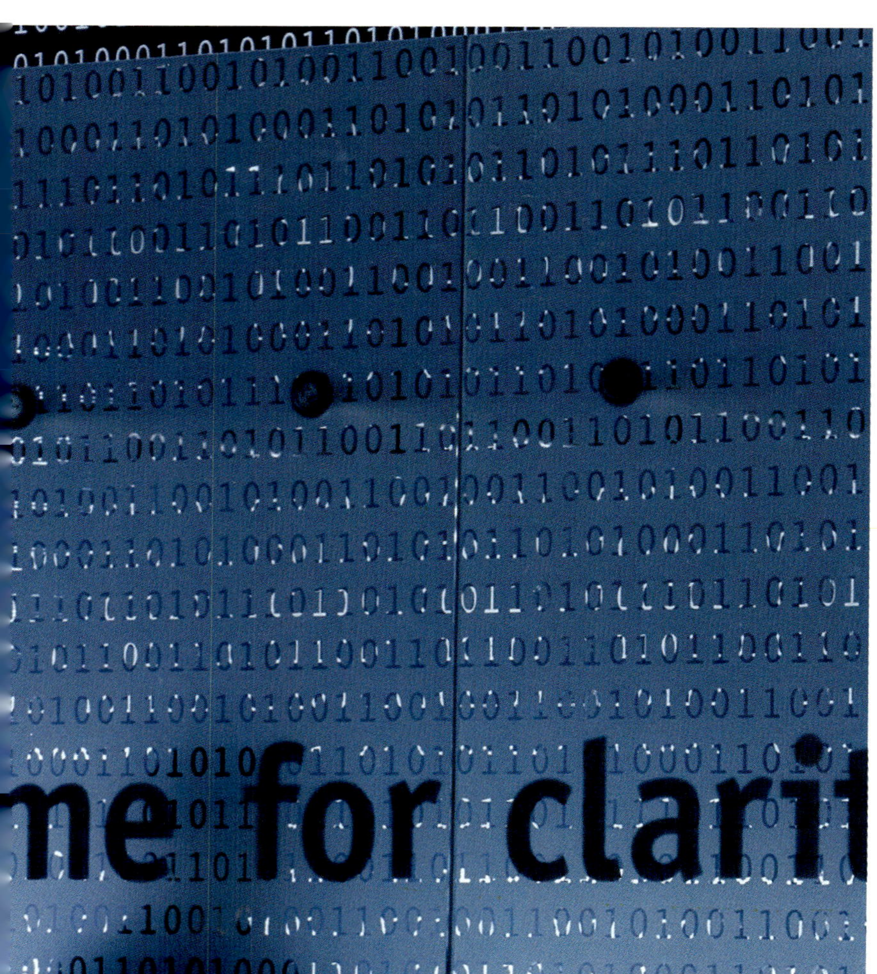

KPMG

Schmidhuber + Partner

This stand is comprised of a system of modules arranged to form different levels and areas of information. For example, the meeting room is located in the center of the upper portion of the stand. These modules are covered in a translucent skin of matte glass, with selective lighting that creates a moiré effect, depending on the spectator's angle of vision, granting a lively optical impression. In succeeding order, the numerals 0 and 1 of the binary code constitute the design's figurative elements.
The actors in this snapshot are the visitors themselves, who, like vague silhouettes, merge with the binary lines upon crossing the corridor located between the translucent glass and the blue partitions bearing the slogan, "It's time for clarity." This is a highly effective aesthetic symbol for the interactive communication between digital processes and users.

Photographs: Stefan Müller - Naumann

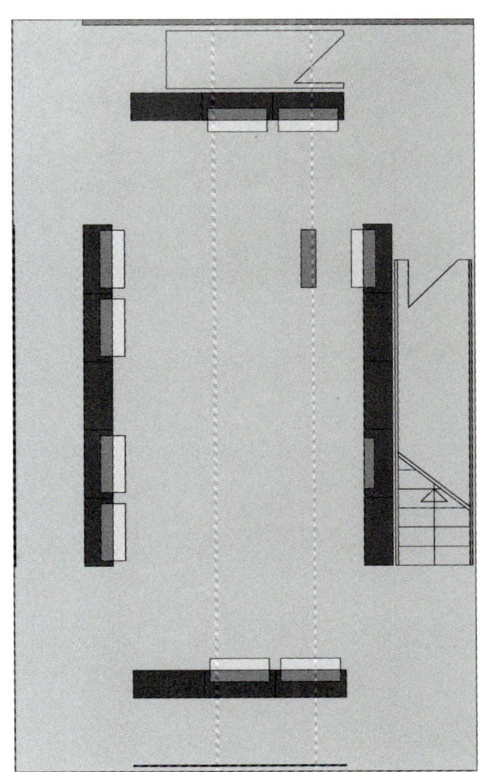

Plan

Design in Zürich

Stefan Zwicky

The lack of well-known Swiss furniture manufacturers in Zurich's annual International Furniture Trade Fair was the basis for the project Design in Zurich. The central idea of the presentation was the visualization and valuation of all products in a single category – an atypical concept as far as trade show stands go.

The stand occupies a surface area of 540m² (27x20m) with an orthogonal transition system whose limits reach the ground floor cafeteria. The primary characteristic is an ordered cluster of 30 light screens measuring 3x3 meters hanging from the ceiling. It is a truncated conical shape made from metal rings, aluminum cylinders, wire and fabric.

The lighting elements, on the other hand, are irregularly distributed throughout the space. A large expanse of white carpeting covers the floor and, along with the lighting, which is directed toward the products on display beneath the screens, plays a clearly leading role in creating the ambience in the stand.

A spatial divider of corrugated cardboard in a natural tone marks the separation between the various furniture manufacturers and serves as a neutral backdrop to the pieces on display. A metal plaque bearing the logo and address of each exhibitor has been affixed to these panels.

Photographs: Stefan Zwicky

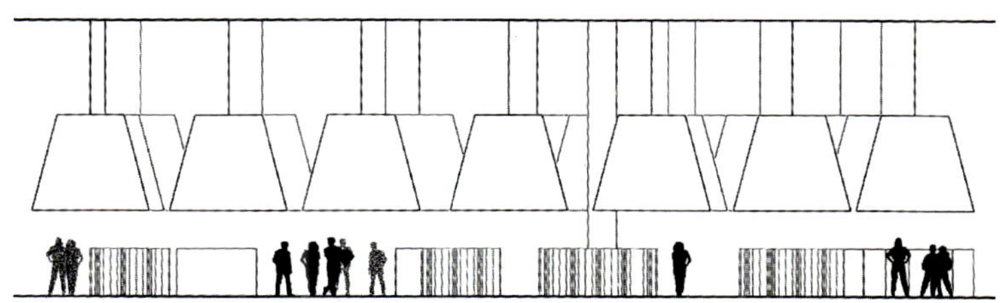

Elevation

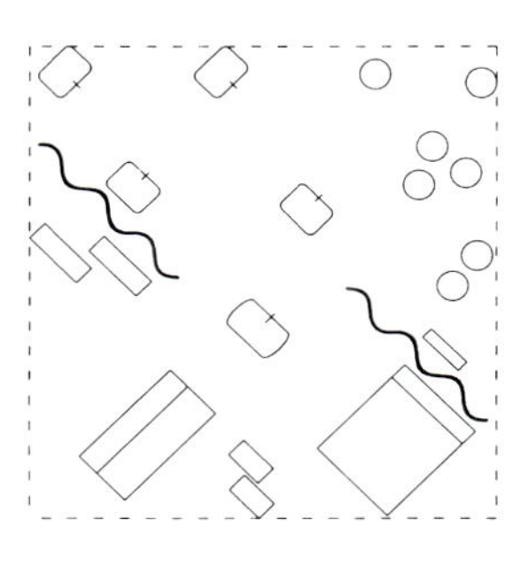
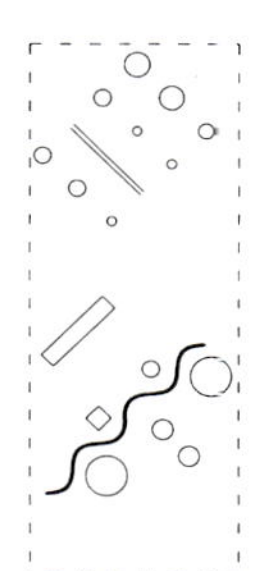
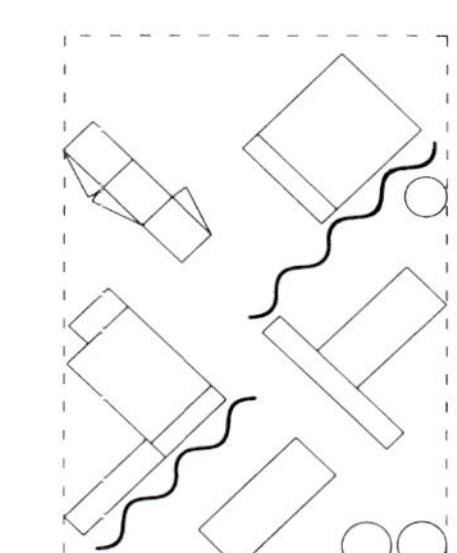
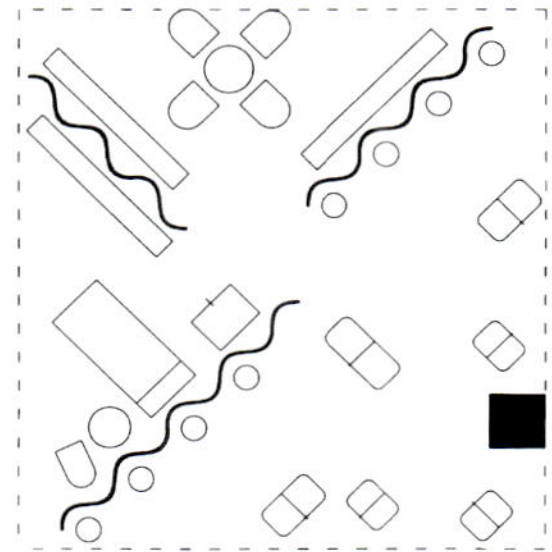
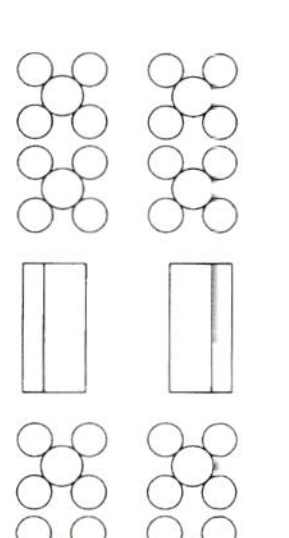
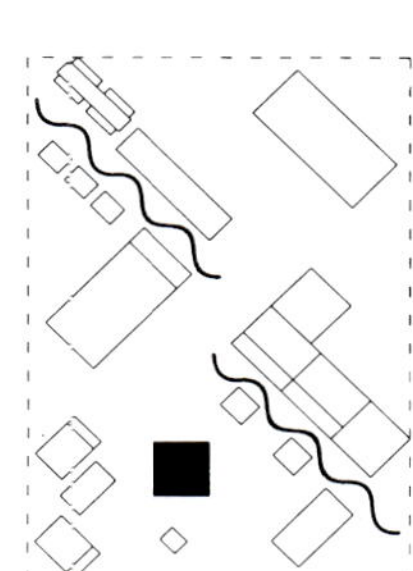
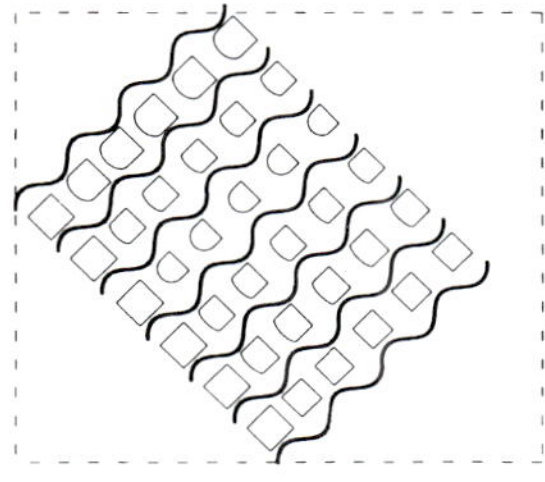
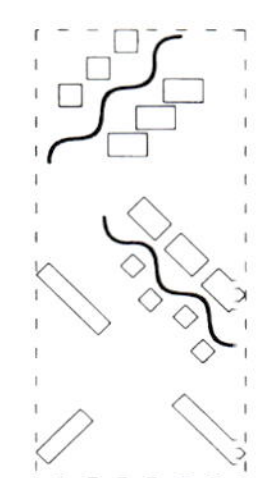
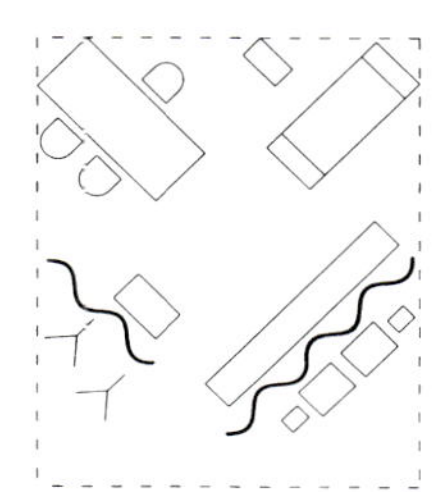

Floor plan

Berker

Schmidhuber + Partner

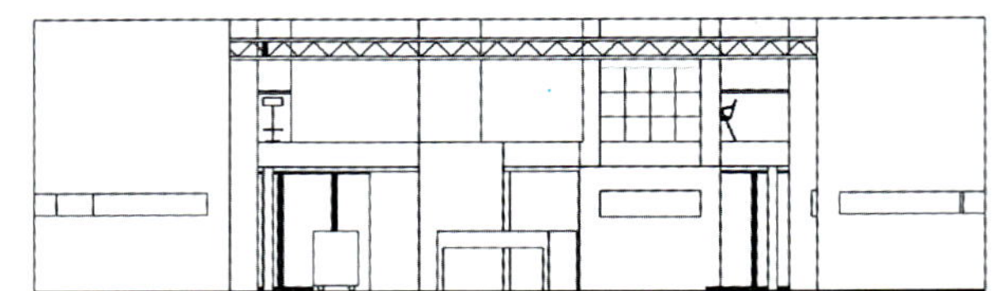

An innovative new line of light switches was presented in this stand at the Light and Building 2002 trade show. The inclusion of a minimal number of objects made for an open, clean design with pure geometric forms.

The stand is made up of white panels, like fragments of a wall, with lighted signs and a large graphic design running throughout the plot. These panels have been fitted with openings which serve as windows and induce visitors to look beyond, toward the interior. The panels, which are also internal spatial dividers with eye-level horizontal openings, show changing presentations of the products.

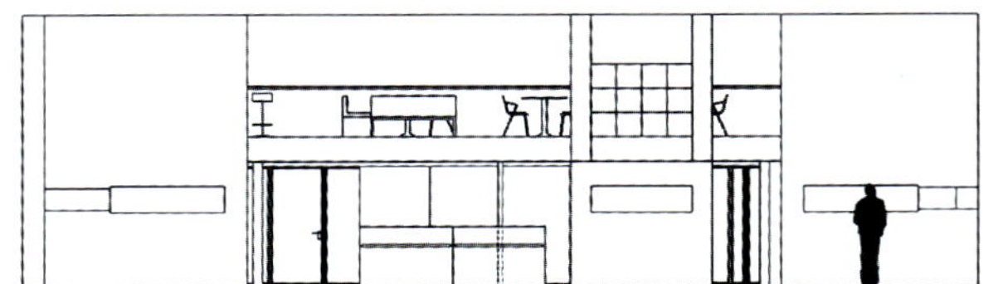

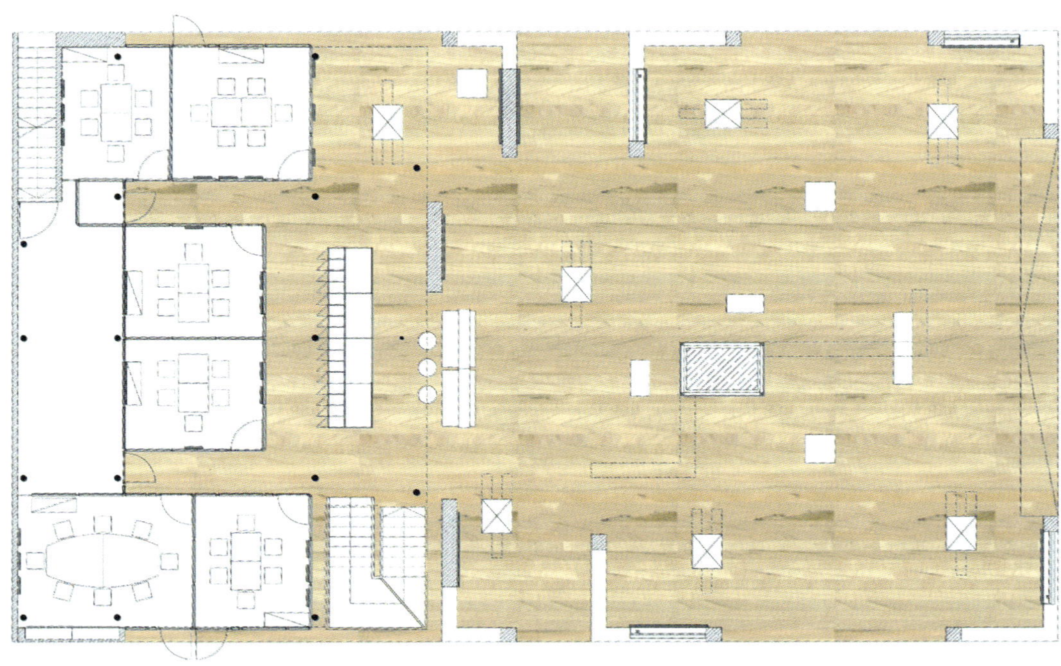

Photographs: Studio Schroll

WHAT'S LEADING
THE RIGHT
WAY?

ART?
LEADING
HEIS

WAS HEISST HIER
INFORMATION
B.

JF DIE EIGENE ART?

Emap

Richard Hywel Evans

Emap's stand for 'Interbuild 2000' was designed to mark the launch of its new Construction Plus website. The prefabricated stand is comprised of four white double-curved fabric canopies set around a 4-meter-high column. Each of the four MDF joints corresponds to a different Emap business area and is finished in bold, eye-catching colors: red for architecture, yellow for contracting, purple for building services and blue for engineering.
Each canopy has been covered with an upper and lower sheet of barrisol white PVC base. The white matte finish gives 80 percent light reflection and the titanium of the barrisol product provides strength. The material was cut approximately 7 per cent smaller than actual size at the Barrisol factory in France.
Set around the central column, and corresponding to the colored canopies, there are four overlapping entrances. This arrangement alludes to the relationship between the central website and its sister sites. For instance, Ajplus, the website for architectural professionals, is a Construction Plus site and can be displayed on a screen set into the column. Emap wished to show that they are the main information provider for the construction industry, their publications ranging from Architectural Review to Heating & Ventilation News.

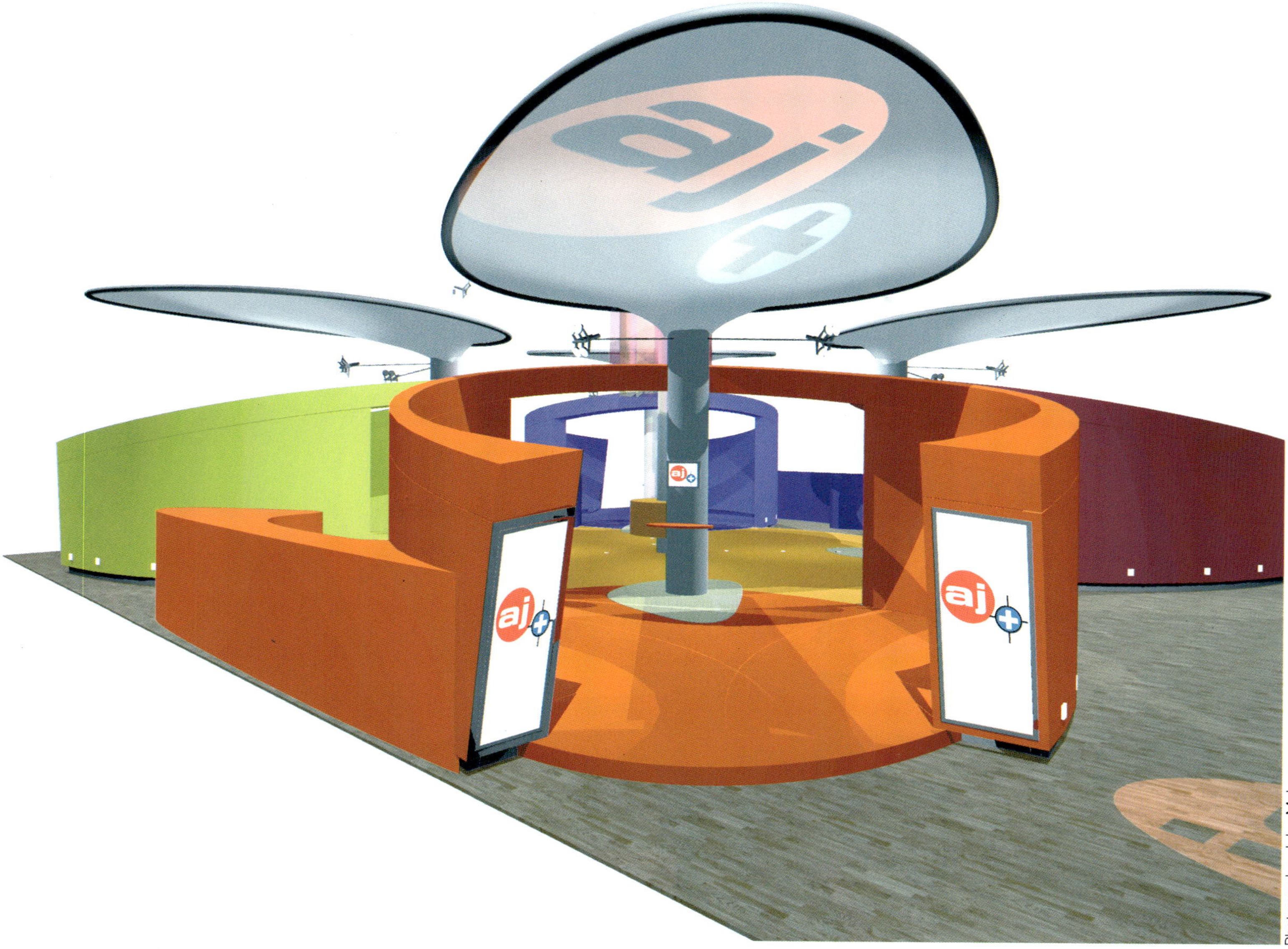

Photographs: John McLean

Plan

Canopy plan

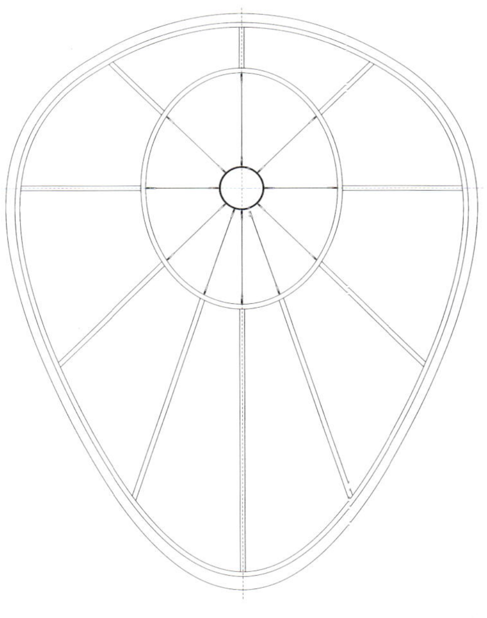

Cross section

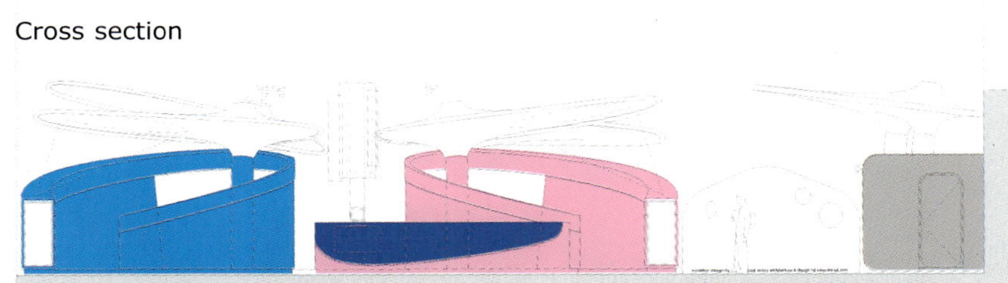

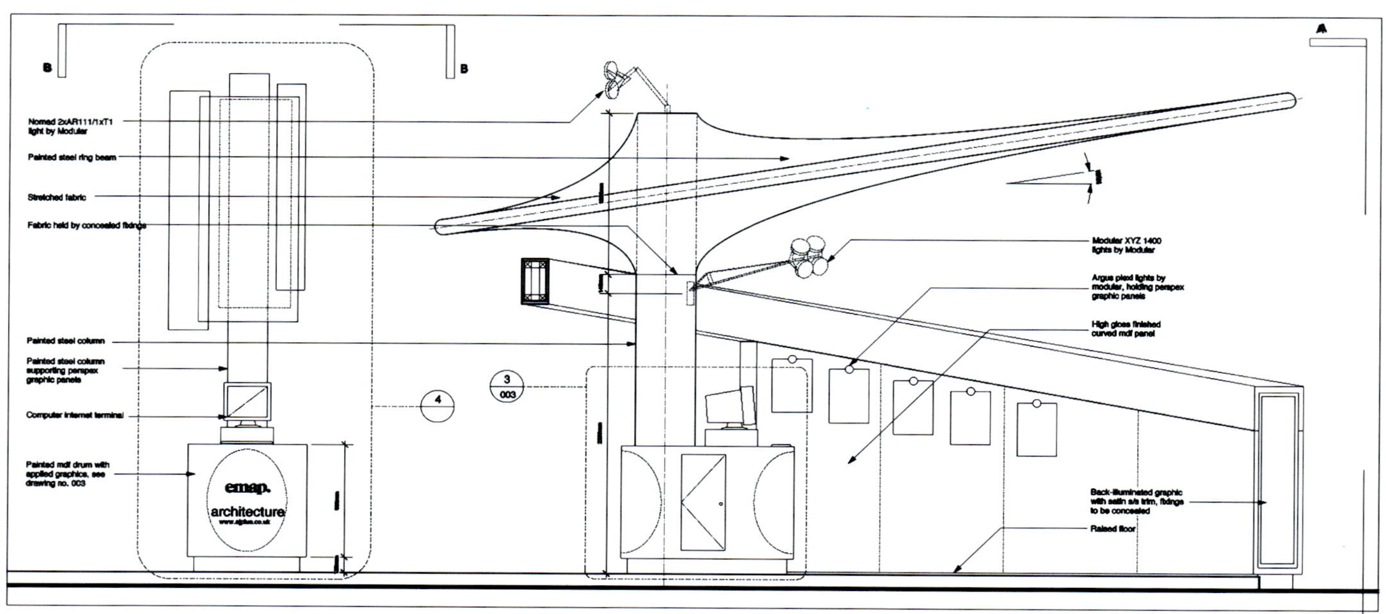

Cross section

Cross section of canopy

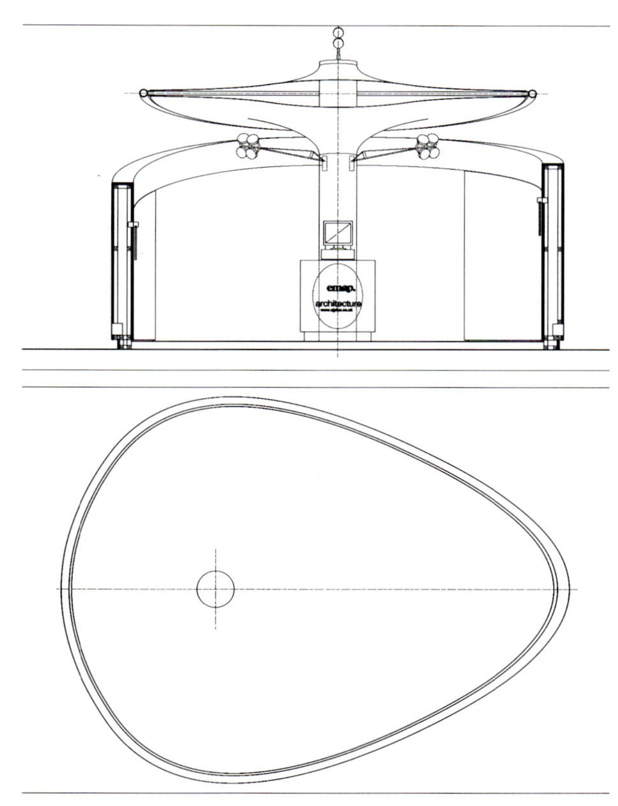

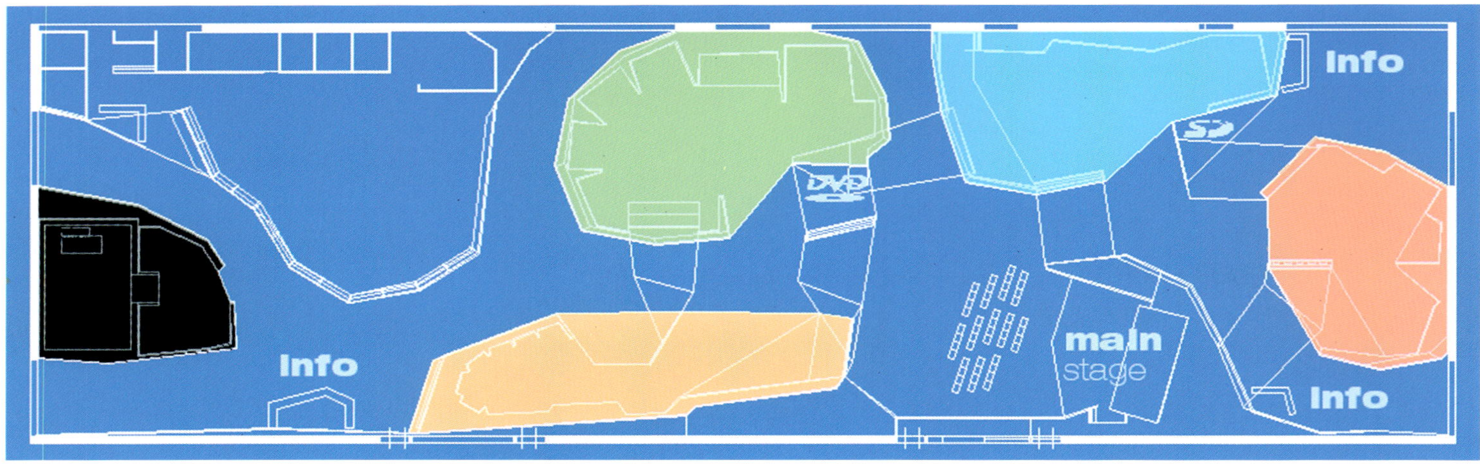

Panasonic

Atelier Brükner

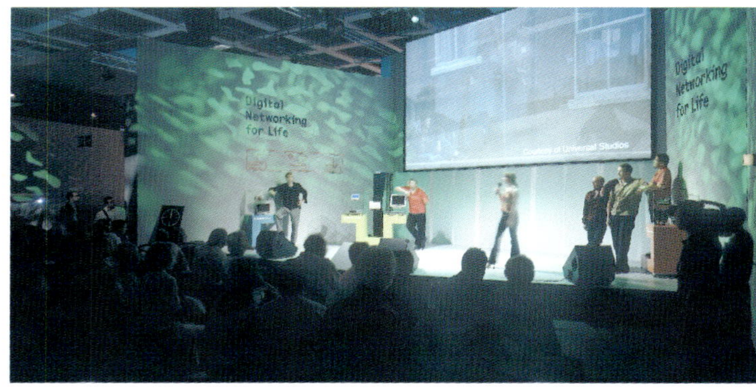

Photographs: bitter+bredt fotografie

Panasonic presented the 'blue garden' at IFA 2001 in Berlin. Occupying over 3500m², this stand evokes the company motto: 'create your world'.

A network solution of different media creates the fascinating and surreal world of the blue gardens. 52 data projectors, each with 10,000 ANSI lumens, project onto a more than 300m long and 4m high screen shaped like a Moebius strip – a movie that becomes the architectural body of twists and loops.

1200m² have been used for islands of 'Network Solutions', where the direct product presentation takes place. This space is divided into themes like: entertainment, creative network, communications and technical worlds (DVD, SD, digital broadcasting)

The visitor travels through a three-dimensional, projected space, a world in permanent transformation. The movement of the images fulfills the function of guiding visitors; they all lead to the center of the stand and into the islands of the network solutions. The blue gardens make use of Panasonic's own resources of high-tech products to create a fascinating and imaginative world of images, sounds and atmospheres.

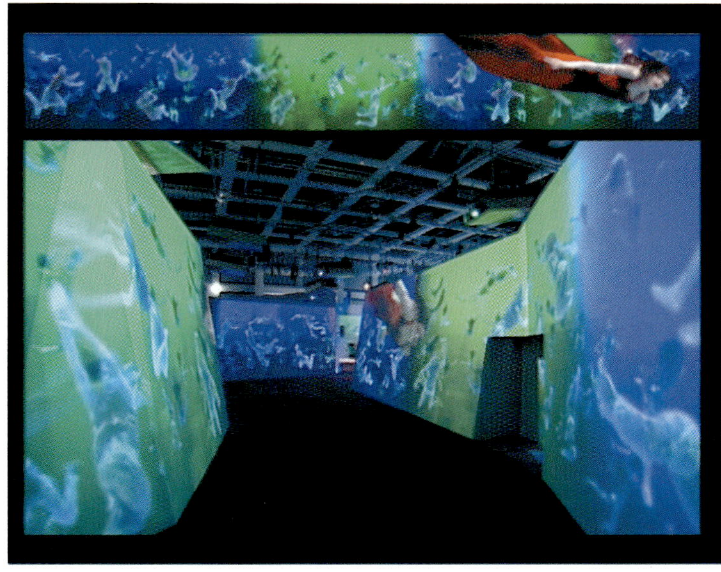

Panasonic
Panasonic

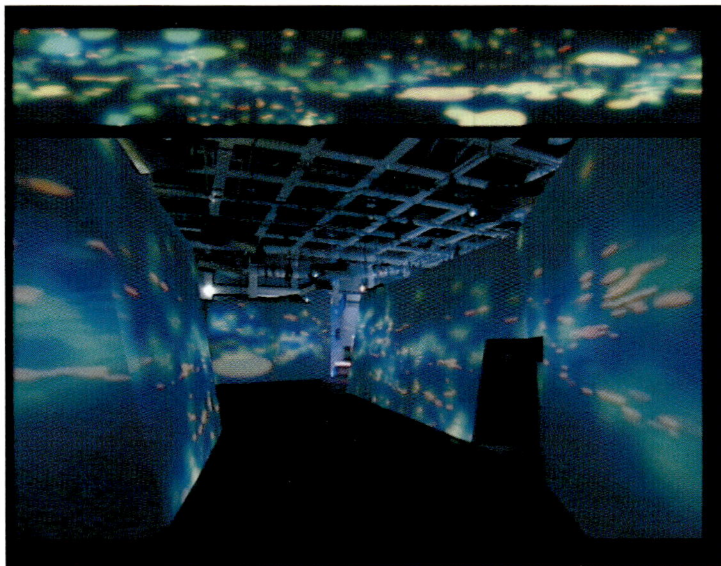

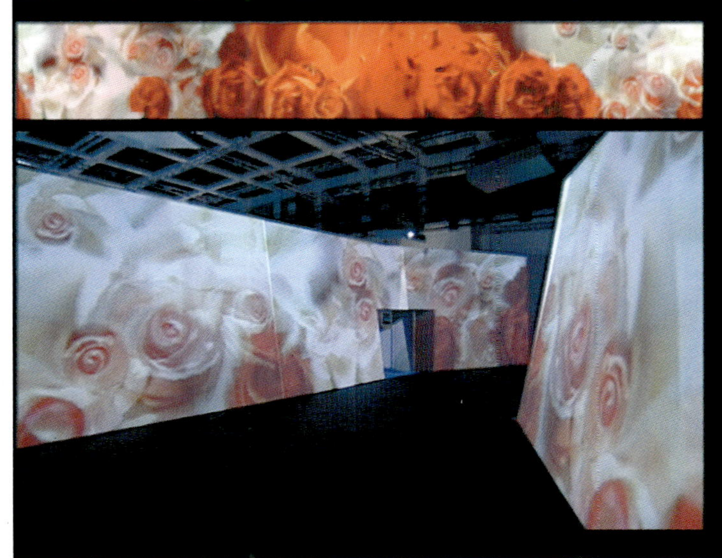

Panasonic

entertainment network
mobile
communication network
corporate stage
digital broadcast world

Floor plan

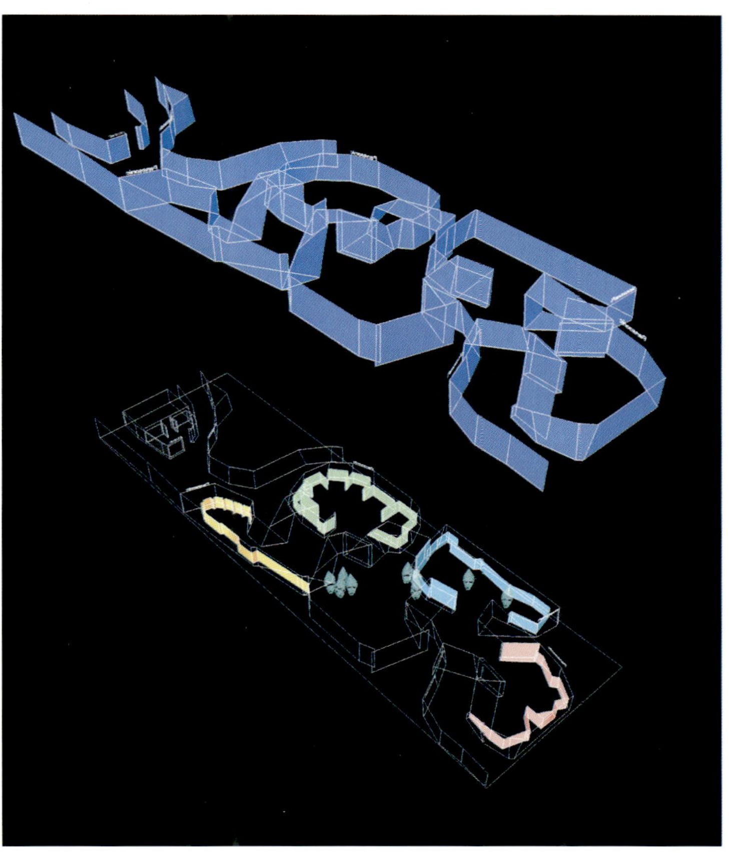

Gin Tonic

Bottega + Ehrhardt Architekten

The slogan "Not So Normal" was developed on the basis of this company's new position in the fashion world and set the tone which their stand had to reflect. Homogenous white in the interior, mannequins from the collection hanging upside down over a mirrored surface in the entryway, objects from the main room as an introduction to the collection and an external wrapping to attract visitors are all part of the design scheme.

An exterior band of reflective concave and convex plates create a distorted image which arouse the curiosity of passersby. In the interior, a predominance of stark white is meant to reflect newness, purity, cleanliness, innocence and clarity. White glass flooring highlights this effect and gives the stand its necessary elegance.

Mannequins wearing the season's most eye-catching garments hang head-down in the entryway; while the floor has been fitted with reflecting tiles that show a right-side-up view of the collection.

The visitor, after signing in at the desk, slips between the mannequins and steps into the stand, thus becoming part of an upside down world. The collections for men, women and children are clearly and neatly organized along two rows of clothing racks filling the space from end to end, thereby accentuating the stand's depth. The furniture (the reception desk and seating in the entrance, for example) has a simple, block-like character and, when compared to the size of the exhibit, seems somehow smaller, almost insignificant – a sensation which highlights the clothing exhibit itself.

Photographs: Andreas Keller / Kirchentellinsfurt

Gaudí

Vicente Sarrablo Moreno

The basic component of the itinerant Año Gaudí 2002 exhibit is a 200m2 air-filled structure, which can be easily inflated in only eight minutes. This plastic cover was made by combining methods used in the manufacture of hot-air balloons and zeppelins and formal and chromatic references derived from work by the architect Gaudí: the sinuous forms of Barcelona's Sagrada Familia are similar to those seen in the floor plan of this blow-up stand; the arch above the fire place in the Casa Milá also gives shape to the entryway here; the oscillating section of the interior space follows the lines of the archways in Parque Güell, while the stand's polychrome "back" recalls that of the dragon presiding over the entry to this same park.

The paradox of forms intended to be executed in stone and brick having been achieved with air-filled textile tubes is a symbolic homage to the iconoclastic nature of Gaudí's work. These air-filled tubes are joined along one side and take on the shape of a sequence of arches, which successively vary in the degree to which they lean. This intermittent pattern, seen along the length-wise axis of the roof, creates variable heights in the route through the exhibit's three main areas without sacrificing visual continuity. Vibrant colors grant a certain unreal, fantastical air.

Photographs: Vicente Sarrablo Moreno

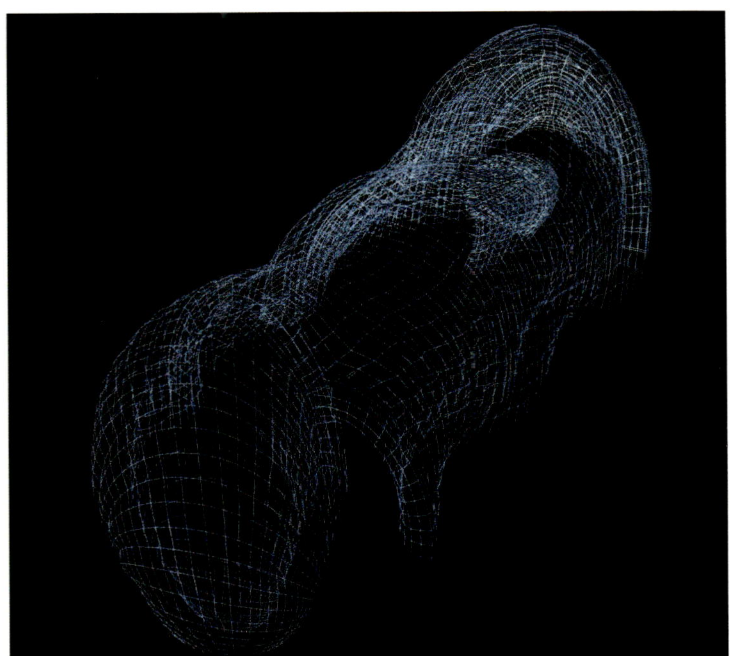

ULMA
ULMA

Durable

Ueberholz Messebau GmbH

The primary characteristics of this open stand, which occupies 528m² (22x24m) of floor surface, are its changing atmosphere and a clear and organized product presentation, for which a system of lighted shelves and display cases were used. A wall consisting of 5m high strips that reflect the changing colors visually separates the exhibit and service areas from the back of the stand.

The stand is made up of very clearly defined areas: the communication zone, which has been placed on an elevated surface in the center for meetings with clients; projection screens enclosing this area display images on given topics and product presentation; the service area, which houses a lounge, the kitchen and storage area; and the exhibit area for the companies Durable, Pagna and Aulfes (the space occupied for the latter two is optimally divided by different decorative motifs).

The flooring is comprised of different types of cladding. The space reserved for meetings features black MDF flooring, while light gray laminate covers the floor surface in the exhibit area.

The floor-to-ceiling projection screens lining the right-hand wall serve as a dividing element in spite of there being a certain degree of contact through its semitransparent weave.

Photographs: Fotoprop

Century nidau

Formpol AG

This stand, designed for the Watch and Jewellery Fair in Basel, was designed for a watchmaking company. The guiding principal behind the design of the stand was that it should express competence and reliability.

The design was based on an enclosed structure with an open concept which is partially double-height and partially two-story.

A custom developed hung facade construction allows a graceful open stand structure. The glass panes of the facades can be arranged in different tilted positions. An interplay of color and light is meant to evoke the sparkling of sapphires.

Photographs: Menga von Sprecher

CENTURY
TIME GEMS

Mercedes-Benz

Kauffmann Theilig & Partner
FreieArchitekten BDA

Barcelona

The elements of this stand at the Barcelona 1999 trade fair originated in a principle similar to that of a theater: a spatial sequence beginning with the foyer and culminating in the theater hall. Rather than separating these areas by closed walls or doors, they have been opened up to the visitor, while simultaneously appearing as individual spaces.

The main design element used to achieve this is a net made from steel cables (diameter 3mm). The net spans two horizontal, free-form steel tubes. Between these two leading curves, the material takes on a winding, sculptural form and appears to vary in degree of transparency and density.

This translucent skin informally separates the foyer from the main space. With the lights in the hall dimmed, this material becomes that much more visible. Depending on its density, the surface may appear to unfold, may be taut or playfully arranged, three-dimensional or incorporeal.

Colored spotlights, positioned according to a defined light concept, model and accentuate the skin, thus making the design idea a material reality. All other built elements, such as the hall, retreat into the background. Their light concept, in combination with the automobiles, is functional, serious and elegant, while the steel net covers the interior exhibition space like a veil, producing effects of interference. Even though the spaces are not strictly delineated, spatial tensions are aroused and materialized solely through the use of light.

Photographs: Andreas Keller / Atelier Markgraph

Si se le acerca
demasiado,
esta perdido.
El nuevo
CL Coupé.
El nuevo
CL Coupé

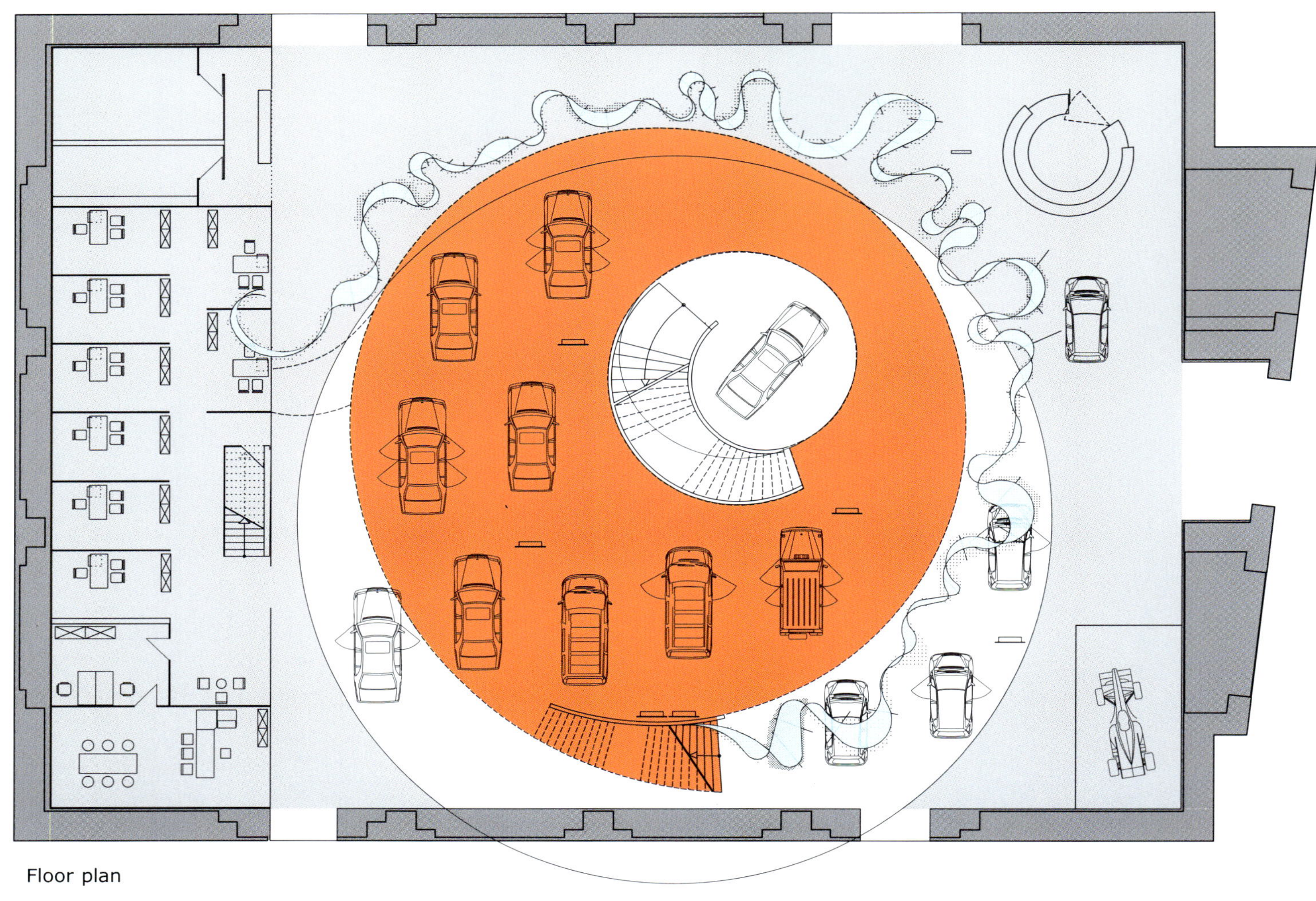

Floor plan

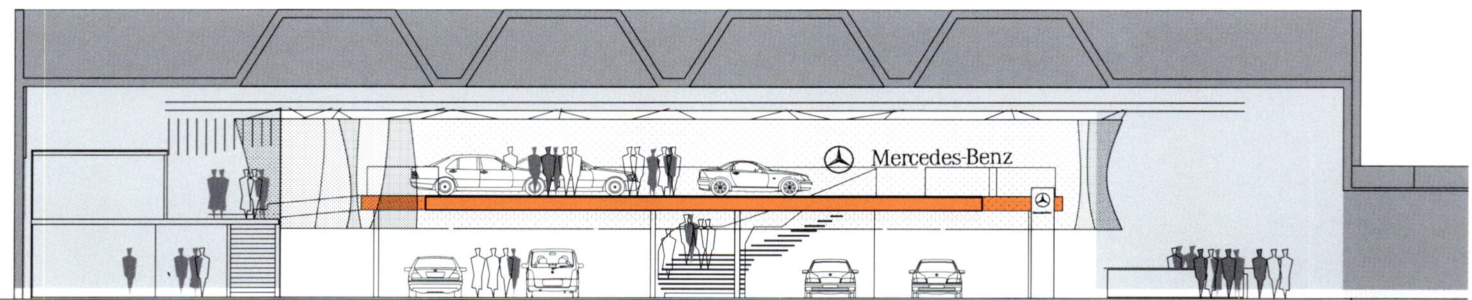

Cross section

Accesorios

Spirit
Courage
Passion
Passion
Strength
Mission
Speed meets Speed

Gira

Ueberholz Messebau GmbH

The 2000 Light + Building trade fair held in Hanover was the occasion for the design of this 17x28m stand.

The Gira trade fair booth is comprised of two very different construction modules, a scheme which poses a conscious, suspenseful contrast. An open, translucent room of lights –the actual presentation area– occupies the larger part of the booth. A closed, two-level construction module is located next to this.

The two-level, six-meter-high building, the ground floor of which is closed, provides a secluded, quiet counterpoint to the activity of the fair. The kitchen, an employee break room, storage facilities, and four conference rooms of various sizes are all located here. A glazed panel on the front of this module and two doors of the same material provide additional lighting on the lower level.

An overhanging balcony just off the upper level conference room presides over the lighting display room, thereby creating the perfect connection between the two spaces. The balcony is open on all sides, with the surrounding railing intensifying its bridging function. The staircase, which is also equipped with a railing, leads from the side of the balcony down into the heart of the display room. This open construction module is enclosed by four illuminated corners measuring over six meters in height. With fluorescent bulbs set into the framework, these corners are a light construction of grey-coated aluminum and square translucent panes, which are attached to both sides of the construction.

With entrances on three sides, the presentation room is bright, clearly divided and spacious. Simplicity and transparency leave lasting impressions here, and also express the central aspects of Gira and their product philosophy.

Another interesting aspect of this exhibition area is a multimedia presentation in the center of the exhibit area. Videos on flat monitors depict the company's latest products and are arranged spirally around a metal pole. Details and additional information are displayed on the bright walls inside the lighting display room.

Potographs: Fotoprop

GIRA

GIRA

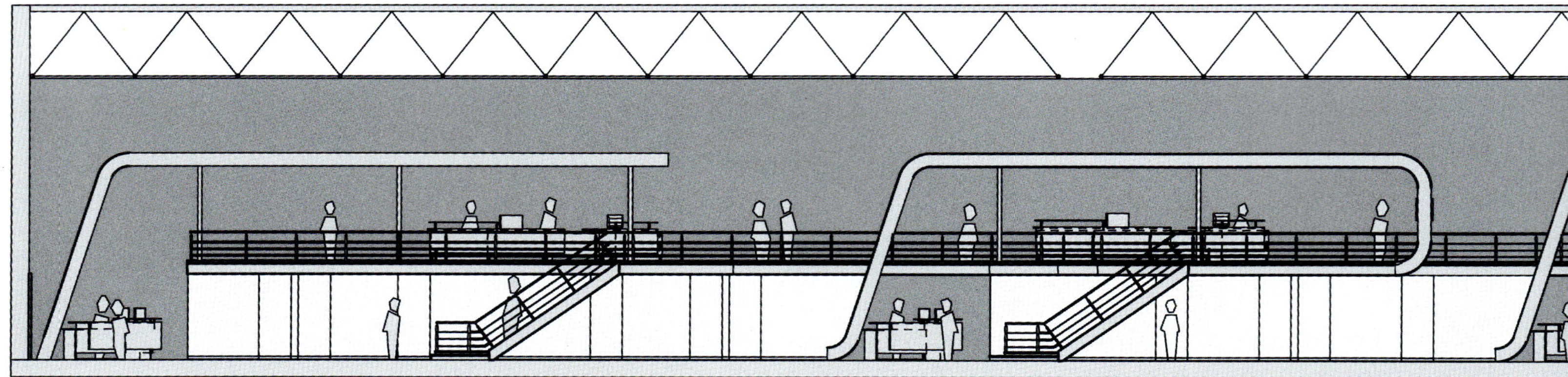

Heidelberger Druckmaschinen AG

Atelier Markgraph GmbH

The project called for the design and excecution of a very large corporate presentation space (at the DRUPA 2000 trade fair) for a traditional, yet highly future-oriented printing press manufacturer. The client also wished to communicate a new brand identity, both within the company and externally, to customers.
This massive, full height space fills two halls, occupying a total of 10,000m² of surface area, and includes an external pavilion, a VIP lounge in the outside area and an adjoined Solution Center.
Here, corporate architecture, the direct use of corporate design, media and communication all form a unified whole.

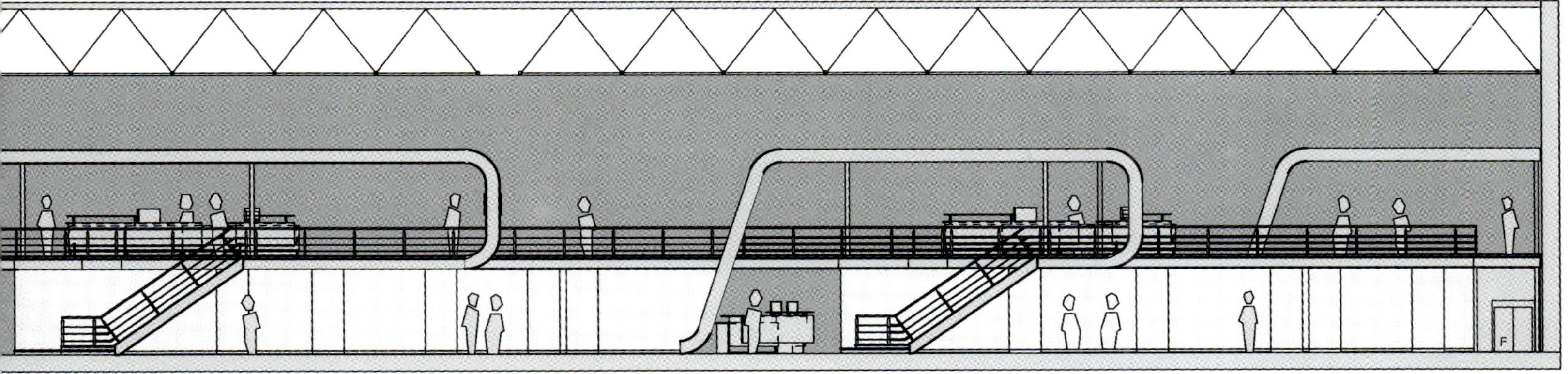

The central design principle is that the architecture should symbolically simulate the movement of paper during the printing process. The easy to recognize, three-dimensional language of shapes creates communication zones, while a generous amount of space has been dedicated to the exhibition of the company's machines within the presentation area. The basic architectural elements can be used flexibly for various purposes.

Rapid new developments at Heidelberg suggested the need for a corresponding new strategy in trade fair communications, one which would be built around comprehensive, long-term corporate communication, with corporate values as the foundation and dialogue with customers at the forefront.

A finely-tuned overall concept of architecture, design and presentation materials was created. The concept provides an approachable, comprehensible scenario which actively supports visitors as they come across the new solutions presented. In the process, it gives a memorable, unique face to both the style and content of Heidelberg's new corporate identity. The concept speaks for the traditional brand values of solidity, trust, strength and proximity; yet also paves the way for a new image as a solution-oriented, forward-looking company.

The concept of the corporate architecture is inspired by the way paper moves through the printing press. A flexible system is created from basic architectonic shapes, and can be adapted as necessary to different locations and demands.

Arranging these architectonic structures creates spaces for products or live presentations, as well as a quiet, pleasant atmosphere for personal talks with clients.

Photographs: Vaclav Reischl

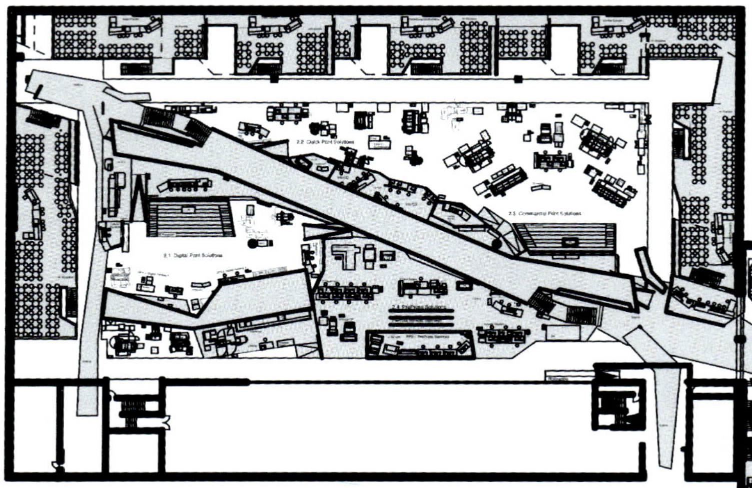

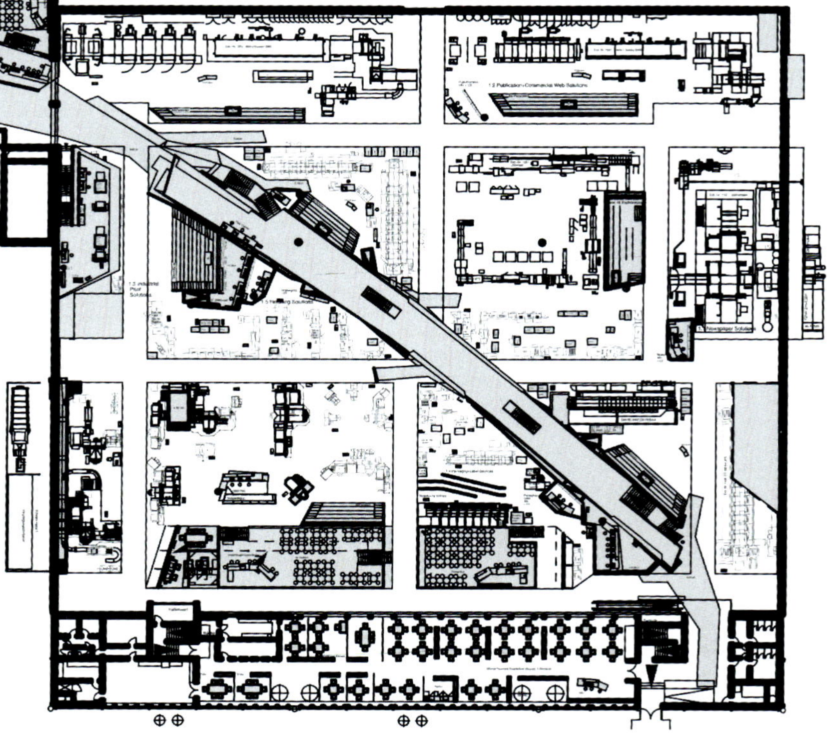

Floor plan

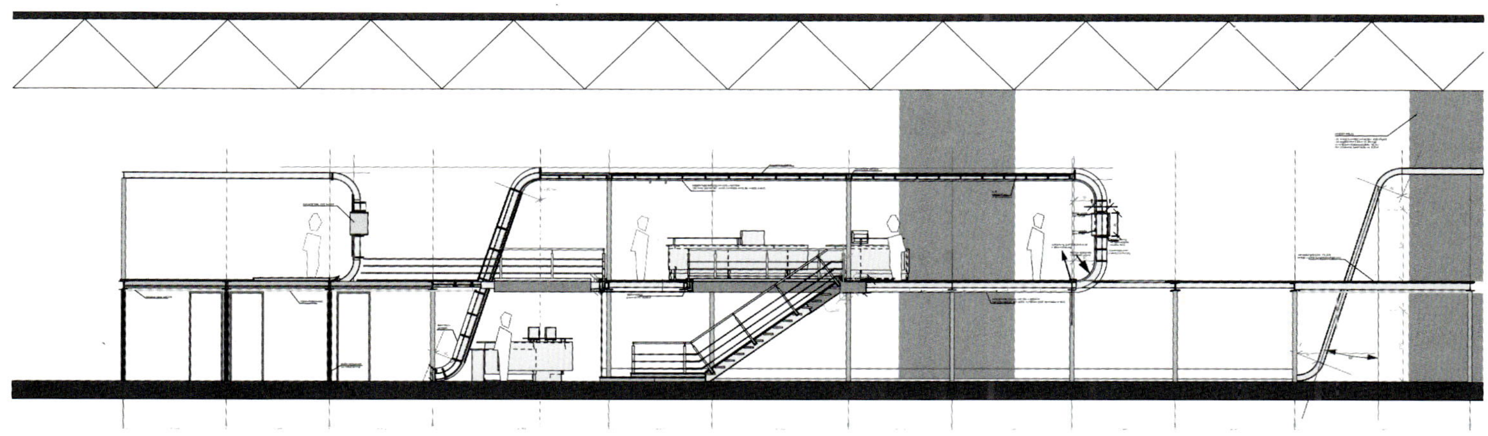

Cross section

Mero

3e-Werner Sobek Ingenieure

The shell of the nautilus consists of a logarithmic helix that grows in the same proportion longitudinally and laterally and adapts itself to the growing animal.
The fascinating complexity and adaptive ability of the nautilus shell gave the idea for the design of the Mero stand at the 'Euroshop 2002' fair.
The central element of this exhibition stand is a 3 dimensionally curved, semi-transparent wall-like shell, which is 28m long and between 4.5m and 5.2m high. The loadbearing structure of this shell consists of individual bars (1306 in total), which are screwed into standardized joint elements (477 in total). The orientation of the threaded holes in the nodes and the various lengths of bar allow an unlimited range of geometries to be produced without compromising the economy of the system. This new system allows the architect to design light, curved structures.
The stand's erected wall shell is covered on both sides with a plastic foil, which was subsequently stabilized by vacuum. The resulting folds in the foil are intentional and produce a specific surface texture. The special effect of this surface is amplified by the use of backlighting. The translucence of the foil produces an impression of semi-transparency; objects and persons on the other side of the wall are perceived only as shadows and contours. The stand can also be used as a projection screen and offers almost unlimited possibilities for image projection. In this way an easily erected basic system can form the basis for an extremely variable exhibition stand with strong poetic effect.

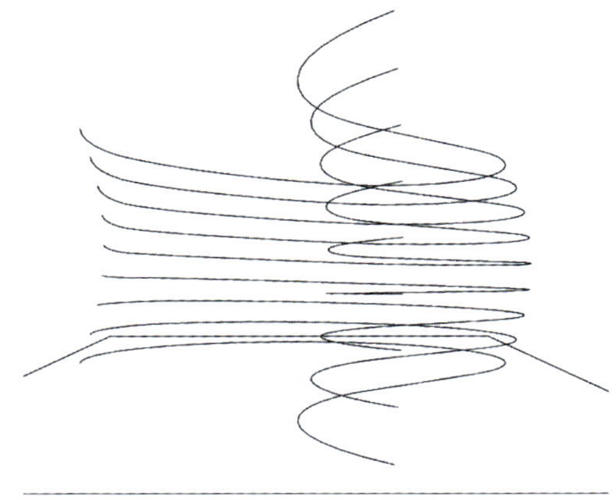

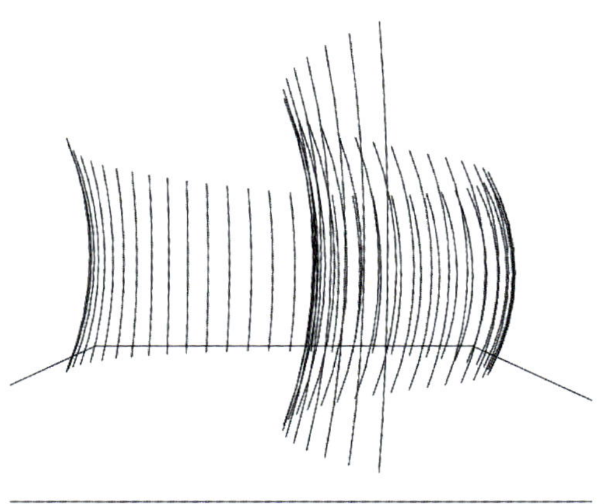

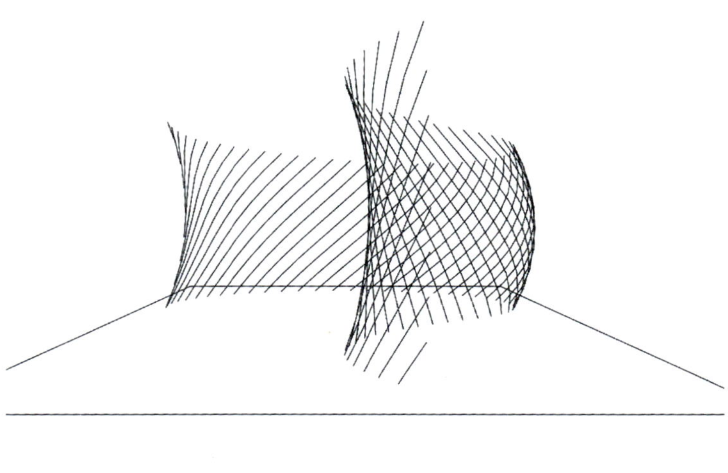

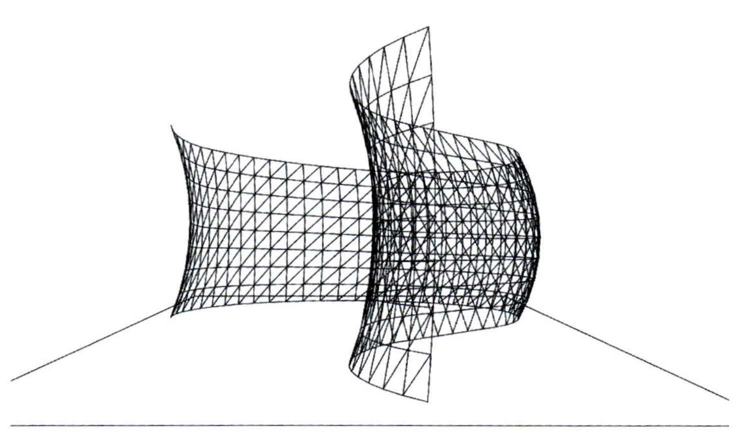

Photographs: Arthur Agency

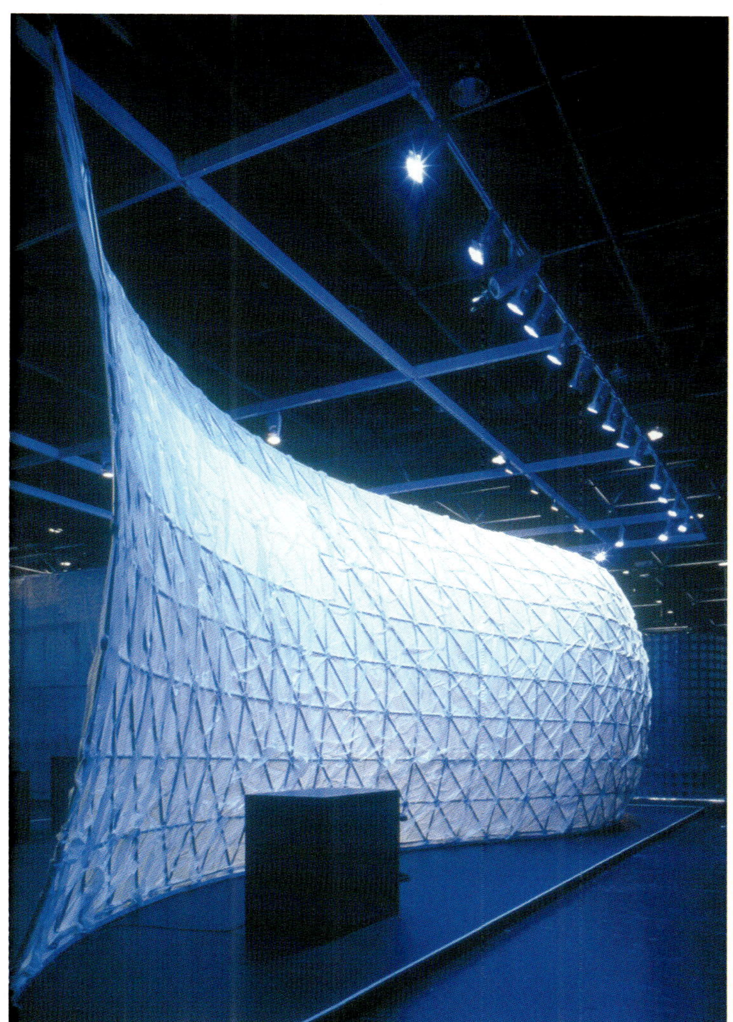

9
A
18

YelloMiles GmbH

Atelier Markgraph GmbH

The aim of this design was to attract the attention of Düsseldorf's GDS 2000 audience to the debut fair presentation for the new brand, YelloMiles. It was essential not only to introduce the new product line but also to clearly establish the brand's image. An atmospheric, brand-consistent space for communication and experience was conceived, with the primary function of facilitating dialogue with potential customers.

The corner location of the stand was emphasized by the straightforward arrangement and implementation of right angles. A sense of steadfastness was achieved through the contrast of the bright display area and the mysterious, reserved black glass around it – solid yet almost floating. Visitors approaching the stand saw a cube clad in black glass on two sides that seemed to be floating within a wooden frame.

The light-emitting display implemented LED and photocomposition to show films, which in both content and form communicated the action of stepping out.

The 10-meter-long, rear illuminated glass bar, which constantly changed its color, was the central element of the interior space. The shoes themselves were presented in anodized aluminum flightcases that were movable and could be opened flexibly. This enabled not only free object compositions of paths and spaces on the inside of the black cube but also adaptability in response to different spatial situations.

Once an hour, the display window for product exhibition was lowered and revealed a show window of unusual format: 11m wide by 50cm high. In cooperation with theater, music and dance professionals, a dynamic show of footwork was performed featuring YelloMiles shoes with yellow lines on their soles.

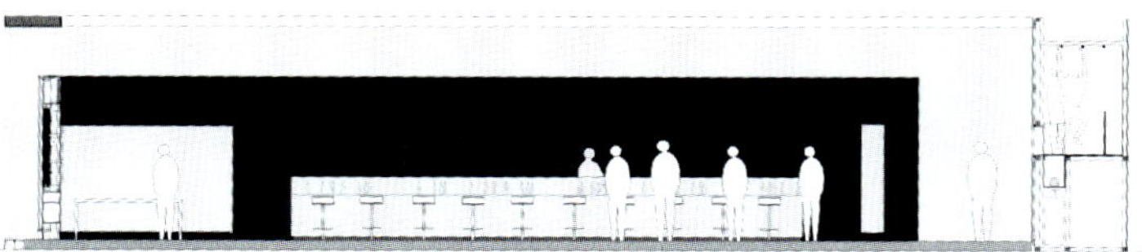

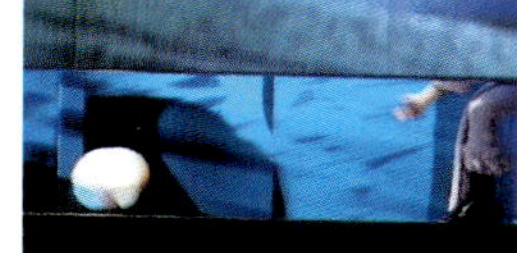

Photographs: Vaclav Reischl

10
ination unknown

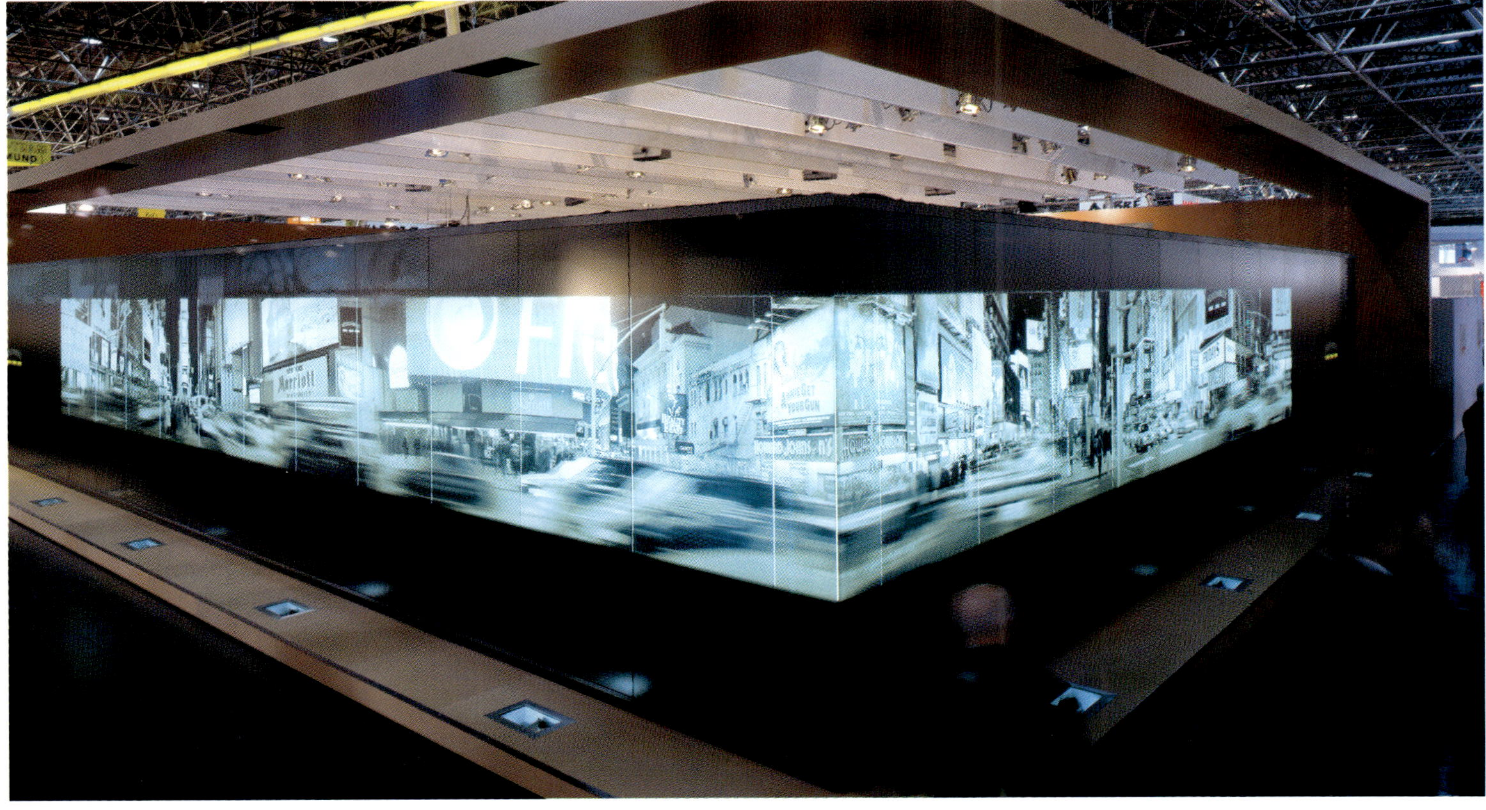
Marriott

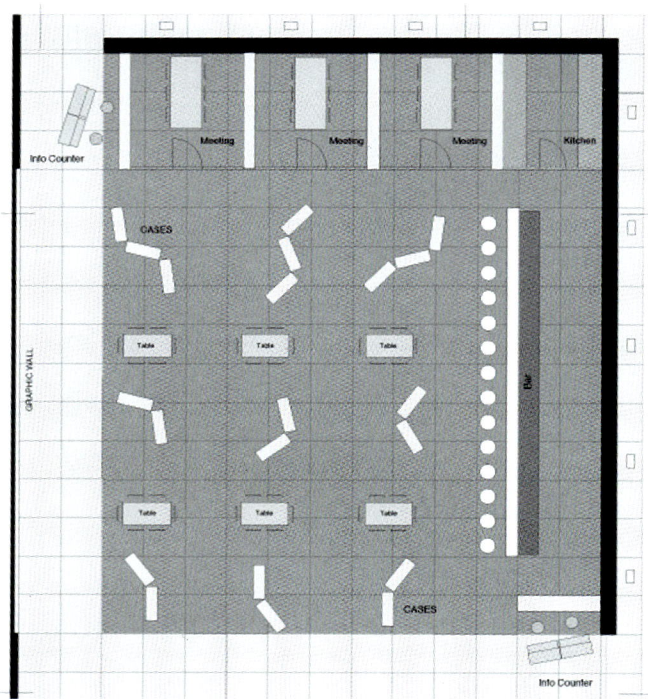

Floor plan

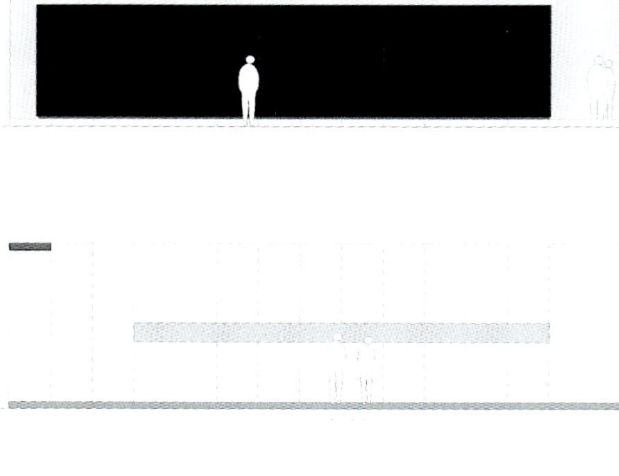

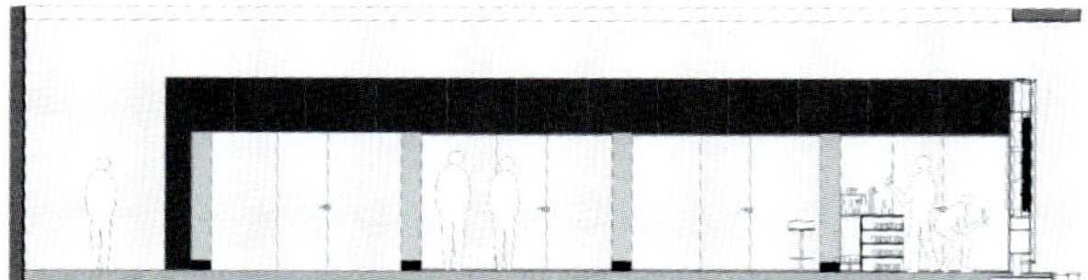
Cross sections

YELLOMILES

An interplay of geometric structures and the application of a range of warm colors are the key design principles behind the stylistic identity for atg's stand at 'CeBIT 2001' in Hanover.

The shape of the mobile structure is based on the company's corporate identity and includes service desks, storage rooms and information counters.

To attract visitors and create a striking visual impact from a distance, the cubes have been colored in warm tones, such as soft yellow, acid orange and light red and have been brightly lit from within.

This display stands out as a sculptural piece and an enhanced three-dimensional space for customers.

atg. Art Technology Group

Kurz + Partner Architekten

Photographs: Andreas Keller, Altdorf

Cross section

Océ

Formpol AG

On exhibit at Drupa 2000 (in Düsseldorf), the world's largest printing and publishing trade show, this stand for the manufacturer of copy systems and printing machines consisted of two very different parts. One was an exhibit area for the machines and the presentation of the company; the other was reserved for the free presentation of a particular theme. The exhibit has been laid out with an interesting mixture of single and two-story volumes.

An exhibit on the theme of "Paper" takes place in a narrow hallway, of which one wall was made of stacked paper. Since this company also runs a paper laboratory, its results and processes in paper research are displayed in graphic form along this hallway. Not only did the theme of paper influence the making of the stand's walls, but also the contents (art objects made from paper) of the cabinets that are integrated into the piled paper wall.

Floor plans

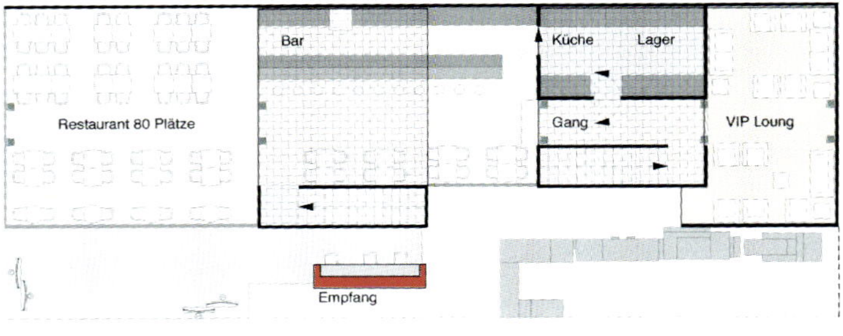

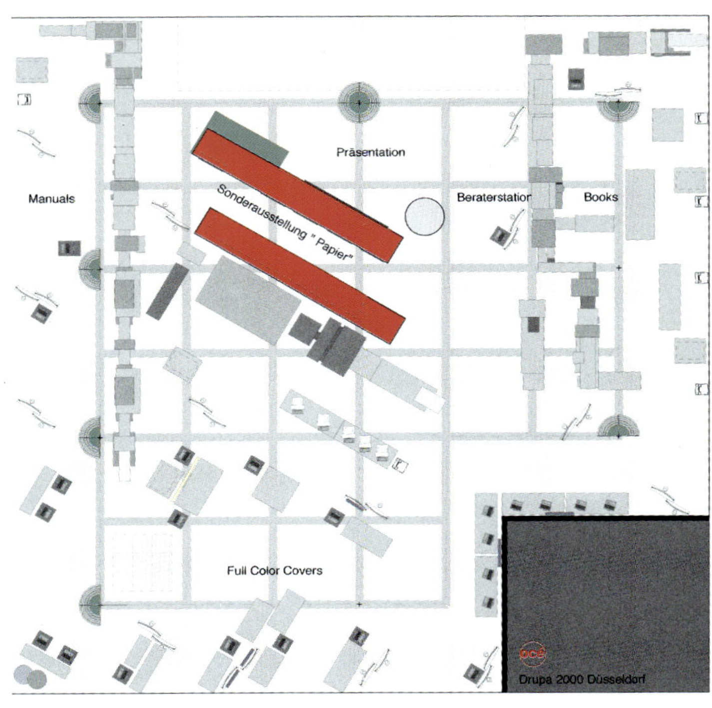

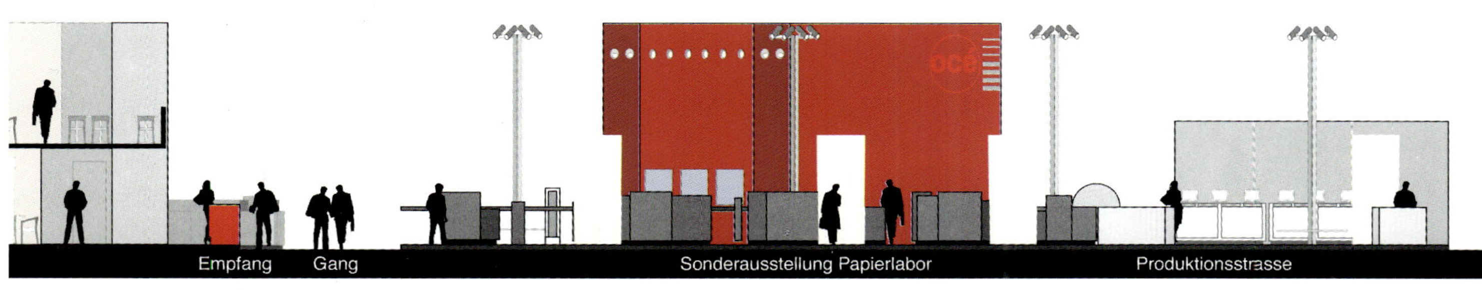

Photographs: Markus Mahle

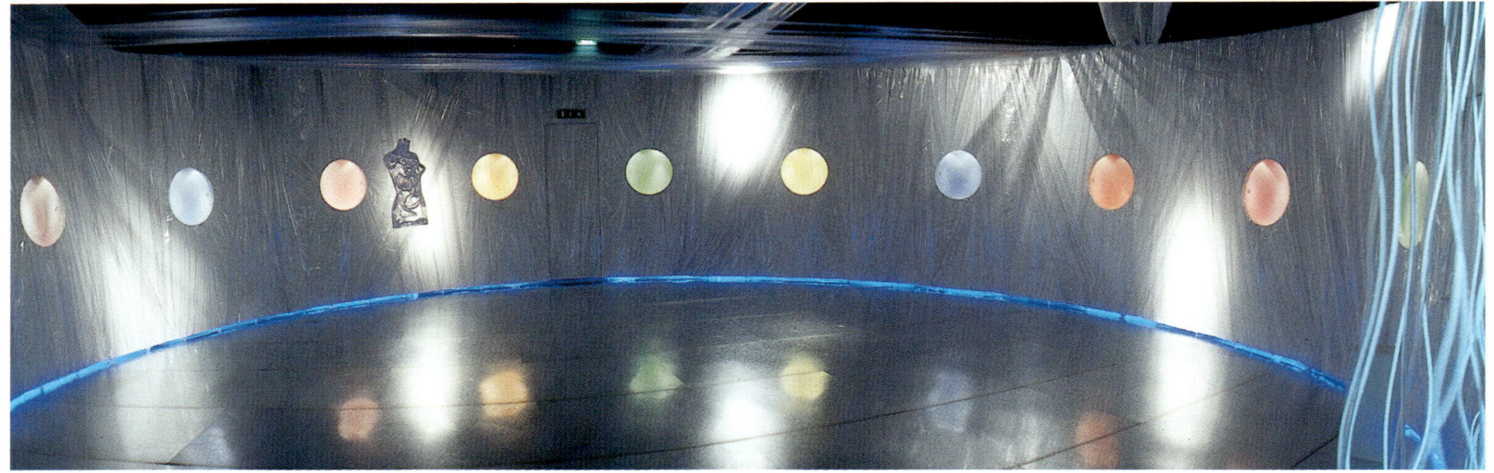

Appendi-Minimo

Simone Micheli

The occasion for this stand was 'Abitare il tempo '98' (in Verona), a trade show for trends and innovations in home decorating. An eye-catching optical fiber curtain introduces the stand, immediately showing its prevailing spirit: 'a declared dynamic of color, light and movement'.
Through this futuristic drapery, visitors are cast into a circular setting where, thanks to neutral colored materials, a zinc-plated iron floor, a ceiling made from broad interlaced strips of cellophane, and dramatic lighting, they are given the improbable and unreal impression of finding themselves inside a larger-than-life iridescent soap bubble. A life-size, transparent plastic dummy is suspended from a central position, acting as a concrete sign of the coat hanger, the fulcrum around which the whole composition rotates. The area is encompassed by a blue neon light that follows the line of the wall, which features twelve 'portholes' with opal-polycarbonate sliding shutters, hiding the proposed objects behind them. Each porthole is defined by varied coloring and emits sound, as if to emphasize the heterogenous elements involved in the display.
The whole setting has been conceived as an attractive showcase for a series of wall coat-hangers, whose designers are quite distinguished for their style, provenance and cultural diversity: a maze of different voices, to be gathered into the same harmonic chorus.

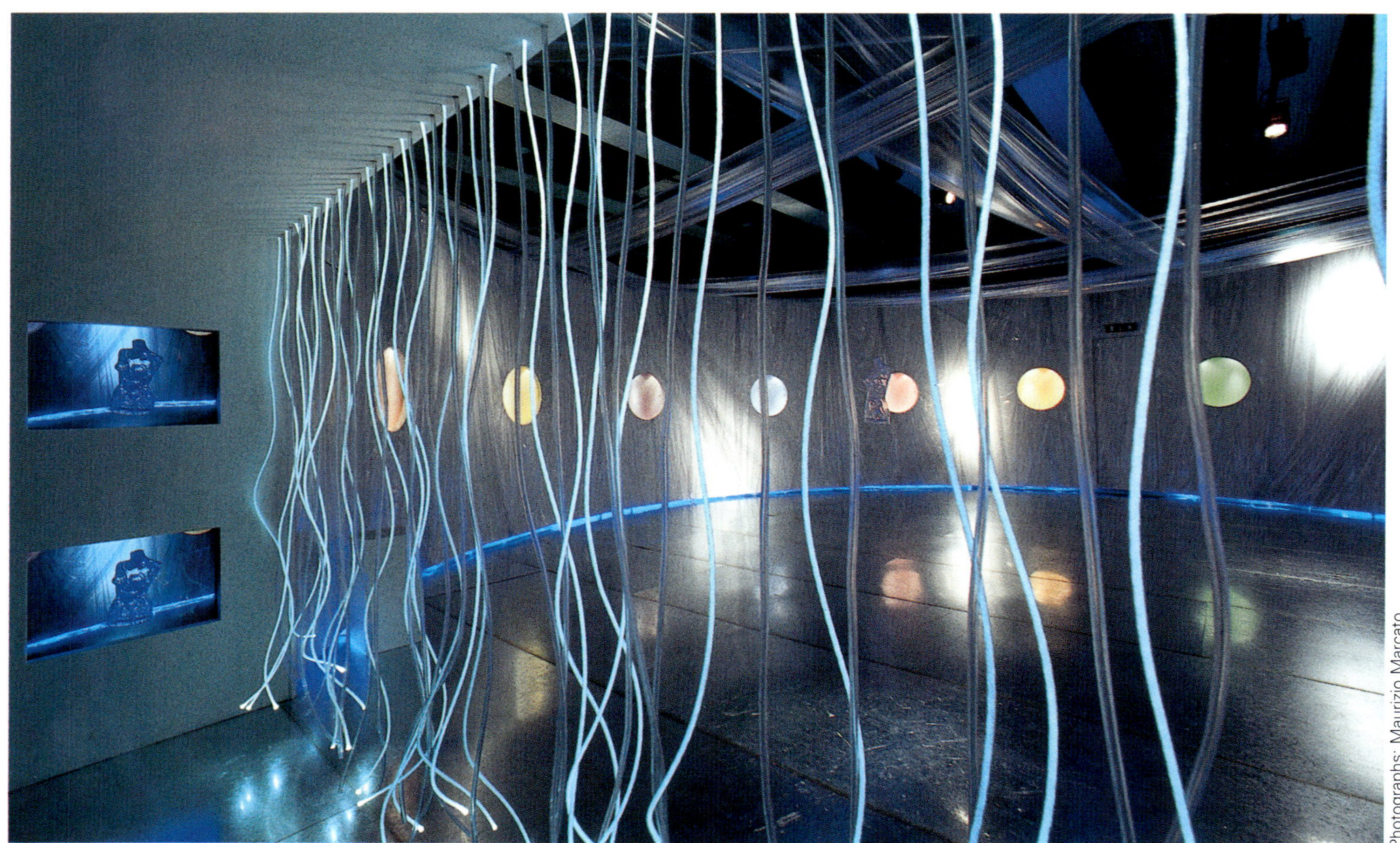

Photographs: Maurizio Marcato

Windsor
Arno design

This stand is characterized by contrasting light and dark tones. It is a transparent and detailed stand which can be varied according to the collection; and its shape can be adapted to different trade fairs.
It is made up of large, luminous, glazed acrylic walls printed with motifs from the print campaign that have been put up in intervals along the walls, and which allow a glimpse into the stand's interior. Inside, there are niches for product presentation. These are complemented by two low presentation tables at the entrance axis, and by brightly-lit, glazed acrylic tables with rounded corners.
The dark, treated-oak back wall and flooring create a contrast to these shining elements. With integrated plasma screens and a prominent high-grade steel logo, the back wall conceals functional rooms such as the tea kitchen and storage room. A peep-in strip has been cut into the exterior face; inside, this strip becomes a pattern on the lounge wall, which is furnished with felt cubes.

Photographs: Frank Kotzerke

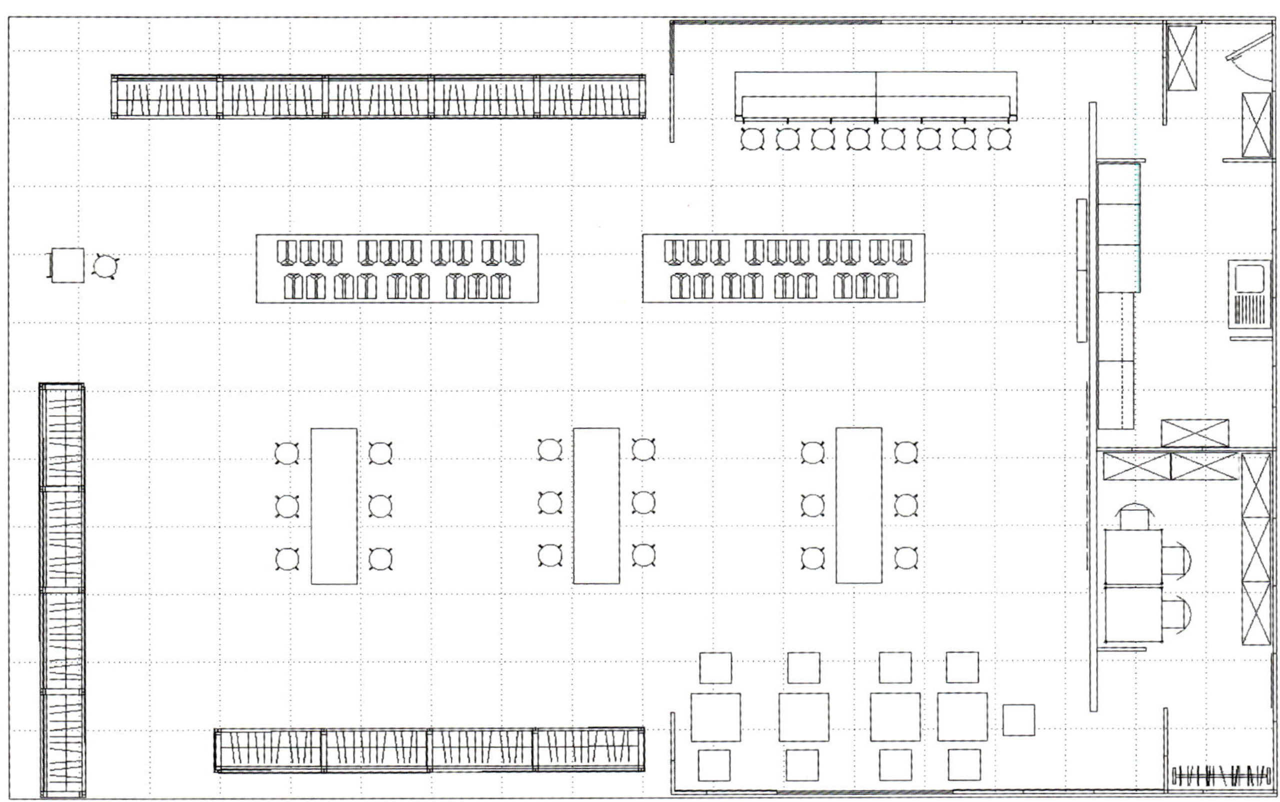

Floor plan

windsor.
windsor.

windsor.

windsor.

Bisazza

Fabio Novembre

The stand for these specialists in ceramic tiles at Cersaie 2002, the international exhibition of bathroom furnishings and ceramics, ingeniously displays the company's product via a walk-in maze of curvilinear walls where color is king.

Although the stand's available floor area was a simple square, Novembre managed to create a fluid, non-uniform and eye-catching stand, which has been divided into two principal spaces: one for the exhibit itself, and a sitting area set along the curved outer wall of the exhibit.

The exhibit space consists of four independent walls which spiral in upon each other. These walls are clad in Bisazza's opus vetricolor tiles, while the floors are covered in geometric designs composed of the company's logos metron line of tile.

At each of the exhibit's three entrances, the walls begin just above head height, but gradually ascend and swirl together toward a higher pinnacle in the center, which is visible even from a distance. As each wall (and corresponding corridor) is composed of a different color (either blue, red or green), the overall visual effect from the exterior of this ascending spiral is an ingenious device for drawing the attention of visitors.

Once inside the exhibit, the visitor is in a visually stimulating world, where the decorative value of the product on display is made manifest.

The company's ceramic tiles also adorn the walls and flooring of the sitting area, although, here, a more subtle color has been chosen in order to avoid sensory overload.

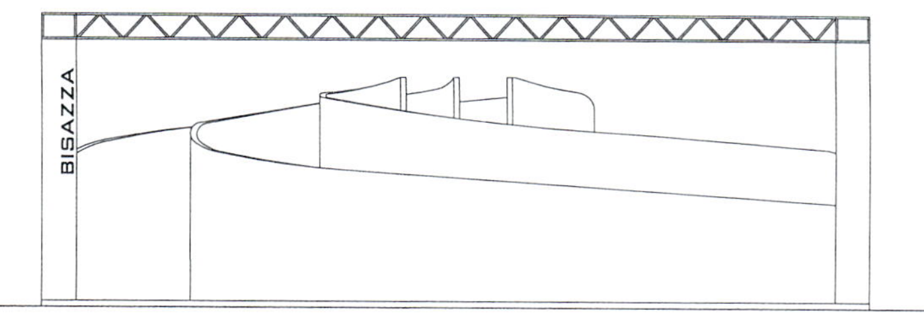

Elevation

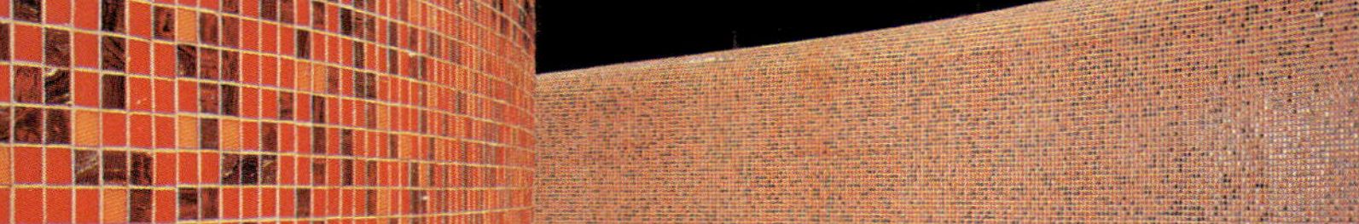

Floor plan

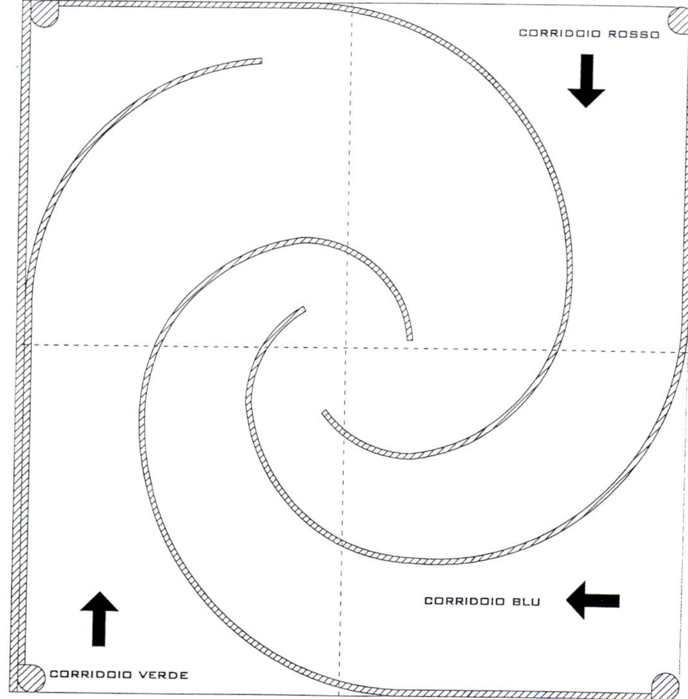

Photographs: Alberto Ferrero

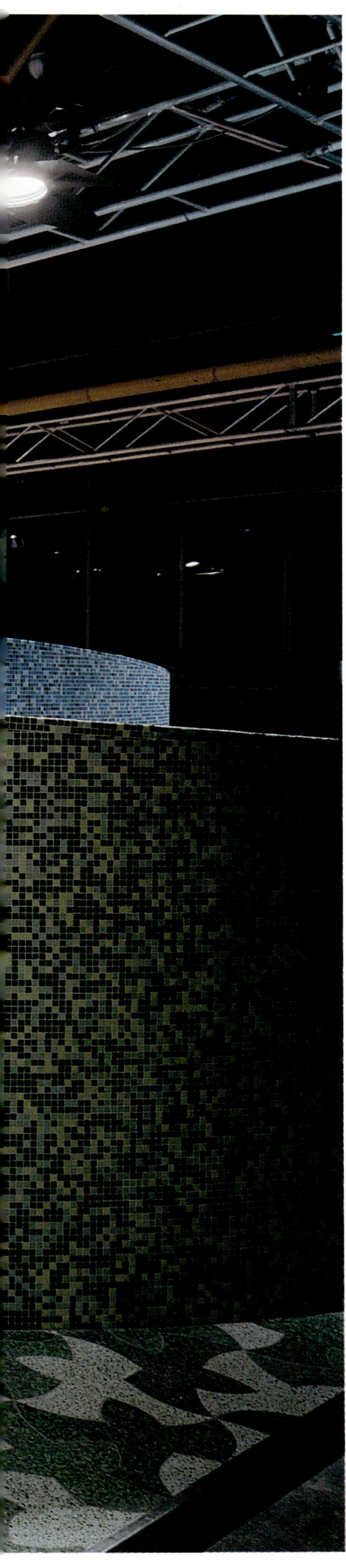

Gandia Blasco

Ramón Esteve

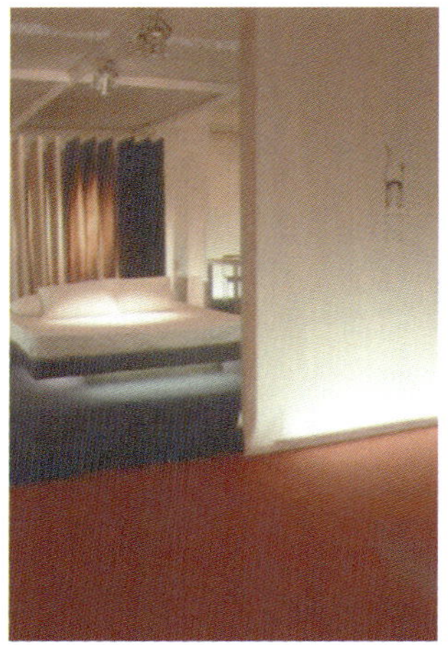

Featuring but a few, highly economical resources, this stand is a good example of the axiom that "less is more". The spaces in this simple, yet effective, stand are defined by floor-to-ceiling expanses of off-white colored cloth which are lit from below.

A metal structure composed of rectangular section profiles, which have been coated in white epoxy paint, serve as a light framework for the decorative elements.

The floor lamps and cloth grant a sense of levity and warmth, making the stand seem to float above the floor of the fair.

The company's corporate information is affixed to these cloth walls, which also allow visitors to glimpse the products on display within the stand, drawing them in to discover what is concealed on the other side.

The different areas of the exhibit and the storage space are uniformly delimited via expanses of cloth, thereby creating a sensual and relaxing atmosphere.

Spotlighting subtly directed toward the products completes the stand's lighting elements. The products are displayed on a base of phenol-treated particle board clad in forest green carpeting.

Potographs: Ramón Esteve

Elevation

Floor plan

Microsoft

Artek

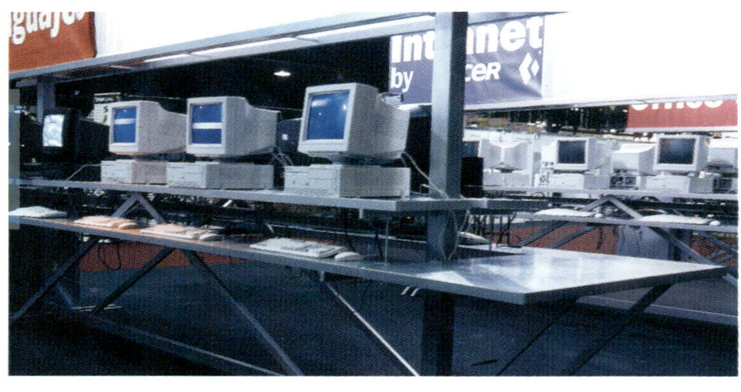

Between 1996 and 2000, all the Microsoft stands were based on the law of 'signs': they resemble giant index cardholders, highway signs or picket lines.
The majority of Microsoft stands are open and do not have interiors. They are almost urban. In fact, they use urban elements, such as streets, parks, diagonals and signalling.
The space stand at 'Computación 1997' was based on the recurrence of an action: the individual who approaches the machine to entering into conversation. The space is long and rectangular and, with fifty computers in a row, divided diagonally. Two triangular courtyards on both sides provide areas where people gather to use the programs.
The Microsoft stands are popular and informal, with no hierarchy, no VIP areas, reflecting the image of their products. However, the stand identity switches gears when it is involved in management exhibits. The design elements are posed at managerial or financial level, delimiting different business areas with closed spaces, different floor levels and the neutral use of colors.

Photographs: Andrea Arrighi

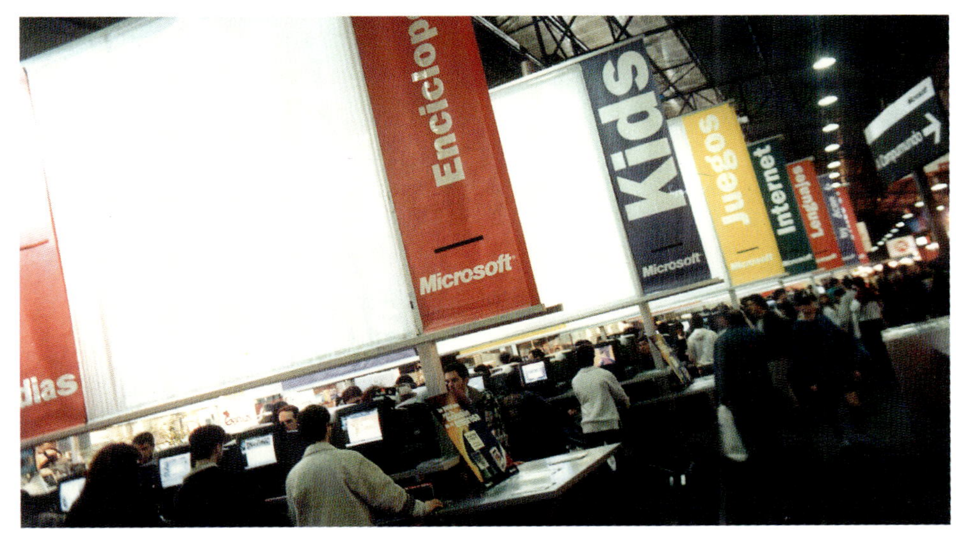

Enciclop
Kids
Juegos
Internet
Lenguajes
Microsoft
dias

Microsoft
Kids
Kids
Microsoft
Juegos
Microsoft
Internet
Microsoft
Lenguajes
Microsoft
Intranet
Texas Instruments

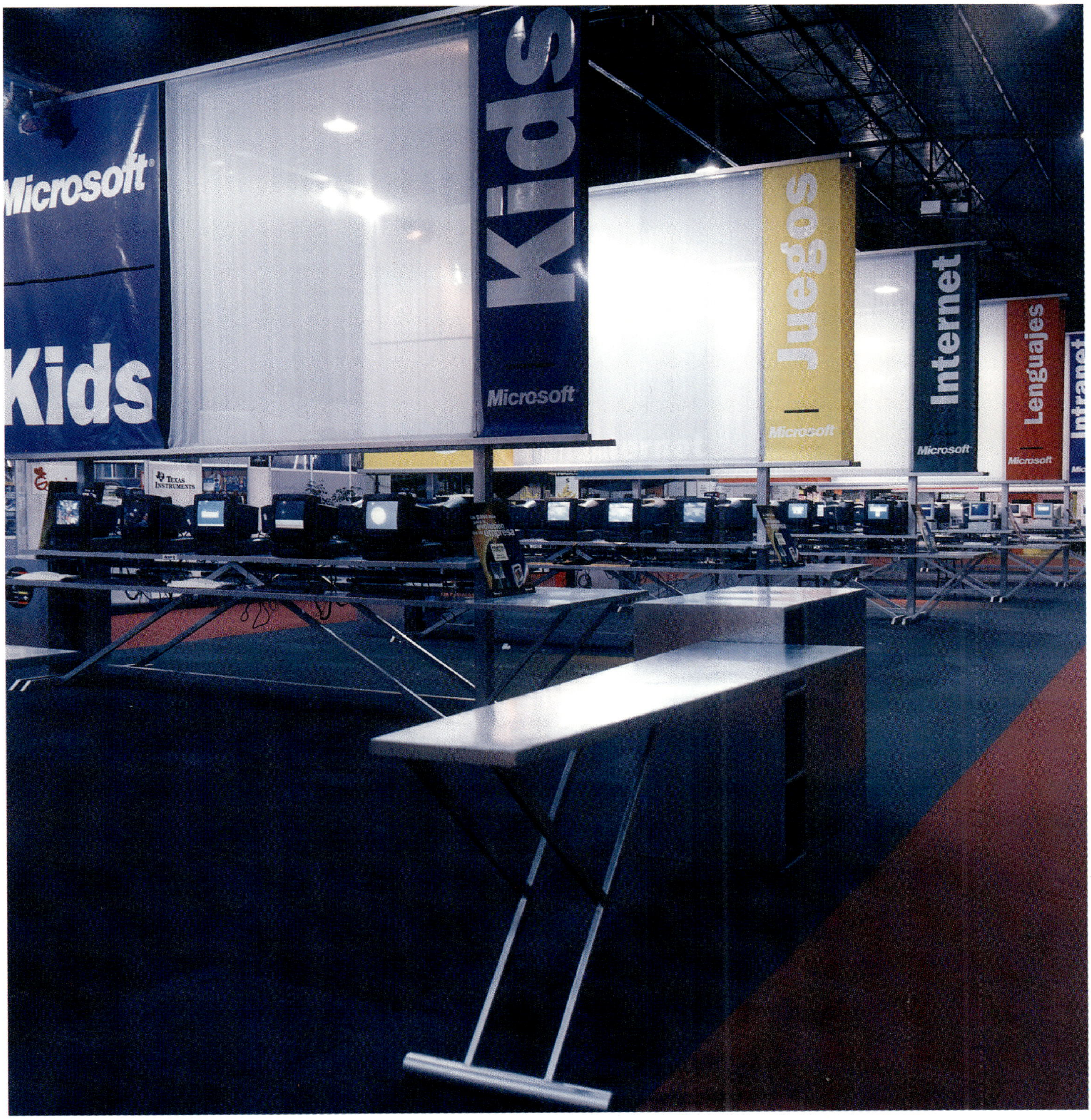

Layetana

saeta estudi. Pere Ortega, Bet Cantallops & Margarida Costa-Martins

The original project was based on the complementary concepts of a "closed box" and of an "interior stage set", both of which would arouse interest and curiosity among visitors at the trade fair.

The final design elaborated on this original idea by proposing a perimetral skin of glowing light. Changing colors and innovative lighting techniques have turned this stand's initial hermetic nature into a box shape, which is nonetheless in continuous communication with the spectator through the interior walkways.

To bring this idea to fruition, a material was sought which would act both as a light emitter and receiver, as well as comprise a high quality facade. The outer skin is a strict modulation of translucent polycarbonate plates, while the same material, here in a bronze color, covers the vertical planes and ceiling in the interior.

In this case, the polycarbonate was directly applied to a support (which has been painted dark brown) which forms a coherent exhibition space, yet one which is different from the exterior. Here, controlled lighting in soothing tones sets this space a world apart from the fair's visual overload.

The company's logo and name had to be substantially separated from the exterior lighting for it to stand out. Six television screens bearing the logo, which vibrates like a video in stand-by mode, have been affixed in an orderly fashion around the stand. This option boldly draws attention to the name of the company and physically separates it from the lighted skin.

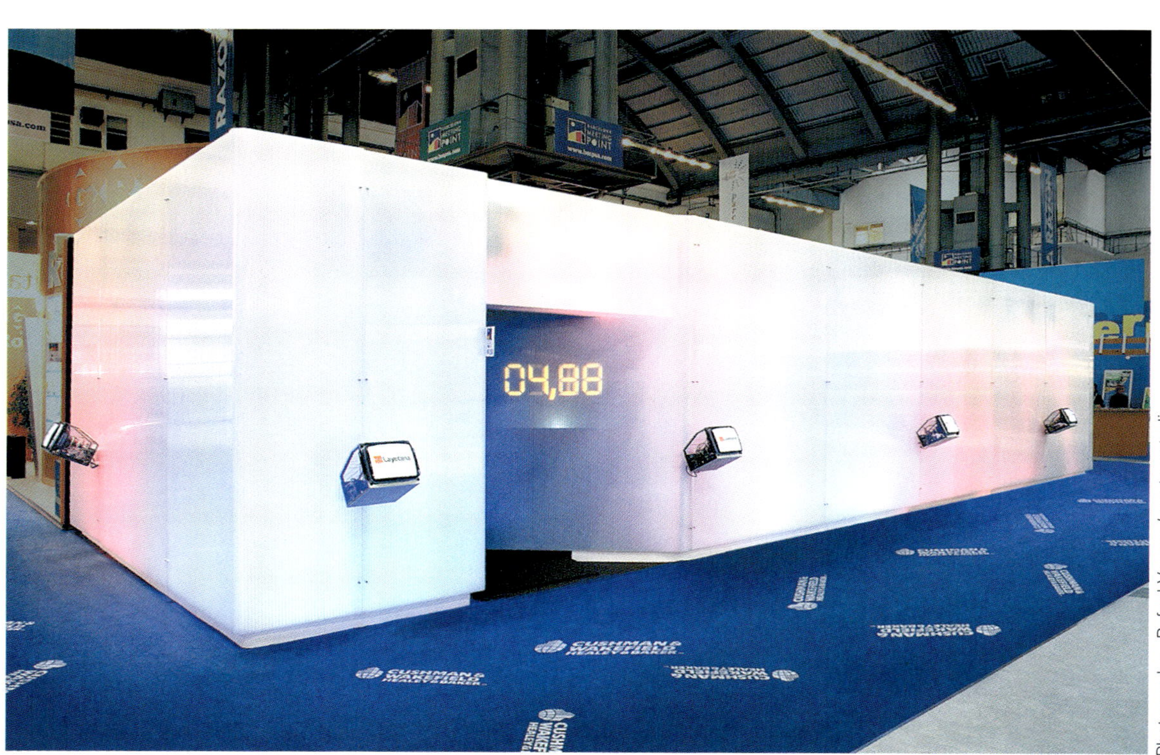

Photographs: Rafael Vargas / saeta estudi

Pensamos que así se hacen buenos negocios.
¿Podemos hacer algo juntos?
We believe that this is how good business is done.
Can we do something together?
Podem fer alguna cosa junts?

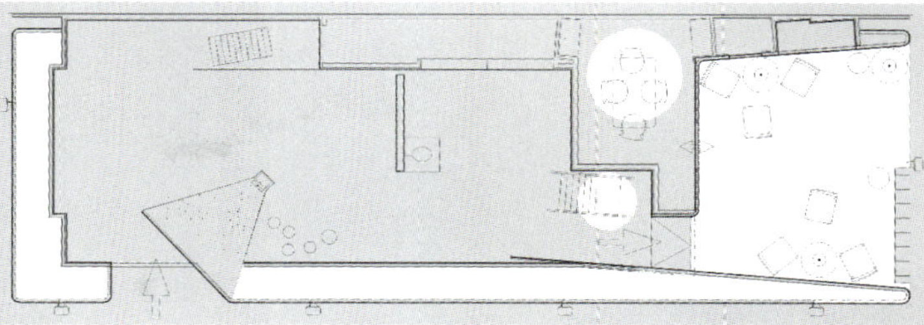

Deseamos que degustes la buena arquitectura.
We believe architecture should be savoured.
Desitgem que degustis la bona arquitectura.

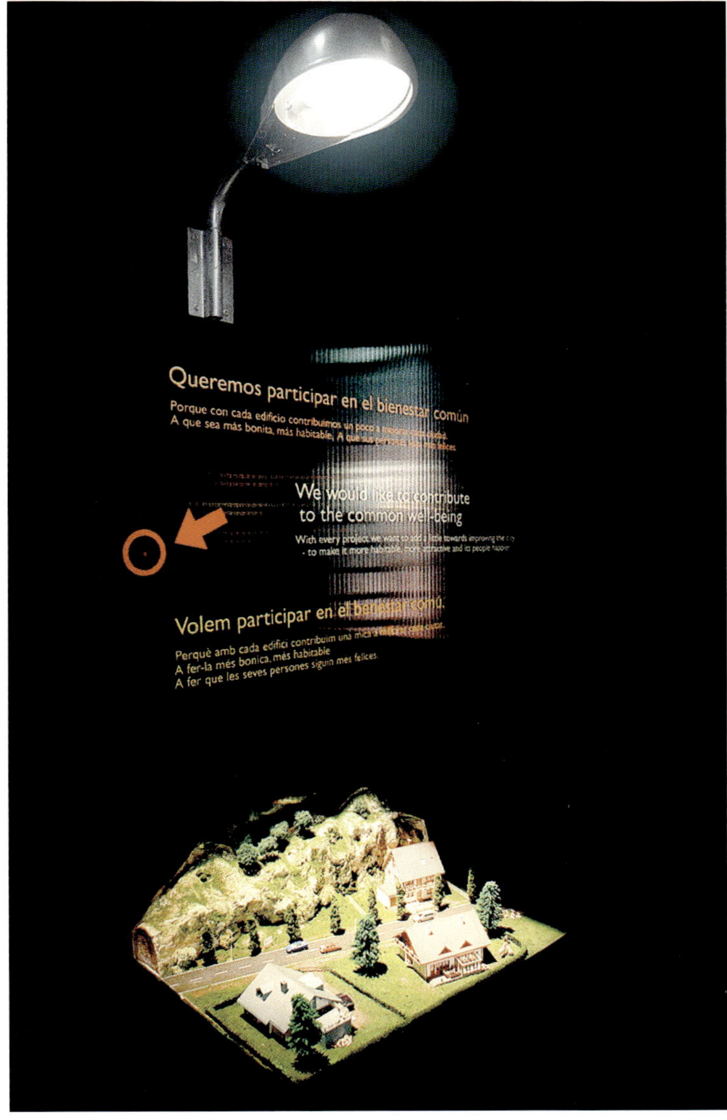
Queremos participar en el bienestar común
We would like to contribute
to the common well-being
Volem participar en el benestar comú.
A fer-la més bonica, més habitable
A fer que les seves persones siguin més felices.

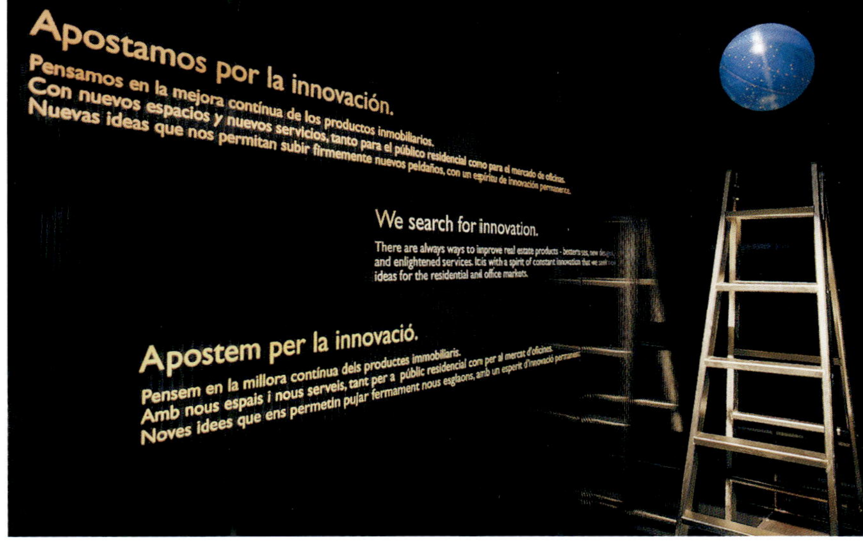
Apostamos por la innovación.
Pensamos en la mejora contínua de los productos inmobiliarios.
We search for innovation.
Apostem per la innovació.
Pensem en la millora contínua dels productes immobiliaris.

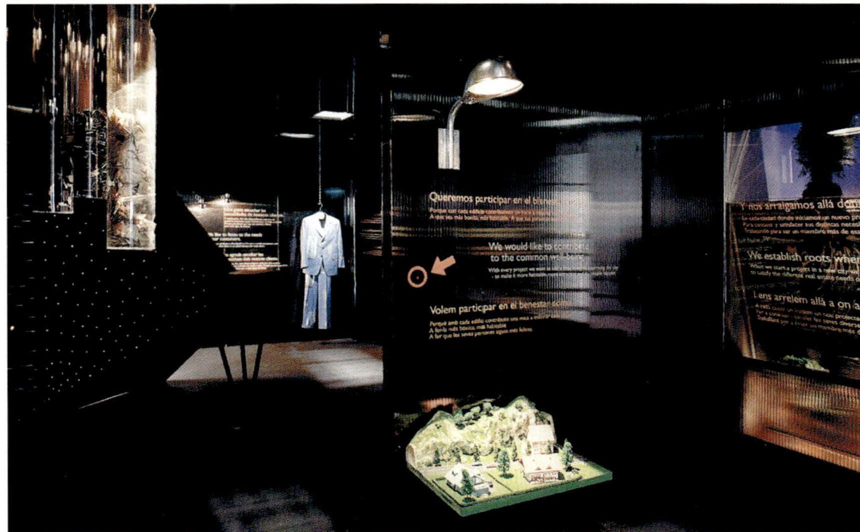

Grundig

Arno design

In spite of this stand's being divided into sectors, the first glance should give visitors an impressive overall insight into the world of Grundig.

The information area has the appearance of an airport lounge in Digitropolis 2020 AD; this space represents the company as a pacemaker in the development of new technologies. The main focus is on the highlights of their latest developments, including the themes: "Grundig goes Digital", "Grundig goes Internet", and "Grundig goes Wireless". The Information Lounge is thematically divided into these three areas. As a consequence, the lounge raises the expectation of heading toward the "digital era".

Long, loosely stacked triangular structures form dynamic improvised walls which, being informational units, prepare visitors for the forementioned highlights. As in an airport, texts, images and monitors provide information on the possibilities and advantages of the new features in a concise and clear manner.

The axially arranged Main Passage is also subdivided into three groups: status, opinion leader, and young and independent. These groups can only be read on the inside; on the outside the entryways have a uniform appearance – a symbol for the "System Thought". Large graphic areas designed according to the respective product groups, using keywords, form the background behind the units. Behind the Main Passage, the worlds of Fine Arts and Accoro can be experienced live, with sound and image technology, in two enclosed areas.

Photographs: Frank Kotzerke

GRUNDIG GOES WIRELESS
GRUNDIG

GRUNDIG

GRUNDIG GOES DIGITAL
GRUNDIG
FASZINATION DURCH
NEUE DIMENSION
FASCINATION IN A NEW DIMENSION
GRUNDIG
GRUNDIG GOES DIGITAL
GRUNDIG
WENN SICH DIGITALE TECHNIK
ZUM SYSTEM VERBINDET
WHEN DIGITAL TECHNOLOGY
CONNECTS TO FORM A SYSTEM

GRUNDIG GOES INTERNET
GRUNDIG
GRUNDIG
GRUNDIG

Bodegas Azabache

Alfredo García Gotós

The creation of this 100m² stand for the Alimentaria 2002 fair was based on spatial rationality and an absolute order. A continuous 16m display window runs the entire length of the space so that the product is visible from any point. With the lights of the stand's general space dimmed and the bottles lit, the sensation of having the product always present is heightened.

The 160 bottles transmit an inviting feeling of being in a wine cellar, while the contrasting tones –red, white, and rosé– provide a soothing hint of color in an otherwise neutral space.

One of the external walls has an opening with the same dimensions as the display window, thereby creating an attractive transparency and providing an enticing glimpse of the goings on inside. The customer service counter and wine-tasting podiums also play into the formal scheme of the stand because they are mobile, enabling quick and easy rearranging, depending on the public's needs.

In order to achieve the total simplification of the space, the design moved away from any architectural stereotype and tried to create a clean, formal, rational, and ordered micro architecture, avoiding the typical fair constructions that contribute very little and seem to repeat the same solutions year after year.

The objective was to create a serious space for a high quality product, where the structure itself would express the desired message.

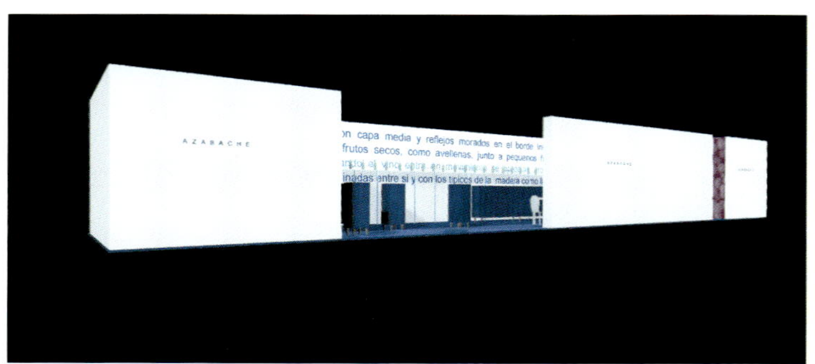

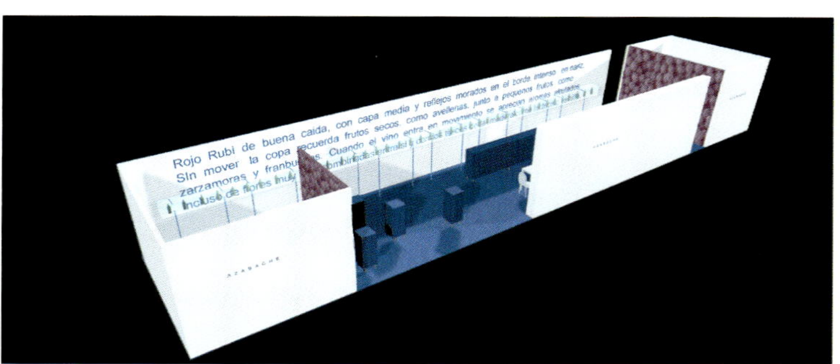

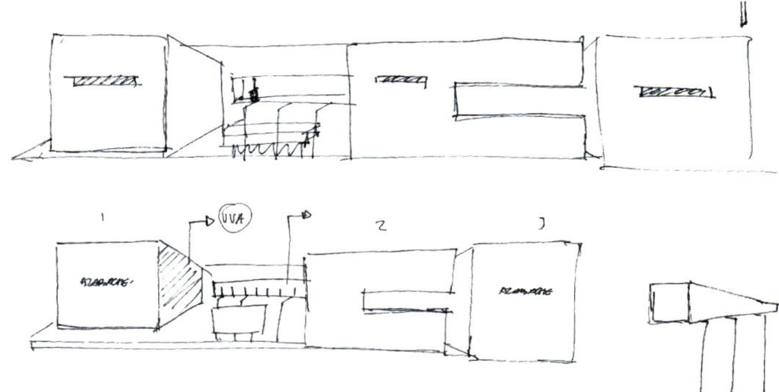

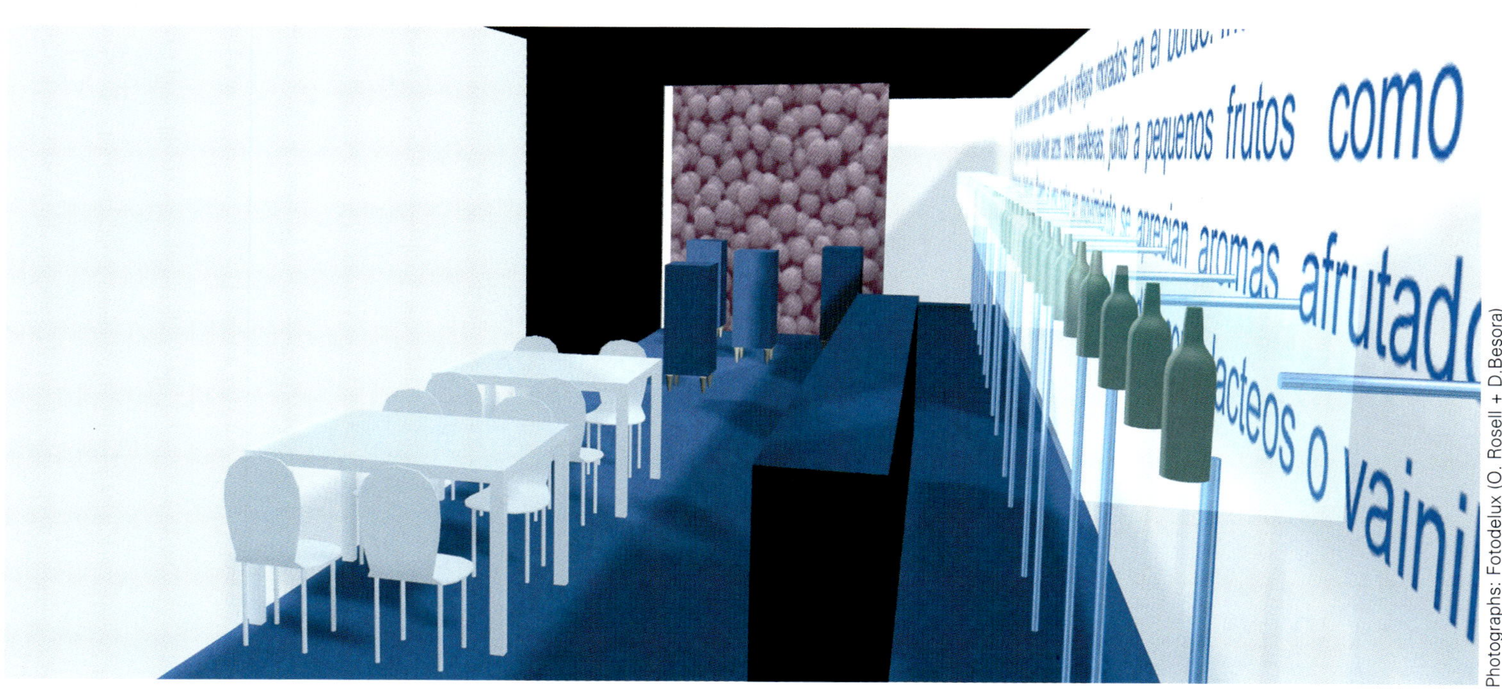

Photographs: Fotodelux (O. Rosell + D.Besora)

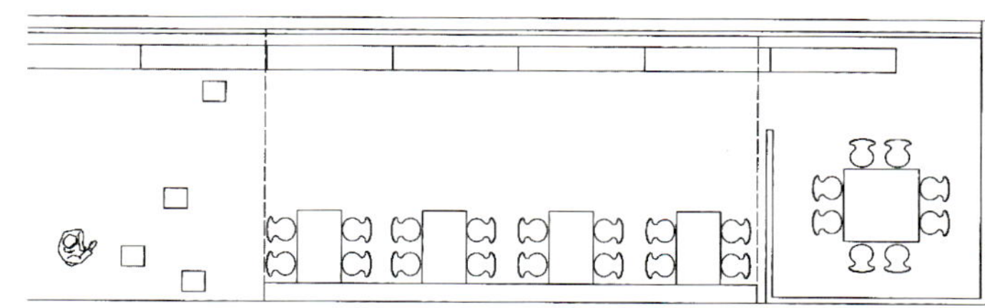

Floor plan

Telefónica

OMB diseño y comunicación visual

This company's work in communications and services (with a high degree of research) formed the basis of the development of a stand for the Fitur '97 trade fair. The decision was thereby made that a bare minimum of physical supports would be sufficient: a container with a short interior labyrinth combining image, text and sound, all displayed via screens and Internet connection terminals.

The final project consisted of a black prismatic box which would be accessed via a white, luminous hall with glass flooring. Large murals help compose this clean space, which is perceived as an interplay of orthogonal lines. Behind the exterior "stage set" is a compact nucleus with a translucent, under-lit floor which marks different routes and discriminates between the different areas.

Projected onto this surface, screens in varying degrees of opacity articulate the different spaces, which finalize in interactive terminals and minimalist fixtures.

An easy to assemble and flexible modular structure serves as the support for a complex technical installation.

Photographs: OMB diseño y comunicación visual

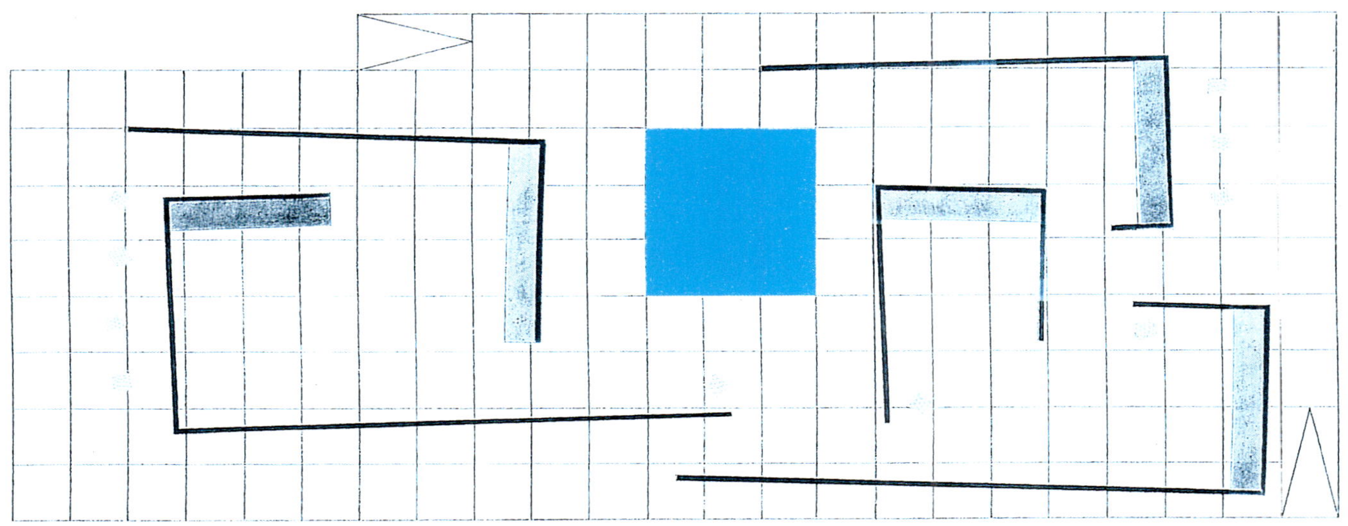
Floor plan

Grupo Telefónica

uestra compañía más grande

medios son
ciones de
alguna
facultad
humana,
psíquica o
física

BMW

ABB Architekten
Bernhard Franken

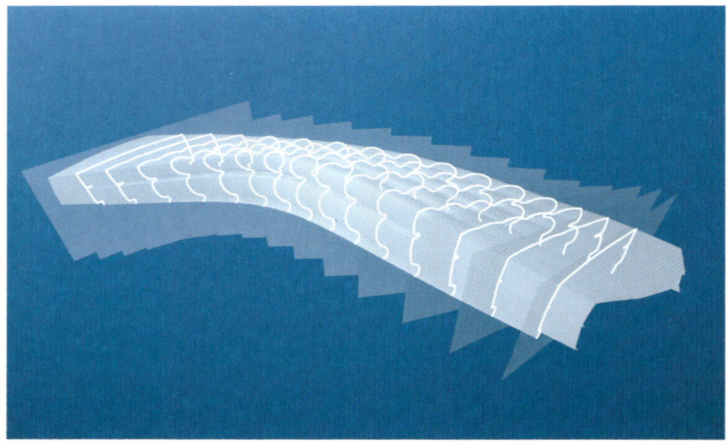

The new BMW exhibit hall is intended to express the company's trademark philosophy: the joy of driving. Although the end purpose of an automobile is movement, they are presented and communicated as stationary objects. To counter this paradox, the space around the automobiles is accelerated so that a sensation of driving is conveyed. To achieve this the Doppler effect was used in the form of passing vehicles; as the car approaches a high tone is heard, replaced by a lower tone after it has passed.

To achieve the framework, intersecting planes are generated in the master geometry and defined as dynaframes, intersecting lines used as a basis for the beam construction. The beams, hollow rectangular structural tubing, were finished and cut using a computer controlled focal ray. To combat the lateral forces in the basic form, all the frames were linked horizontally with tubes and a common one-story space framework that serves as an exhibition area.

The building's skin was stretched horizontally from frame to frame in the pre-given form. Due to the semi-tranparent membrane covering around the base area, the upper two tubes seem to be suspended in air. In contrast to the transparency of the upper area, the form of the base is a reduced area "sucked" firmly between the ground and the first tube.

Despite the complexity of the form, the "Dynaform" (as the exhibition hall was named), appears in its exterior reduced and minimalistic. The topological surface folds upon itself from the ground up to the roof and back down again. All protrusions are clearly detached from the skin of the building by ducts.

In the interior, there is a dramatic linear crossing from east to west of the exhibit area. From the foyer, a staircase leads to a mezzanine level, were the BMW 7-series is revealed shooting out of a quasi space-age tunnel. Behind this, a monumental LED wall display creates a virtual world around the vehicle.

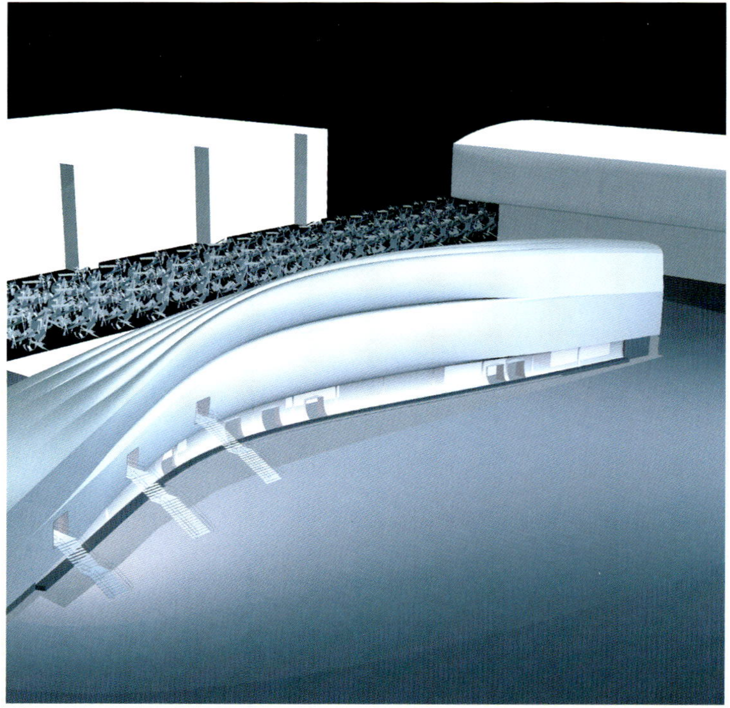

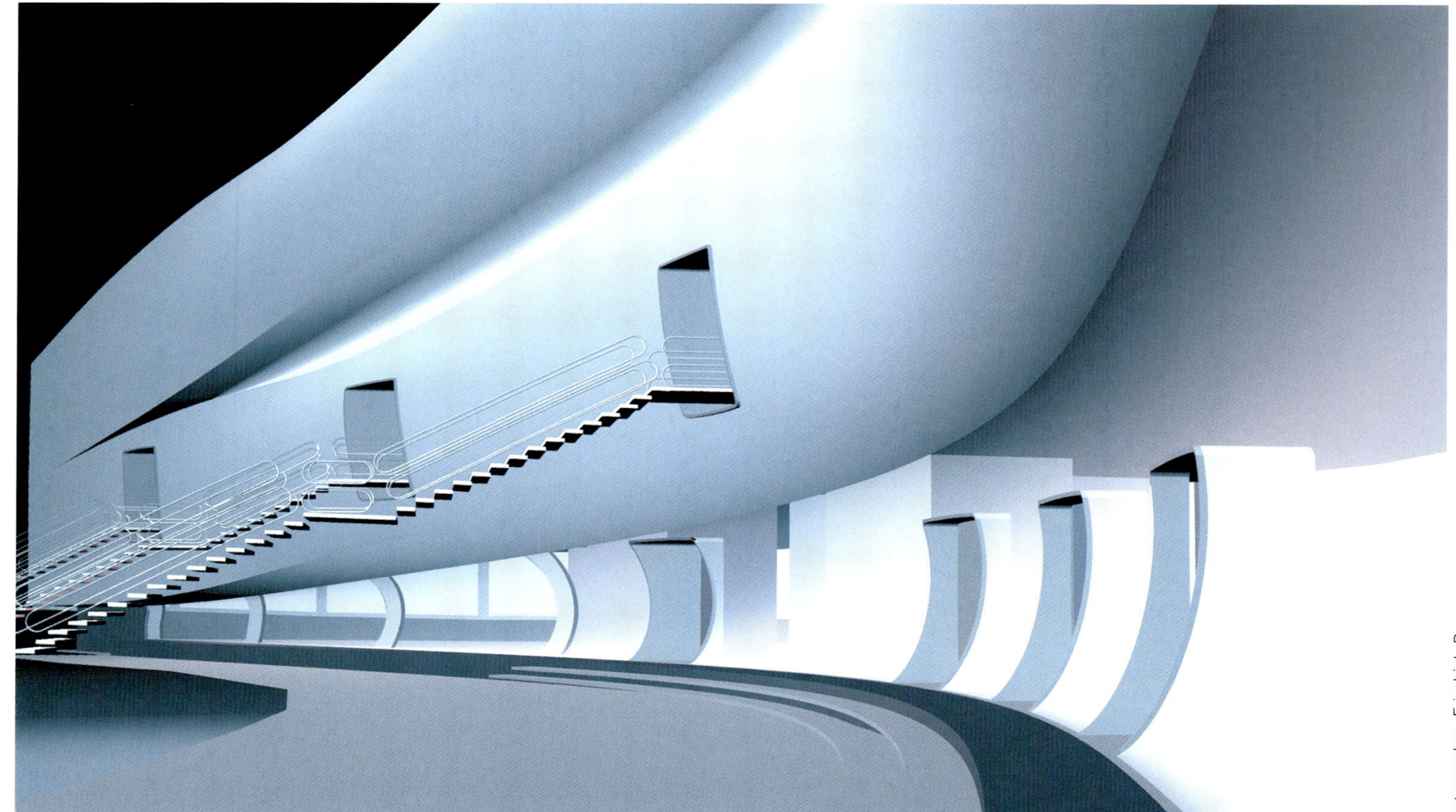

Photographs: Friedrich Busam

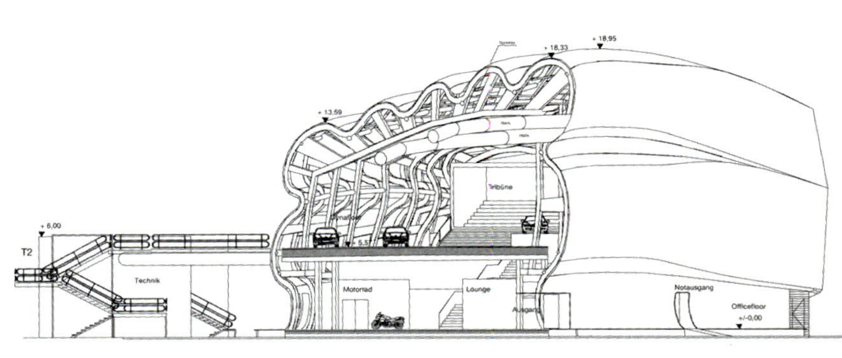
+ 18,95
+ 18,33
+ 13,59
+ 6,00
T2
Tribüne
Technik
Motorrad
Lounge
Ausgang
Notausgang
Officefloor
+/-0,00

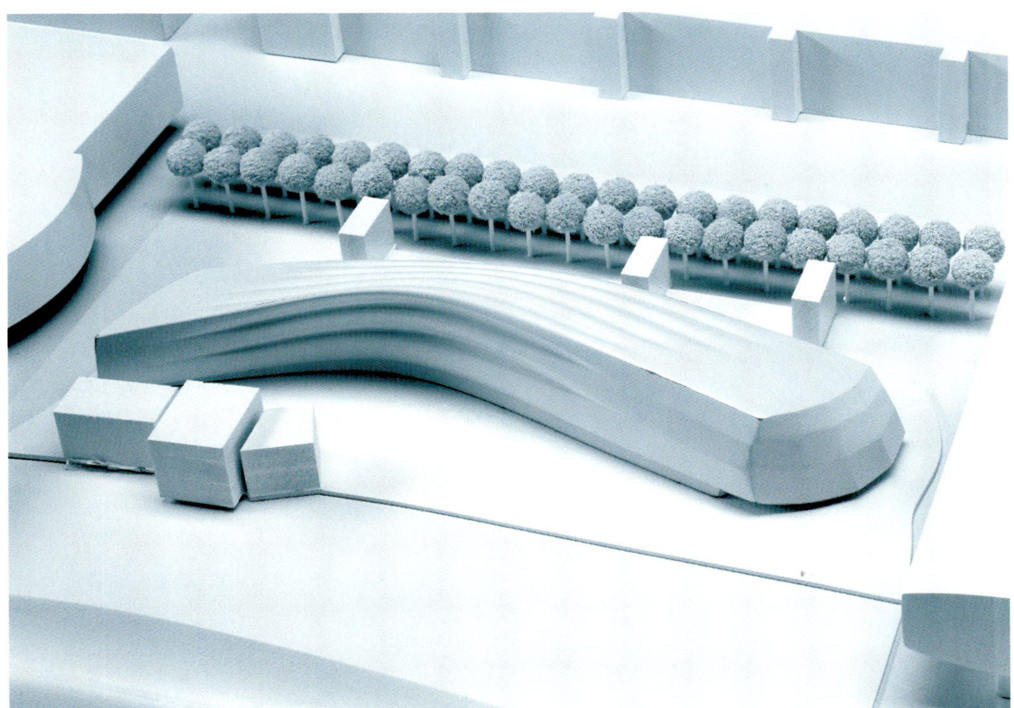

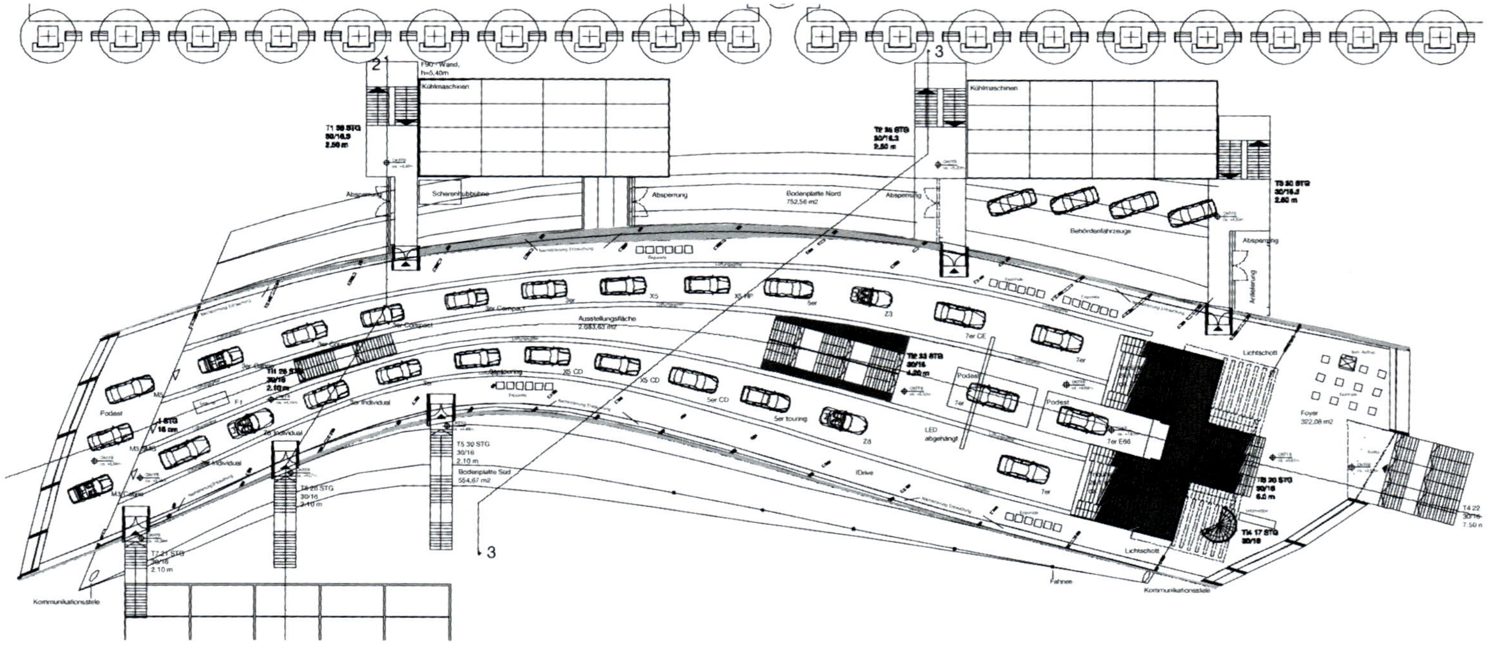

Floor plan

The exhibition area is reached by ascending a baroque staircase, where the automobiles are displayed on three "streets" following the 7-series. The rhythm of the frames and the interaction of the curves in the floor plan bring the automobiles to "acceleration".

The sloped floor means that visitors not only experience the space virtually, but also feel it in their whole body. After the crest in the middle of the area, one falls into the horizon. The reduction of the successive frames and their centralization through piers emphasize the force of suction. The entire north wall is covered in a projection screen on which an 80m film functions as the main communication element. The film, supported by audio and lighting, transforms the space into a complete communication experience.

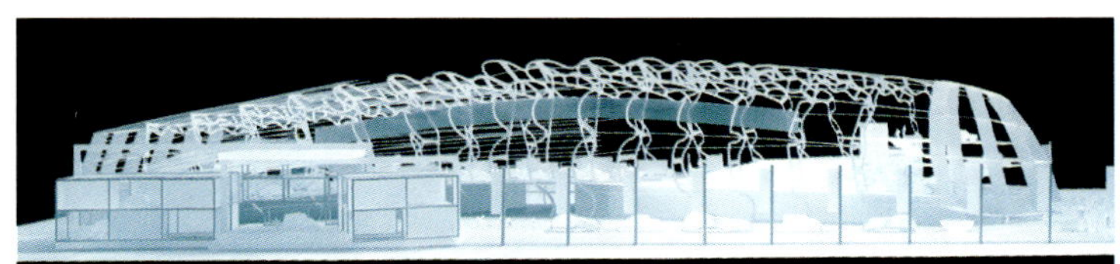

VELTINS

BMW X5 3.0d

drive.

BMW X5 3.0d

Siteco
Atelier Brückner

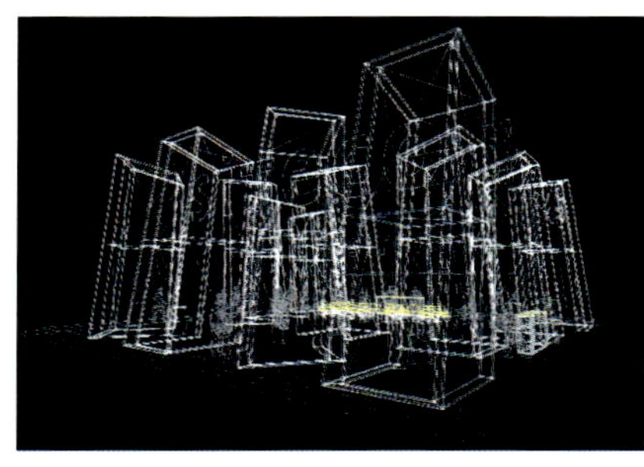

A preliminary study of the contents to be displayed at this stand for Frankfurt's Light and Building 2002 trade show led to an emblematic design. Light has been used here as a design medium in and of itself: light as structure, as architecture.

A total of eleven glowing towers nearly brush the ceiling of the host building, calling to mind the image of a city skyline. Each tower stands 8m high and is clad in a skin of translucent film, thereby granting a sense of subtlety and fragility.

A series of heterogenous products, from wall lamps to street lighting, is on exhibit within the bases of these illuminated pillars. An interplay of light and changing colors creates a striking ambience in this stand, while at the same time demonstrating the quality of the product on display and the fascination of light as a mood enhancer and source of inspiration.

Photographs: Bernd Eidenmüller, Victor Brigoleit

siteco
siteco

VDP

D'art design gruppe

Verband Deutscher Papierfabriken's (the German Papermaking Association) work consists of keeping a changing industry informed about the advantages of paper and cardboard as packaging material.

At the Interpack trade show, since their presentation was to be concentrated on providing services, the stand was centered around communication with visitors to the stand. Their primary objective was to spark interest in the quantity and variety of applications of their product: paper.

The design of the stand made use of a peculiar treatment of this material and limited the space to its essential communicative function. The basic form of the stand is an enormous sculpture of cardboard boxes, which can be seen from even the farthest corners of the show. All of the construction modules are white so that, through the additional application of light, an interesting interplay of shadows is projected onto the back wall behind the sculpture. From the visitor assistance area, one has the sensation of being beneath a tree being blown by the wind.

Photographs: D'art design gruppe

papier, karton, pa

Ellesse

Arno design

On the occasion of the 'ISPO Spring 2002' trade fair, the intention was to promote the Ellesse image and reposition it as a leading label in the areas of tennis, ski, shoes and leisurewear. Bearing this in mind, the most natural and effective solution was to design the stand in accordance with the color and contours of the 'half ball' logo.

The main stand, which is open on three sides and has a floor area of 252 m², is the Center Court, where everything revolves around the Ellesse brand. A curved ledge, patterned after the shape and color scheme of the company's logo, frames the rear area, where meeting rooms, storage, logistics and services are located. The bold, warm tones of the logo, ranging from red to orange-red, stand out against the stand´s dark blue rear wall. An elegant design and fine materials, from red, backlit Plexiglass to steel, distinguish the bar area. To one side, several groupings of seats with bistro tables offer the ideal, informal atmosphere for further discussion in the Lounge.

Shining white dominates the rest of the stand's surfaces, reflecting an era when it was a breach of etiquette to appear in a tennis match in any color but white. Inspired by this tradition, four over-sized bright white cut-out tennis balls seem to be growing out of the floor. These four product islands were deliberately positioned in order to evoke the excitement of an intense doubles match.

Selected pieces of Ellesse clothing and shoes push out from the interior toward the upper surface, thereby drawing the attention of visitors to the stand.

The roaming spotlights of a professional light show conjure water and snow motifs on the upper exterior surface of the shell. This diffused interplay of light and shadow is reflected in a floor of white-coated synthetic plates, while the company's colorful logo has been appliquéd onto the outer surfaces of the four tennis balls.

Photographs: Frank Kotzerke

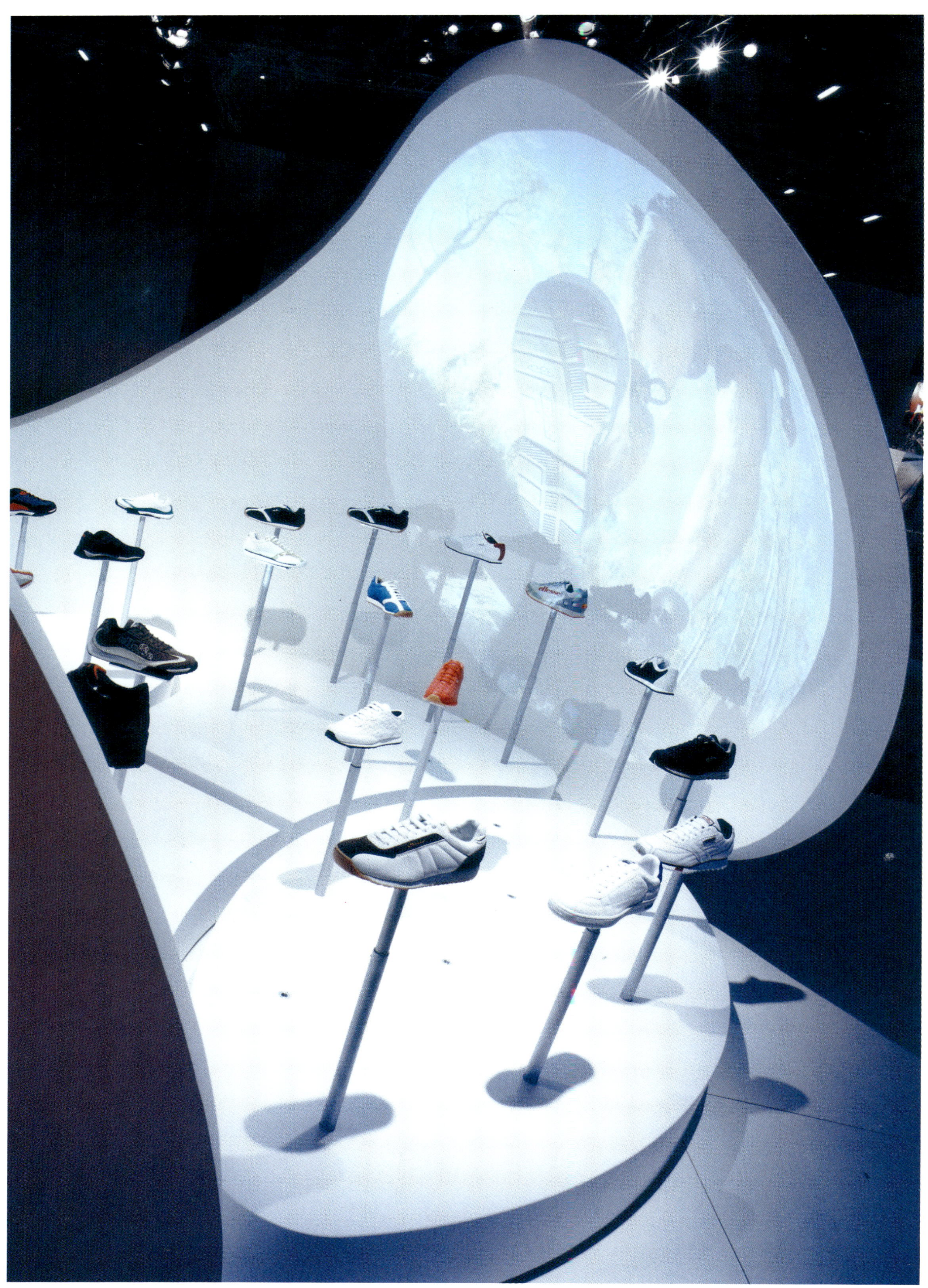

ellesse

La casa en forma

Agustí Costa

Barcelona's Colegio de Arquitectos Técnicos designed this 10x7m stand, with open entrances on three sides, in which a computer provides information on the supposed future of the house. This space had to be enclosed, yet at the same time transparent.
The stand's function is three-fold, acting at once as a display space for photographs and written texts, with recommendations on the various components of houses (structure, roof, installations and facade), an exhibit of time-worn elements, poorly used material or improper manufacturing (aluminous beams, tubes damaged by electrolysis or poorly conserved windows) and, lastly, the reception area, where a computer analyzes the topic of "the fit house".
Display cases with posters bearing the company's slogan are set into the sides of the perimetral columns. A series of obsolete domestic objects exhibited on a triangular platform clad in black velvet take on a certain abstract, sculptural air. The graphics exhibit was organized along a number of white corridors lying parallel to one another and opening onto the central display case. White Copenhagen style ashtrays are placed at the end of each wall and silver arrows on the ground point the way through the exhibit.
The customer service area features a single desk which also serves to distribute the space. Light emanates from 63 warmly colored, non-diffused fluorescent tubes set into boxes, which form narrow grooves in the false ceiling.
Made from MDF panels, the floor has been painted red, the ceiling yellow, and the back wall is in indigo blue, while the pillars and the rest of the booth have been done in silver.

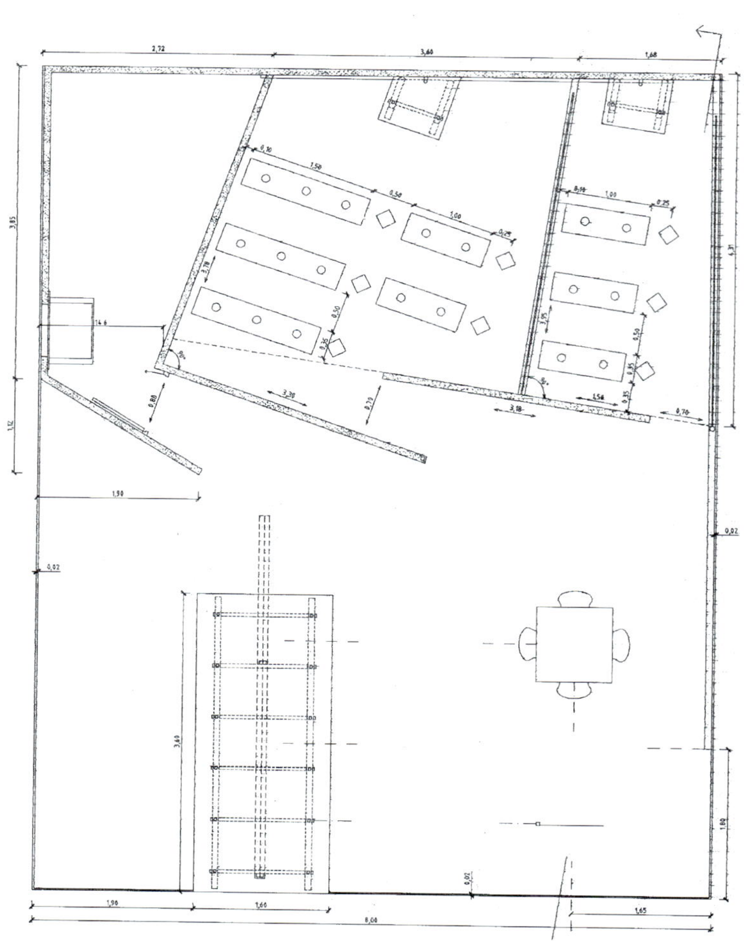

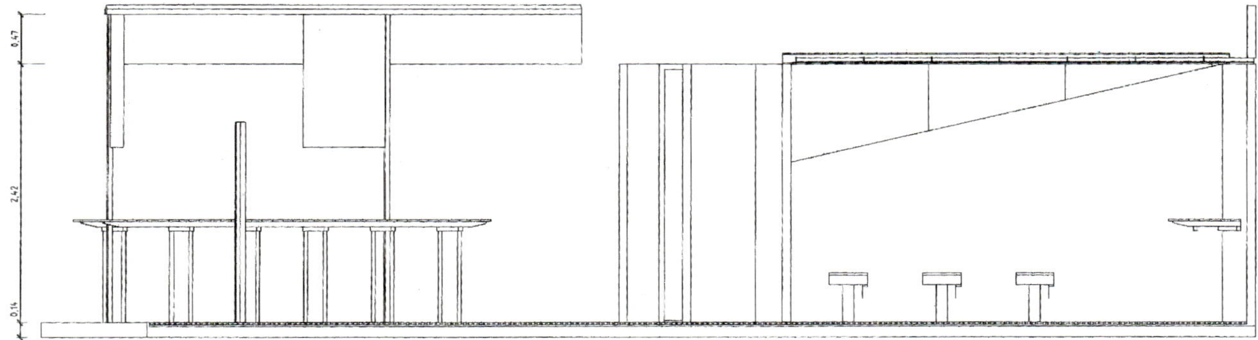

Cross section

Photographs: Jaume Much

Space

Richard Hywel Evans

Space magazine, the weekly design supplement which comes with The Guardian newspaper, presented a stand at 100 % Design 2000, the UK's biggest interior design show in London.

The Space stand was conceived to showcase the best student designs of the year, picked from the recent graduates at UK design schools, ranging from wall fabrics to street bollards to a WC.

In order to adhere to a very tight budget of just 4000 pounds, a unified black display case with individual compartments was created for each piece so they could be viewed at the same time.

The whole stand was pre-fabricated in 7 parts that could be easily assembled on site. The space available to display the work was also restricted, being just 2 m wide and 11 m long. By setting the stand away from the wall, the viewing public could walk around it and observe the work from both sides – essential for three-dimensional objects. Low voltage spotlighting would highlight the work against a neutral black background.

A huge Space magazine logo was printed in yellow vinyl along the stand's long side to catch attention where it was intersected by the oval display spaces.

The logo was also printed in reverse on the backside of the stand, and the remaining parts of the logo that were 'punched through' by the holes were carried through onto the back wall, creating a playful game of solid and void.

The result was a dynamic, youthful and fun design that grabs the attention of visitors.

Photographs: The Guardian, Philippe Moseley

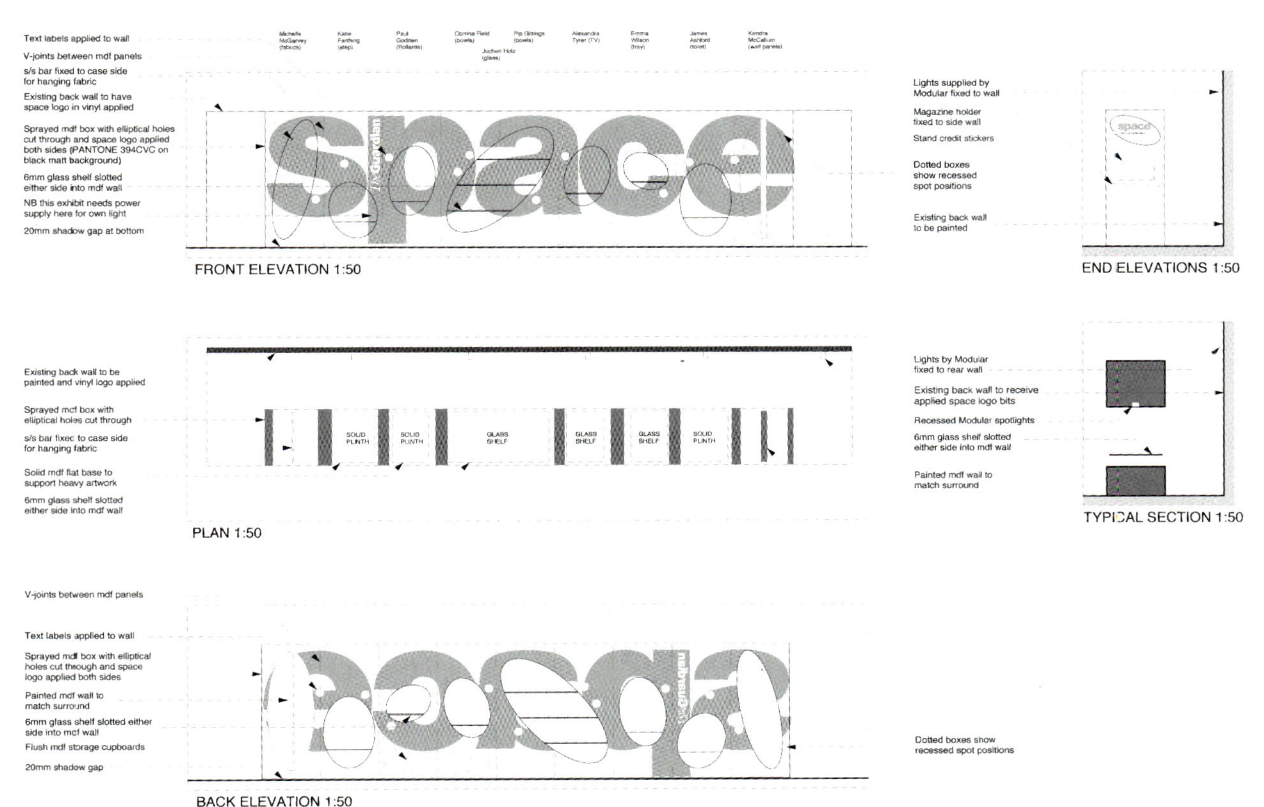
Text labels applied to wall
V-joints between mdf panels
s/s bar fixed to case side for hanging fabric
Existing back wall to have space logo in vinyl applied
Sprayed mdf box with elliptical holes cut through and space logo applied both sides (PANTONE 394CVC on black matt background)
6mm glass shelf slotted either side into mdf wall
NB this exhibit needs power supply here for own light
20mm shadow gap at bottom
Michelle McGarvey (fabrics)
Katie Farthing (step)
Paul Godden
Corrina Field (bowls)
Jochen Holz (glass)
Alexandra Tyrer (TV)
Emma Wilson (tray)
James Ashford (toilet)
Kendra McCallum (wall panels)
space
FRONT ELEVATION 1:50
Lights supplied by Modular fixed to wall
Magazine holder fixed to side wall
Stand credit stickers
Dotted boxes show recessed spot positions
Existing back wall to be painted
END ELEVATIONS 1:50
Existing back wall to be painted and vinyl logo applied
Sprayed mdf box with elliptical holes cut through
s/s bar fixec to case side for hanging fabric
Solid mdf flat base to support heavy artwork
6mm glass shelf slotted either side into mdf wall
SOLID PLINTH
SOLID PLINTH
GLASS SHELF
GLASS SHELF
GLASS SHELF
SOLID PLINTH
PLAN 1:50
Lights by Modular fixed to rear wall
Existing back wall to receive applied space logo bits
Recessed Modular spotlights
6mm glass shelf slotted either side into mdf wall
Painted mdf wall to match surround
TYPICAL SECTION 1:50
V-joints between mdf panels
Text labels applied to wall
Sprayed mdf box with elliptical holes cut through and space logo applied both sides
Painted mdf wall to match surround
6mm glass shelf slotted either side into mdf wall
Flush mdf storage cupboards
20mm shadow gap
Dotted boxes show recessed spot positions
BACK ELEVATION 1:50

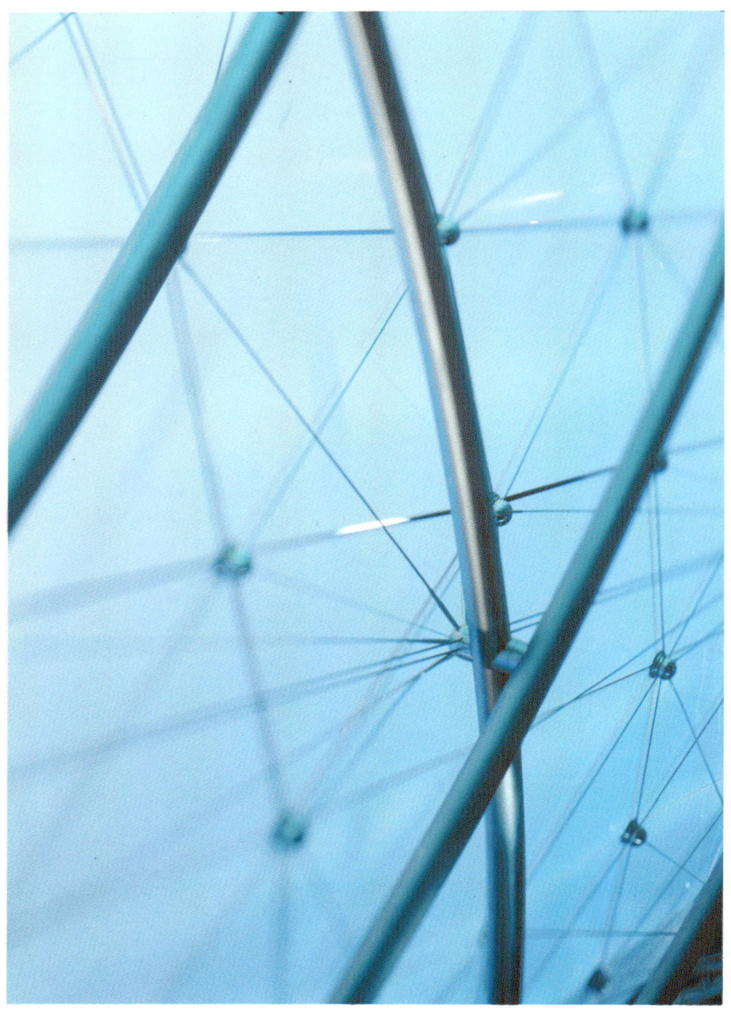

Audi

Ingenhoven Overdiek & Partner

This well-known car manufacturer have presented their vehicles in a completely new exhibition environment, enclosed within a specially designed engineering structure – the Loop. The exhibition area in the new Audi stand is enclosed within a three dimensional multi-curved façade, known as the Loop, made from stainless steel, nets of wire rope and glass.

The layout in plan and the curved section of the Loop form a spatial continuum. Directional lighting, image projection and a floor sloping slightly upwards define a special environment. The exhibition space spreads into an extensive landscape. Arched doorways link the functional zones of the exhibition spaces within the stand. The surface of the Loop is formed with triangular glass panels clipped onto the structure at the net nodes. A wire rope net hangs from the corundum-blasted, stainless steel frame and supports the nodes. The modular timber floor has a white, oak-finished surface. On the outer surface, areas of transparent and satinized glass alternate in the transition areas leading to the functional zones beyond. The transparency of the glass allows an interplay of views, providing glances between vehicle displays, exhibits of engine technology and hospitality lounges.

Photographs: H.G. Esch / Andreas Keller / Ingennoven Overdiek & Partner

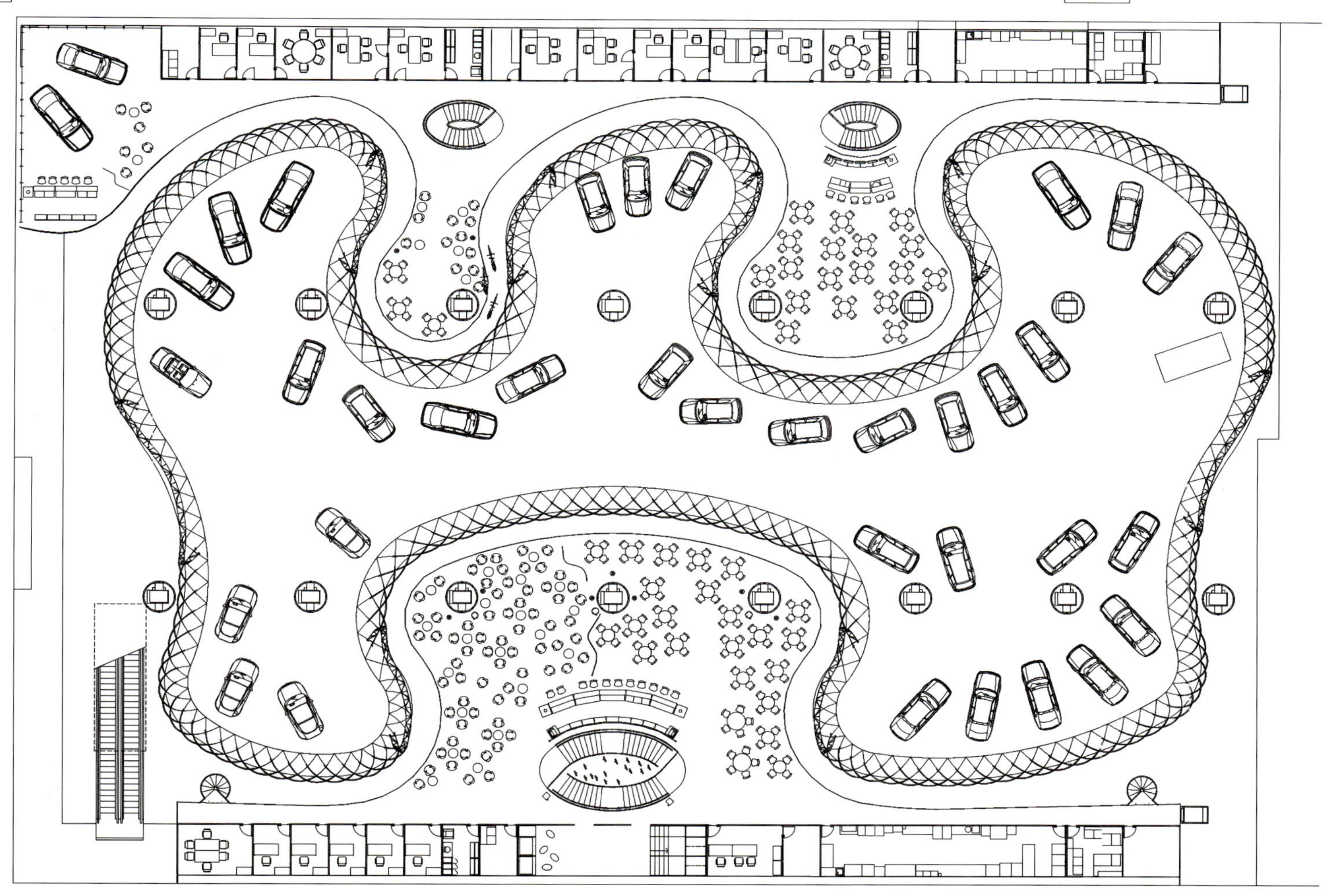

Floor plan

Continuously changing images are projected onto the Loop throughout the day. Software-controlled video projection is complemented by colored lighting blended smoothly at the edges of the Loop. A large arched doorway provides the main entrance to the stand along its centerline. The concept is a continuous thoroughfare linking the different environments of vehicles, engines and design technology.

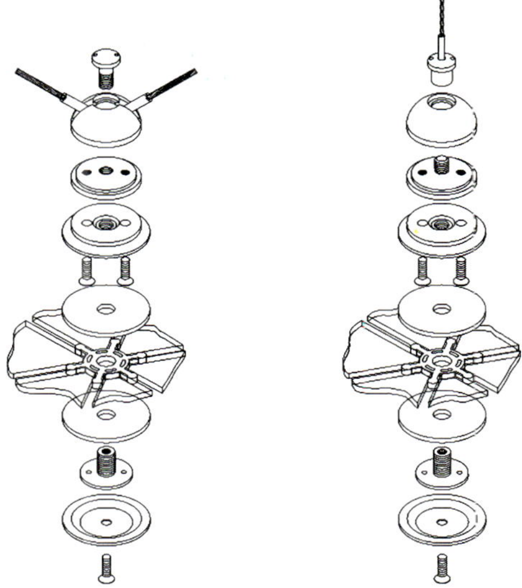

Covering a surface area of 160m², this stand was designed and built for the Alimentaria 2002 trade fair in Barcelona. The sheer amount of products that were to be displayed made this a very complex space. Florette Vega-mayor is a company dedicated to the commercialization of salads, soups, and a fairly wide variety of vegetables - all washed, cut, packaged and ready to consume. Based on these characteristics, the decision was made to display each product individually through a virtual gallery. The gallery would start where the product starts: the field, followed by a photograph of seeds, then a few lettuce leaves, and so on, until reaching the final product: the combination of several of these vegetables.

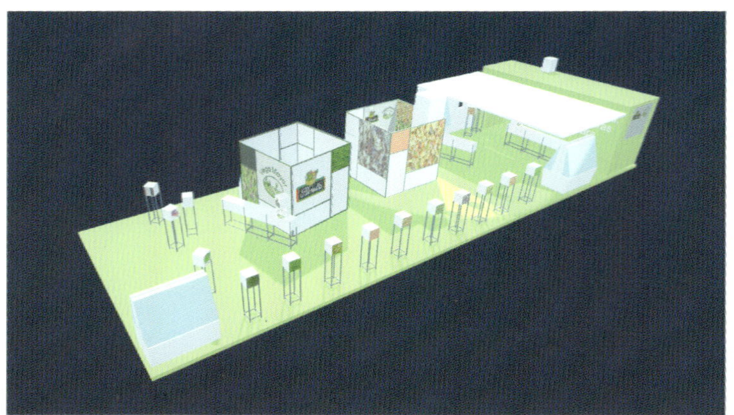

Florette / VegaMayor

Alfredo García Gotós

This virtual gallery was designed using 40x40cm cubes, lit on two sides and placed atop stainless steel supports. This display covers the entire space prior to the tasting zone. It is an almost mandatory reading, during which visitors are acquainted with the entire process, until reaching the final product.
The entire space has been patterned on the dimensions of these 40x40cm cubes. The meeting rooms and tasting bars, also cubes, have been built to the same scale.
The basis of the design was a template which was applied to all the elements in the stand, scrupulously respecting the initial measurements and creating a display of perfectly scaled dimensions. Although this detail is not immediately perceived, viewed as a whole, good architectural balance has been achieved.

Photographs: Fotodelux (O.Rosell + D.Besora)

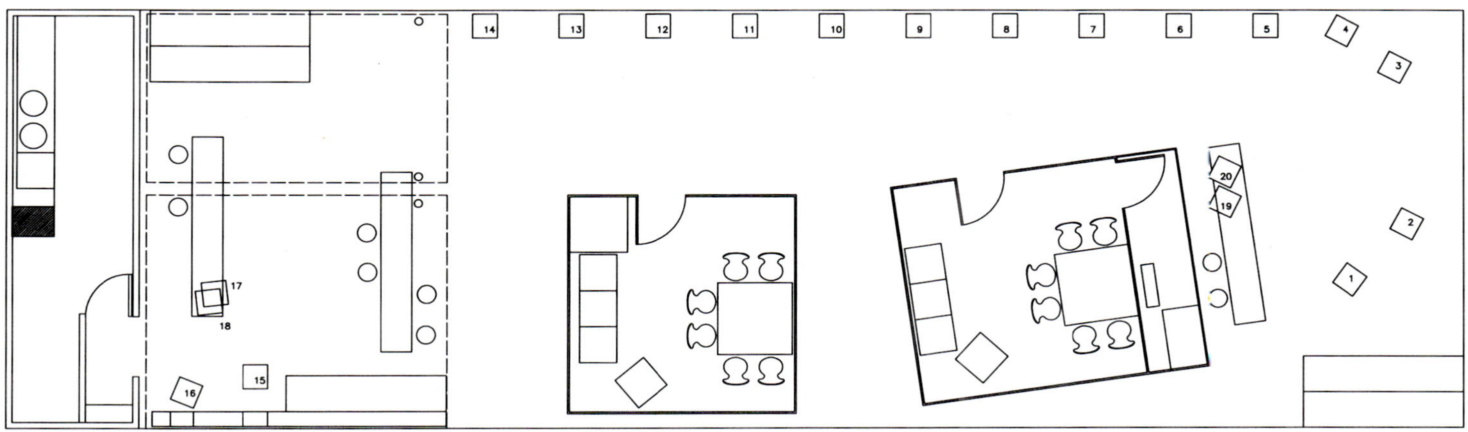

Floor plan

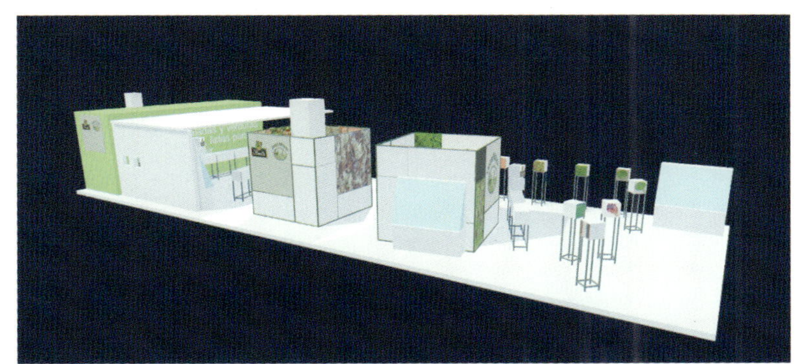

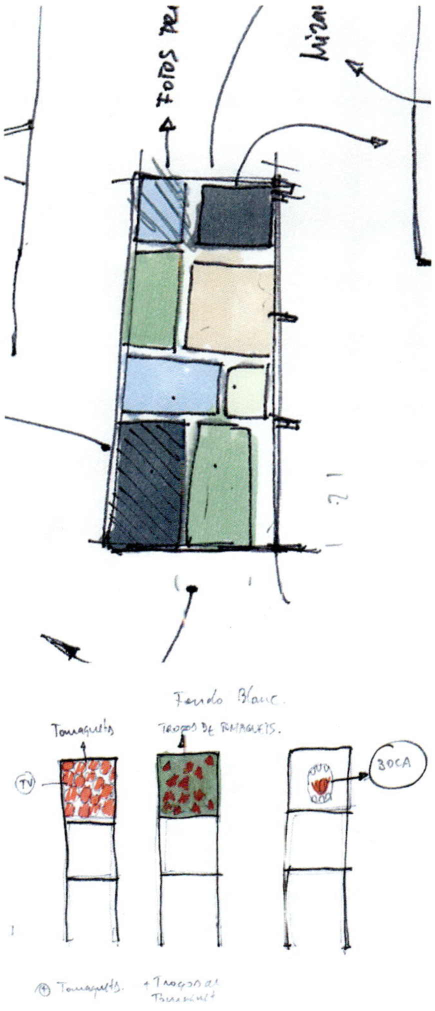

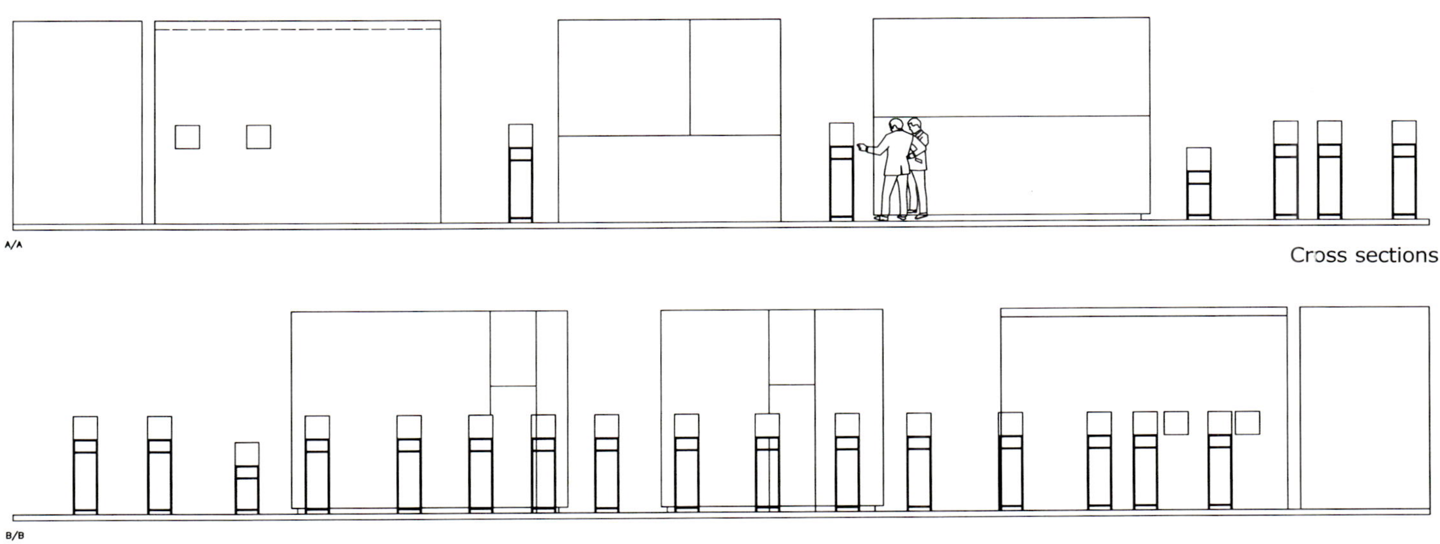

Cross sections

Ingersoll-Rand

Ochs.Schmidhuber.architekten

The stand for Ingersoll-Rand, an American corporation dealing in street tarring machines and road rollers, was built for the 'BAUMA 2001' trade fair in Munich.

The idea was to create a stand that would support the position of the company in the market. The importance of creating an easily interpreted building that would be found without difficulty was translated to a clean shape and design, the use of natural materials and the minimum but necessary graphic design, such as the exterior logo.

A freestanding, exterior pavilion opening outward toward the main exhibit thoroughfare was the end result. The pavilion is designed as one solid block, which is curved in two directions, thereby calling to mind the roller, which is the most important part of the machine made by this company. This curved form also creates a certain dynamic, which represents movability and innovation.

The front of the building is entirely glazed and the elements of the facade are filled with street paving material, such as gravel and sand. The visitor can see inside the pavilion and discern a ground-floor lounge area with a long bench and relaxing furniture, two information desks located on either side of the entrance and a meeting room on the upper floor.

The building is made primarily of form-wood, very little steel has been used to hold up the first floor and all the facade elements are prefabricated.

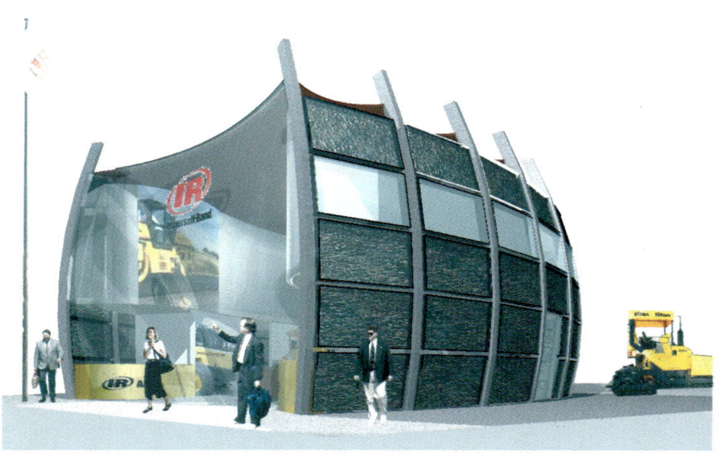

Photographs: Ochs.Schmidhuber.architekten

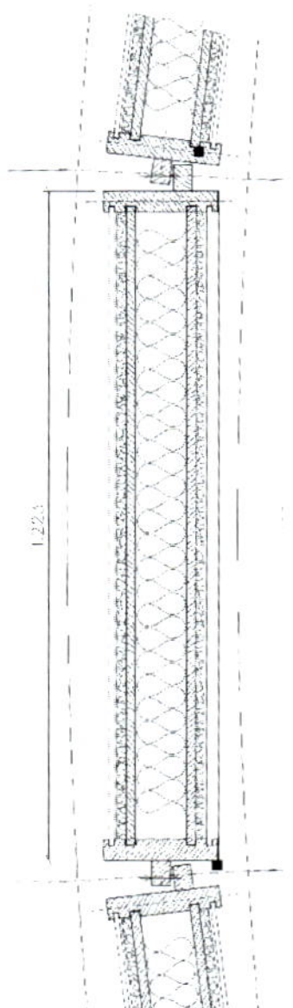

Constructive detail

Renault

Couvert & Terever + Bernac & Gonzalez

The guiding principle behind the design of this stand is that the car is a continuation of the dwelling, "a home in motion". To give tangible form to this concept, the interior of the stand, designed for Barcelona's Salón del Automóvil 2001, was patterned after car terminology.

With a floor area of 2500m2, the basis of the structure is a box-like form with a revolving floor, walls and skylight all finished in elm wood panels for a homogenous, continuous interior.

Projectors and spotlights in varying intensities and colors create an ongoing rhythm and an intriguing chromatic pattern. The cars take center stage on revolving podiums of stratified metal. The reception counter, offices, a bar and VIP lounge (with capacity for 80 occupants) are all located on the ground floor.

Photographs: Lourdes Jansana

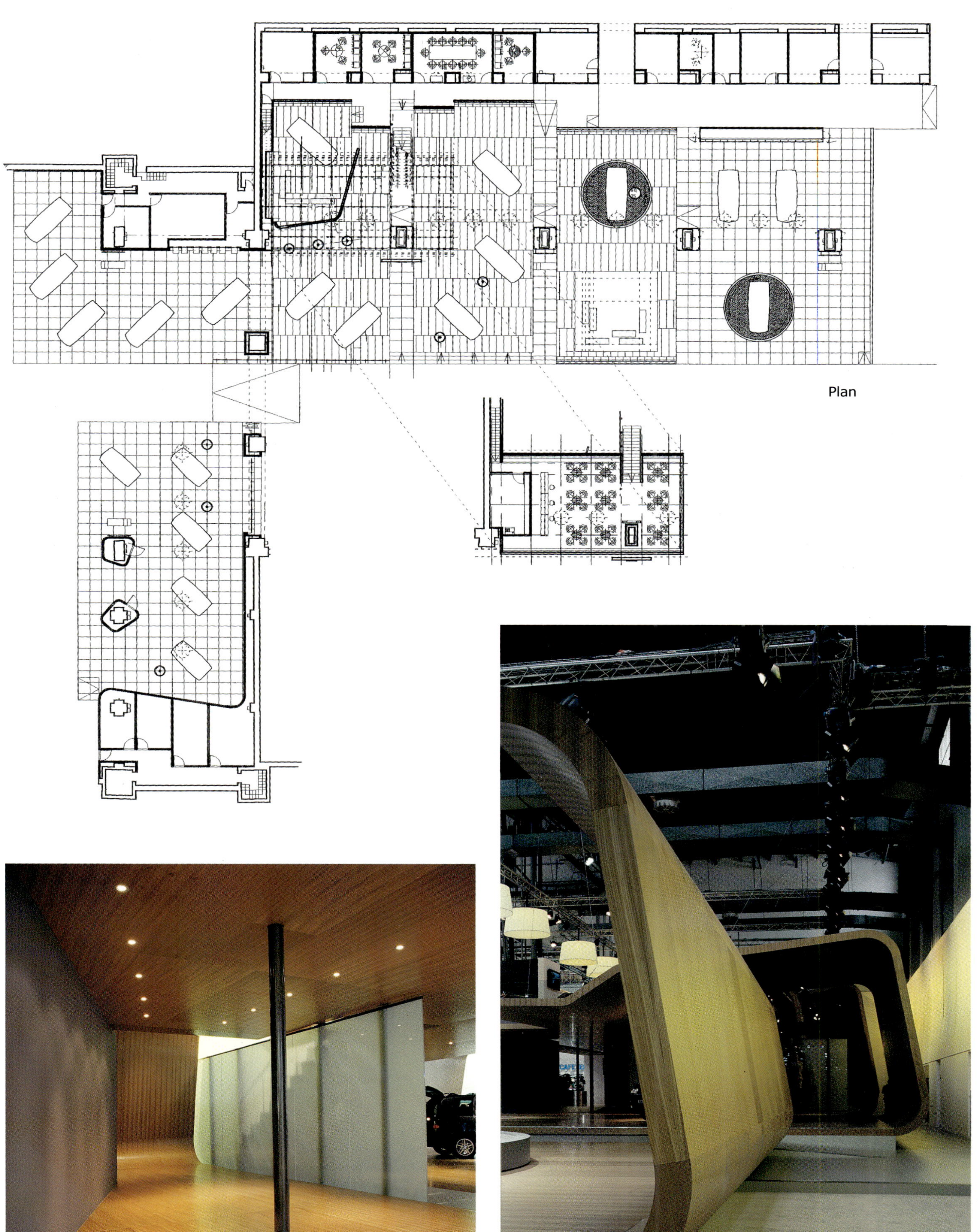
Plan

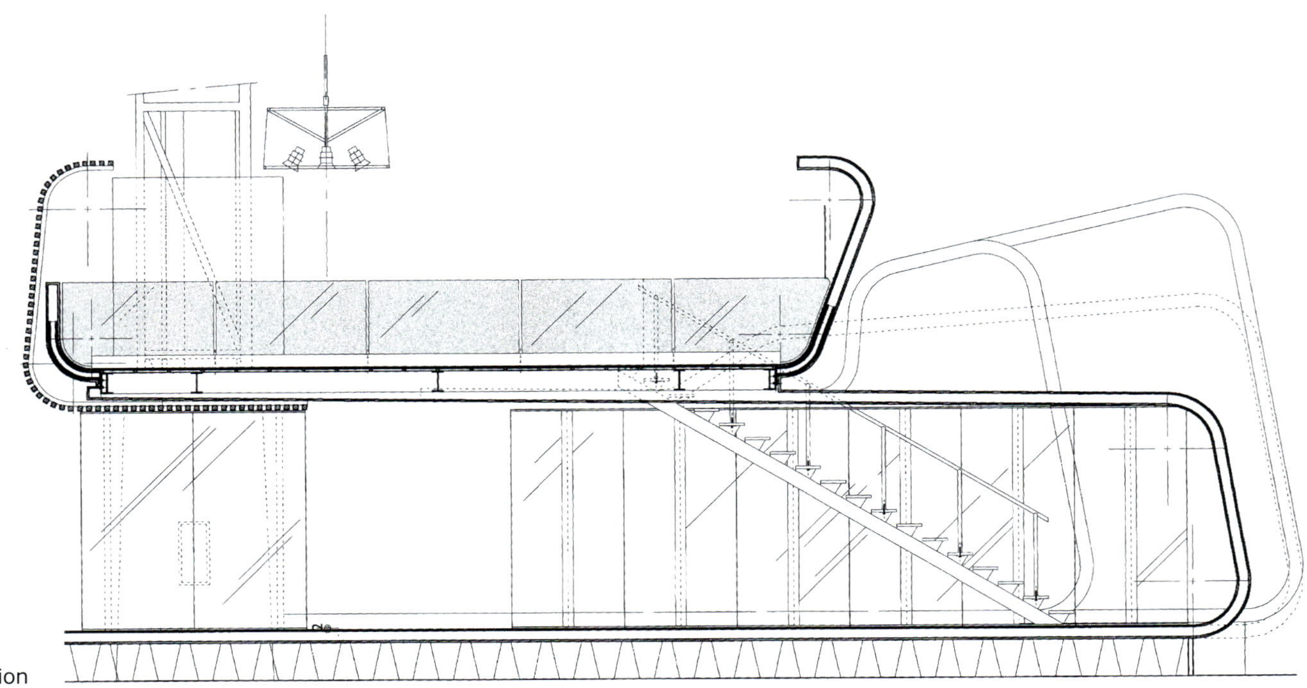

Cross section

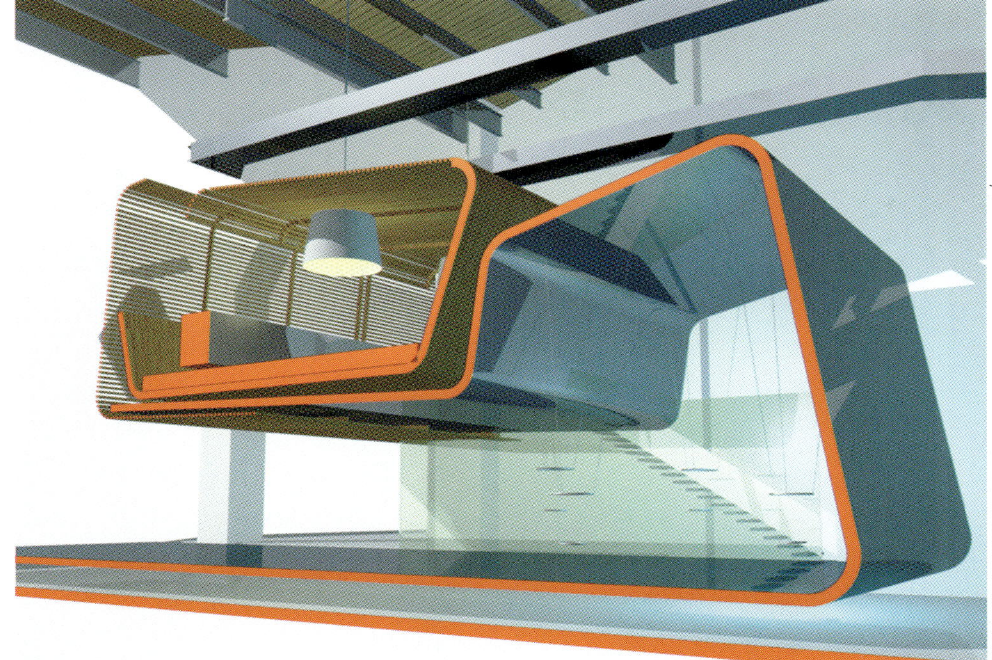

PEUGEOT

Innoval

Estudi Arola

2000 Innoval is a contest held inside the 'Salón Alimentario de Barcelona', a fair dedicated to product and packaging innovations in the food sector. In its 2000 edition, a differentiated space dominated by an intense warm red light was created.

An immense showcase with a wood structure lined in plastic and lit from within organizes the spatial distribution. The display cases representing the different families or sectors are arranged elliptically to facilitate circulation.

Four raised 3x4m projection screens arranged in the form of a cross have been placed in the center of the room; here, audiovisual information pertaining to the foods sector is projected. Providing the background to the exhibit is red carpeting interrupted here and there by 1x1m white rectangular modules which serve as impromptu seating. The exhibit also features a video wall displaying the ads of the various participating companies.

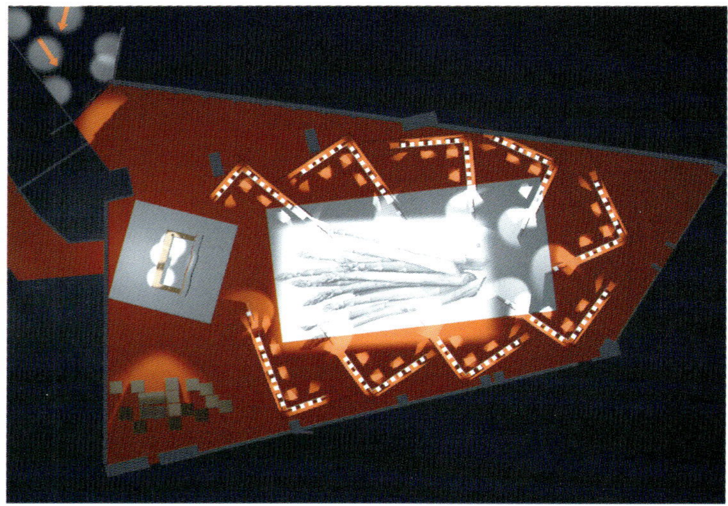

Photographs: Javier Ties / Laia Roviras

i
i
h
h
g

i
h

g

i
h
g
d
c
b

2002 For the 2002 edition, a great anteroom was arranged. The visual bet of the set fixed an entrance, unmarked of the expositive space. The central part was presided by a great helicoidally mobile of orange methacrylate that endowed of dynamism the reception zone. A great projection in panoramic format completed the visual proposal. The distribution of the interior space was quite marked by a circular circuit sense in which were distributed the food sectors by groups (in both sides of the course). A single methacrylate skin like fluorescent lamp formed the showcases. The graphic part was content in a rear fabric screen linked with the ground stiffness trough a welded wedge. The final result obtained a background curtain effect. A cylinder with applied graphic retro illuminated culminated the centre of the circuit.

Photographs: Eugeni Pons / Laia Roviras

sweets.

frutas y verduras
fruits and vegetables
nova
frutas y verduras
fruits and vegetables

arroces, sopas y pastas
multiple foods
aguas, refrescos y cervezas
arroces, sopas y pastas
rice, soup and noodles

vinos y espirituosos
wines and spirits

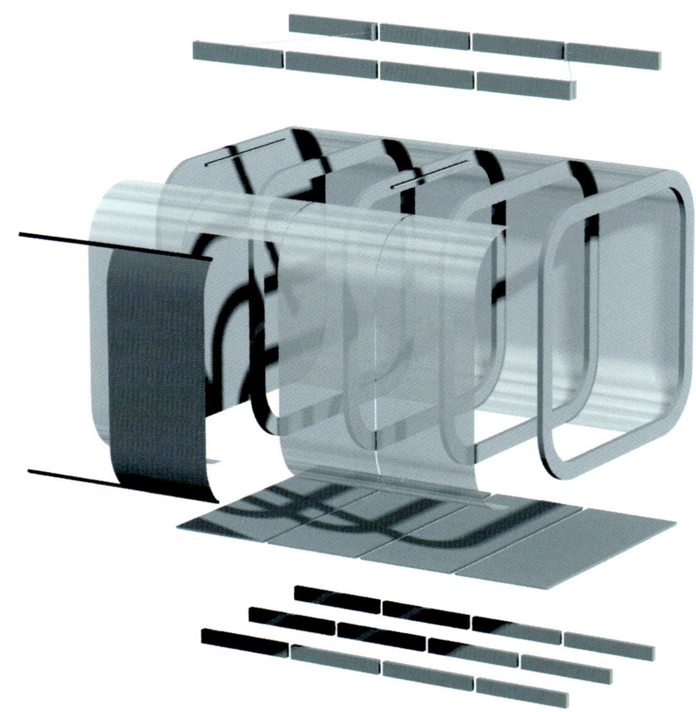

Bertrandt

totems

At the IAA 2001 trade fair, Bertrandt, which is one of the largest engineering service providers in the automobile industry in Europe, presented itself to its customers and business partners. The aim of the stand was to express the company's motto, "Engineering with Passion", in a tangible, three-dimensional form. Apart from the stand's lounge-like lobby, there is a separate, enclosed area. Here, apart from the derivatives, Bertrandt's methods of working and technology were presented: digital engineering, physical engineering and engineering management. Distinct lines, lighting and pure design features draw the eye to the essentials – attention to detail and passion for vehicles and technology.
Two studies of potential Audi A2 derivatives provide visitors with an insight into Bertrandt's work methods. Visitors are shown the entire process of car development in three separate areas.

Photographs: Markus Mahler

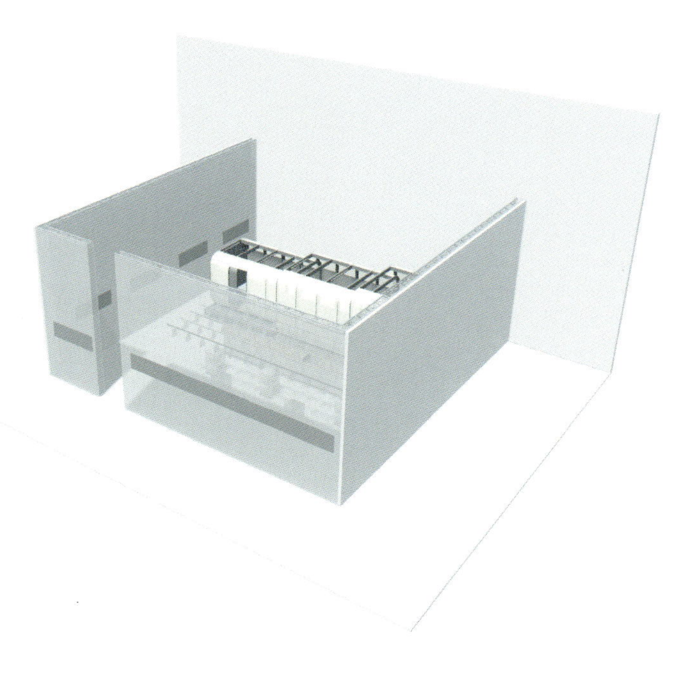

Rendering

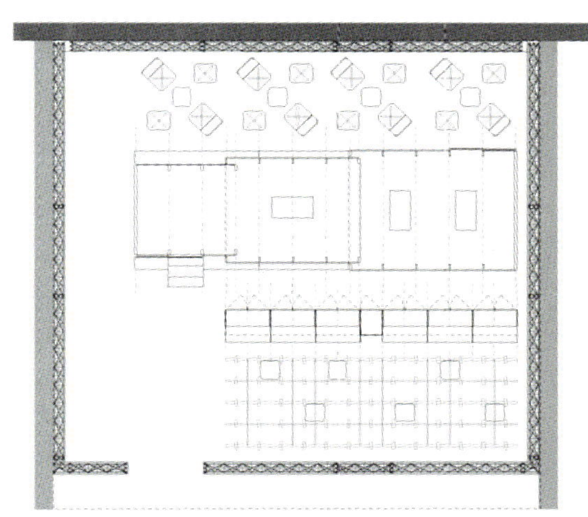

Floor plan

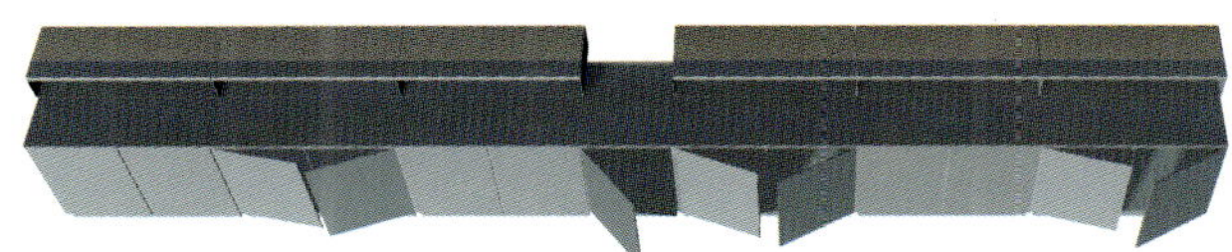

Detail of closets

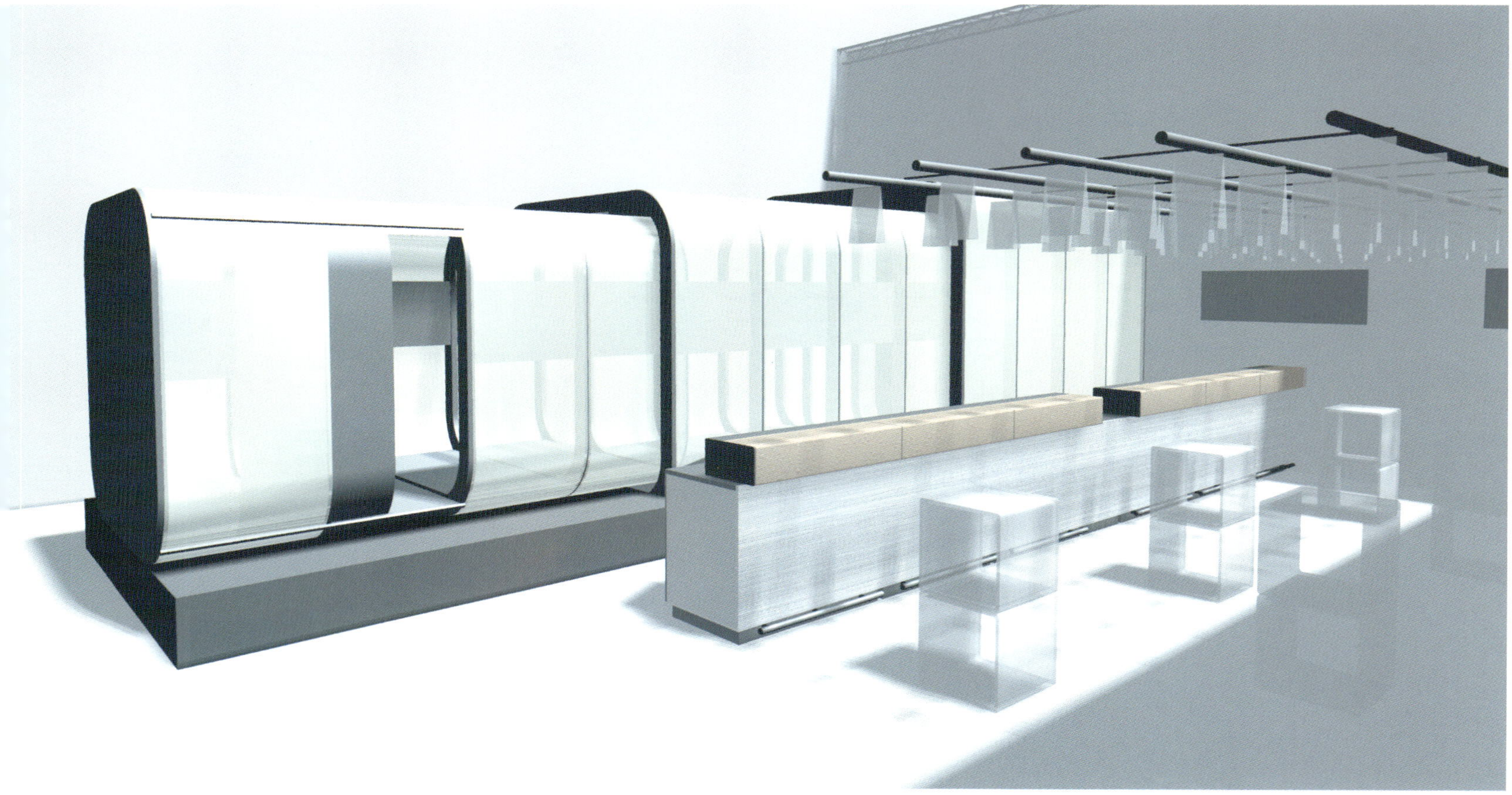

Engineering with Passion

Engineering with Passion

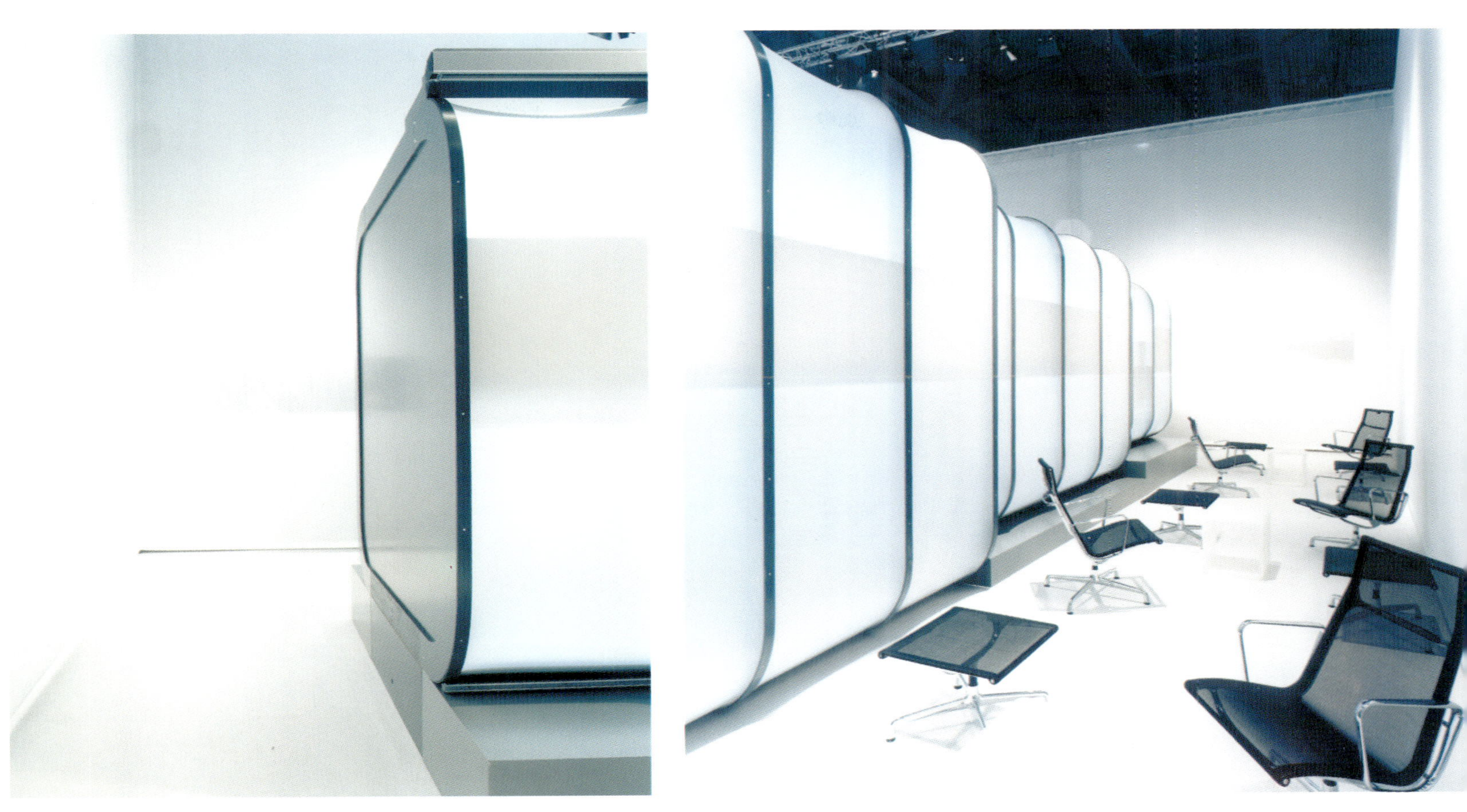

Baumann
Thutundknup

Based on the subject matter of this stand created for the Heimtextil Frankfurt 2002 trade show, almost all of its components have been designed using textiles.
Covering 300m² of floor space, the stand's basic shape is a long rectangle with one rounded end. There are three service modules dividing the space, with the exhibition occupying most of the available space and a café-bar at one end.
There is no single entrance, in the conventional sense, but rather the stand can be entered at any point along the periphery by simply stepping through the textile strips that hang from the six-meter-high structural frame.
This "spaghetti curtain" clearly separates the stand from the trade fair, while also allowing constant, changing glimpses of what goes on inside.
The collection itself is presented on back-lit corner elements, which function as connecting parts.

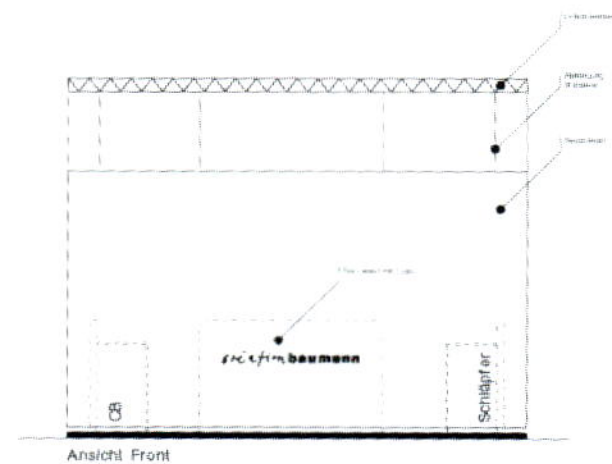

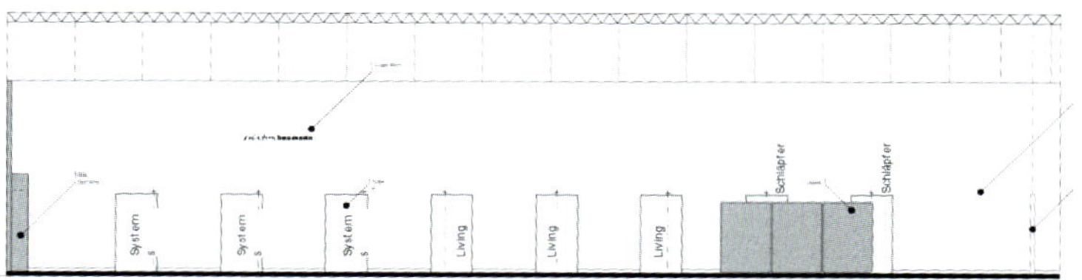

Elevations

Photogrphs: Peter Knup

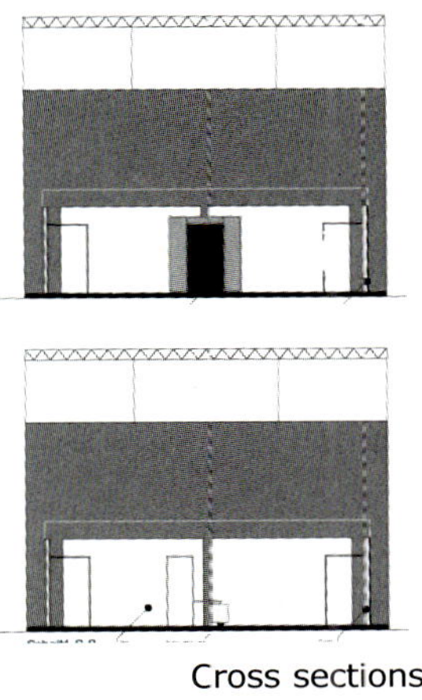

Cross sections

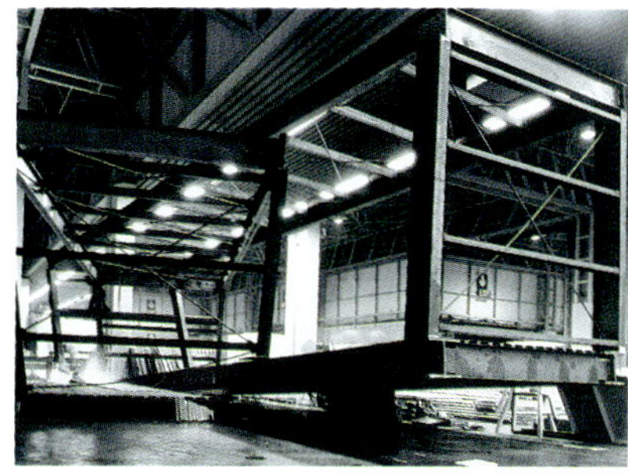

Blueprint

Zaha Hadid Architects

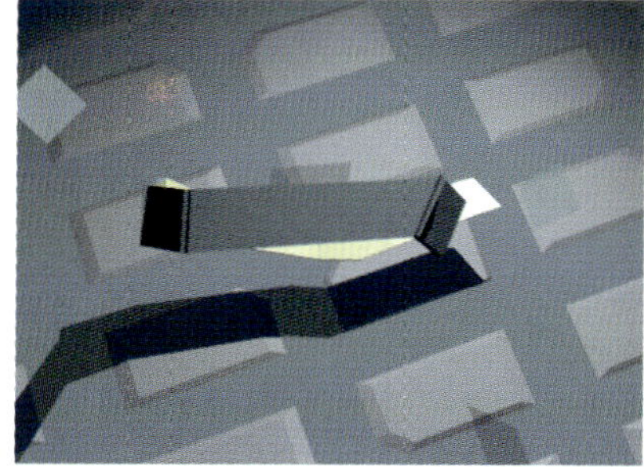

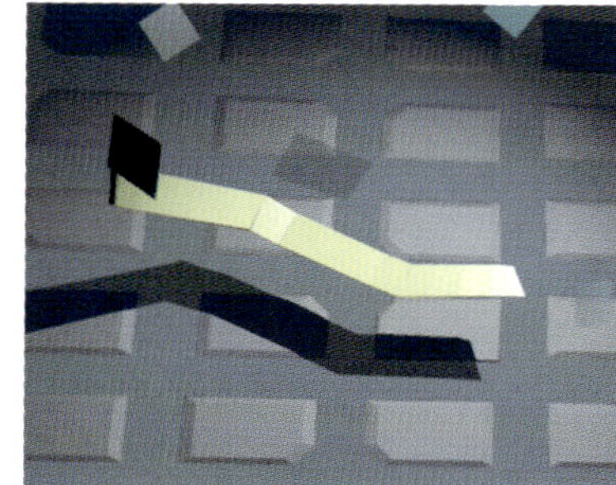

On display at Interbuild '95, in Birmingham, this stand is composed of a single sheet of steel which has been folded over itself. Finishes, lighting and ironmongery have been incorporated into the surface, which, as the plate folds over itself, defines spaces for the display of larger volumetric objects such as furniture by Vitra. Each exhibitor has been assigned to a specific location within the "stand-object", enabling certain exhibited materials, such as surface finishes, to flow seamlessly across one space and into another.

The plate is supported by a chassis of steel beams, which is in turn sandwiched between an industrial skin and an internal cladding material such as MDF, industrial flooring or another finish. The space has been intentionally designed so that finishes can flow along floors and up walls. Lighting is alternately recessed into the plate and suspended from it.

Photographs: Edward Woodman, Helène Binet

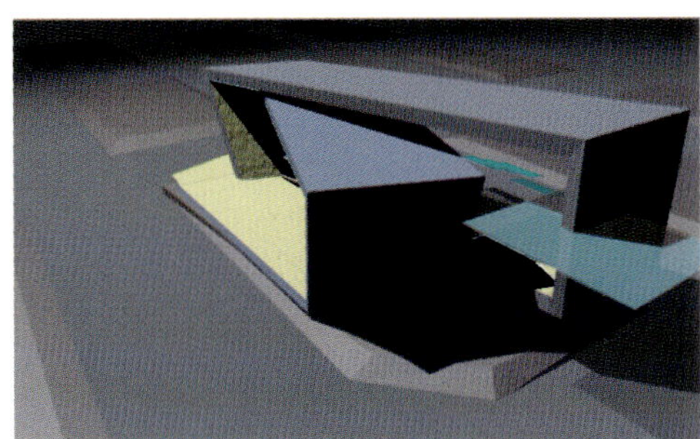

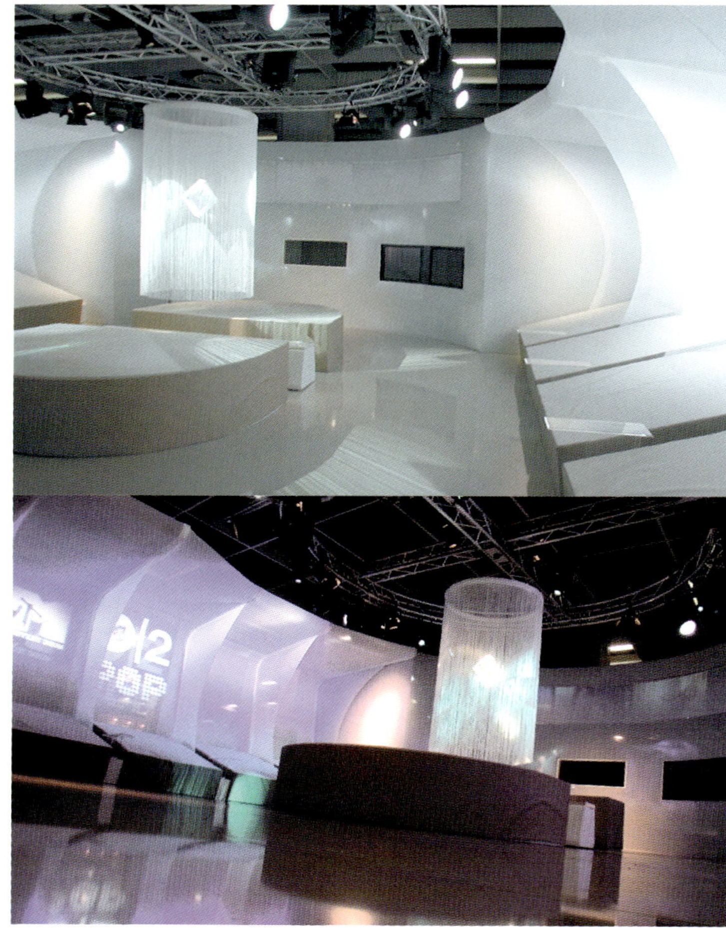

Mtv

3 deluxe

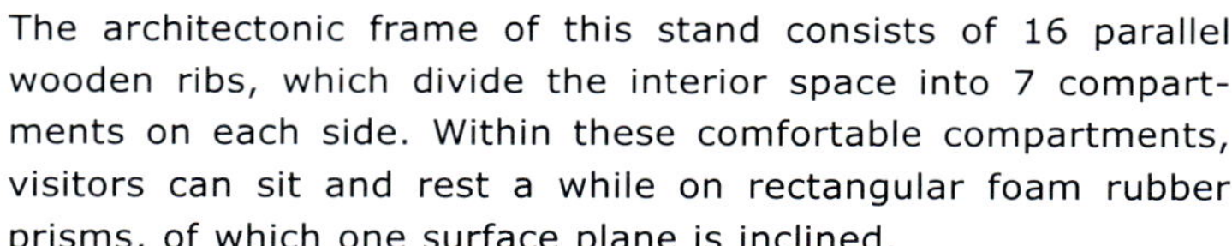

The architectonic frame of this stand consists of 16 parallel wooden ribs, which divide the interior space into 7 compartments on each side. Within these comfortable compartments, visitors can sit and rest a while on rectangular foam rubber prisms, of which one surface plane is inclined.

Three of the exterior faces of the stand are clad in white gauze, which provides visual hints of activities on the other side. This semitransparent skin also acts as a projection screen for various combinations of lights and the company's logo, all of which is visible from both the exterior and interior.

The stand's strictly symmetrical layout is reinforced by a central, circular ceiling. An illuminated sculpture of acrylic fiber hangs from this ceiling, its multicolored, crystalline rays of lights penetrating a curtain of cylindrical strands before being projected onto the surrounding gauze surfaces. This unique space, which is located in the center of the stand, is also defined by two independent lounge areas. At the back of the stand, the private spaces are concealed behind a concave dividing wall, which also comprises the service counter. A cubical structure at the entrance serves as the reception desk for visitors.

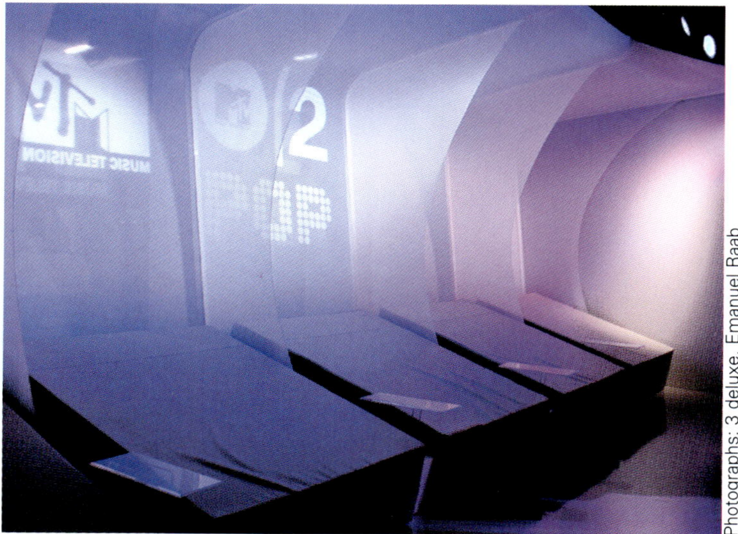

Photographs: 3 deluxe, Emanuel Raab

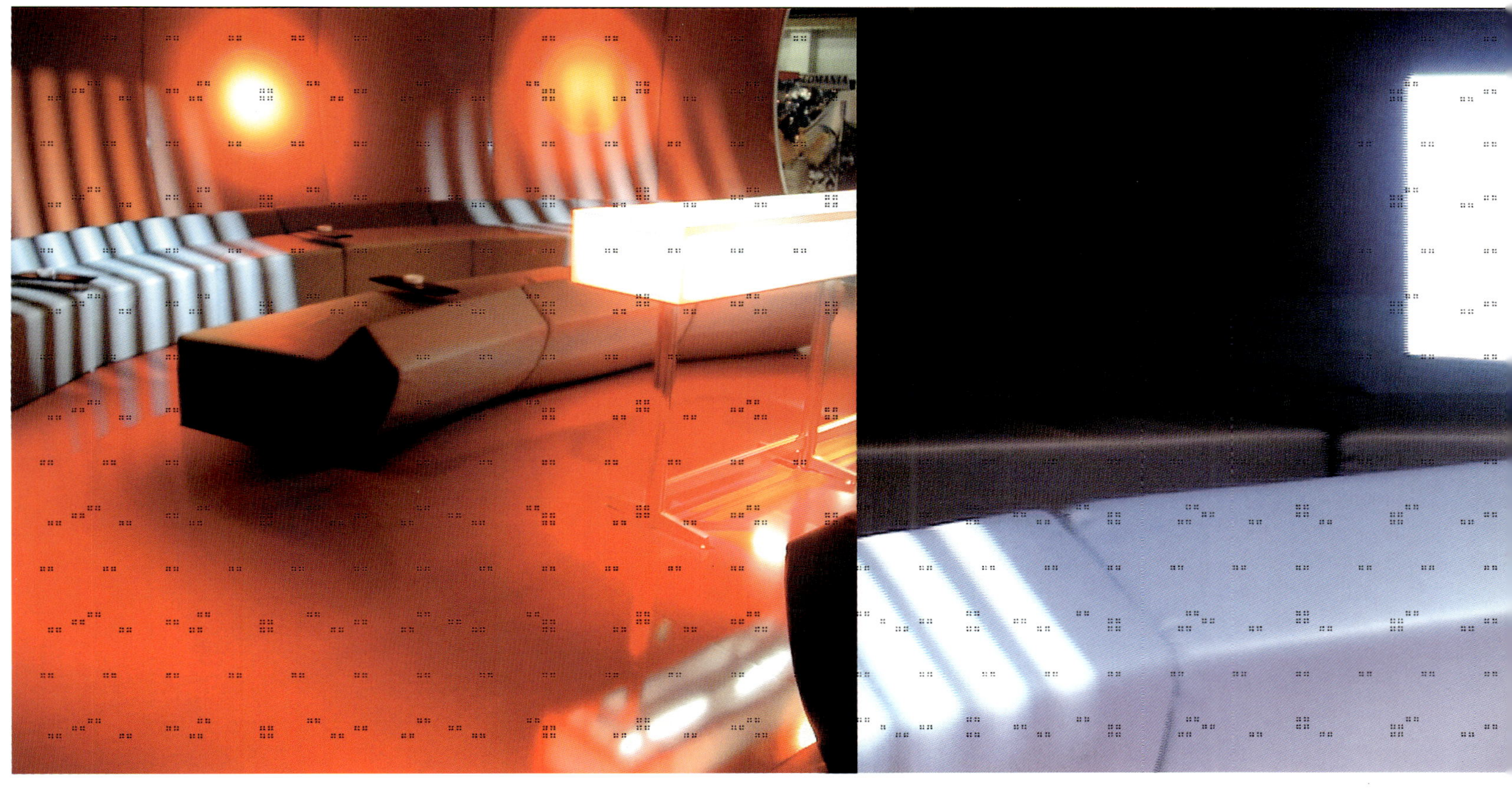

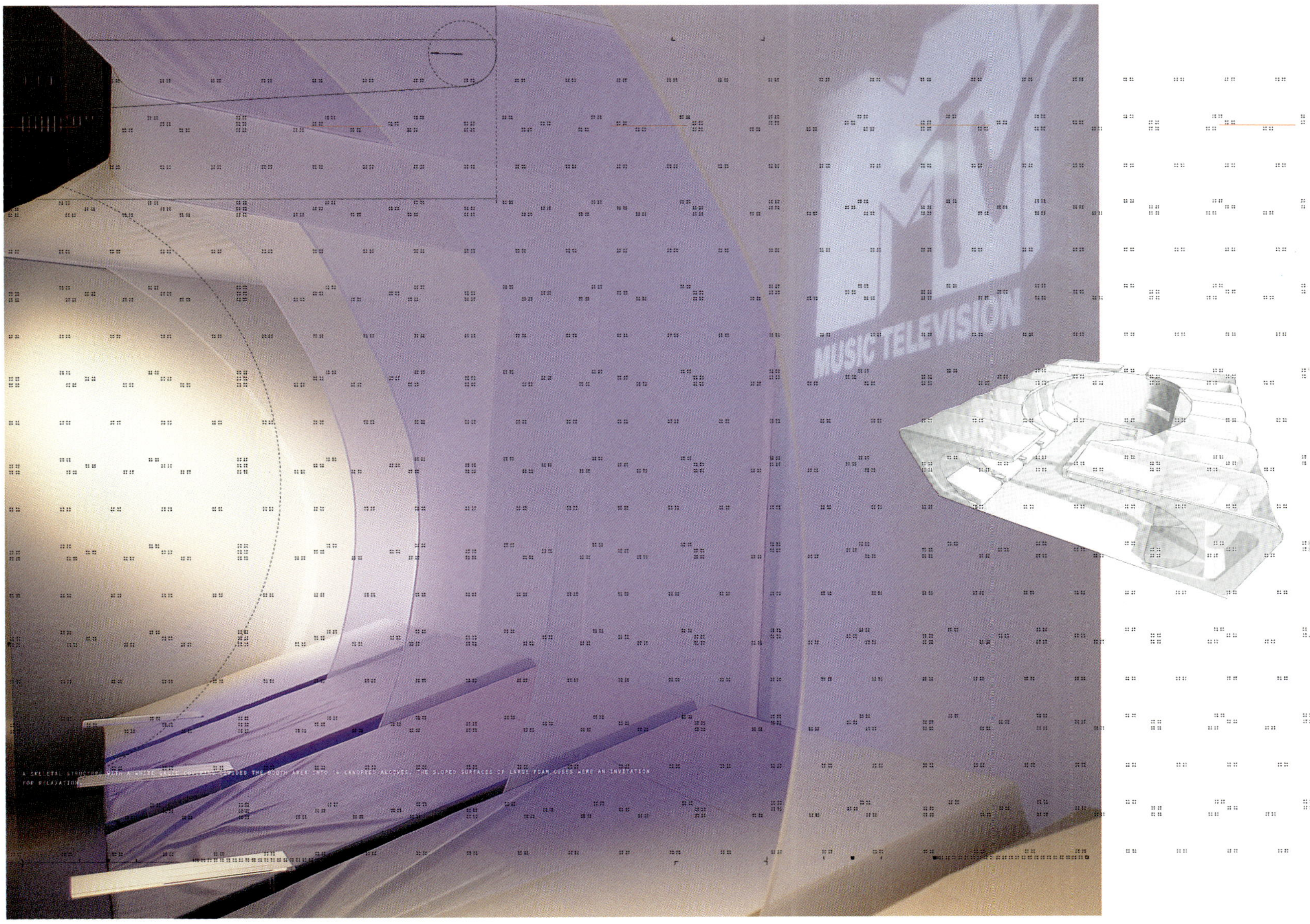

A SKELETAL STRUCTURE WITH A WHITE GAUZE COVERING DIVIDED THE BOOTH AREA INTO 14 CANOPIED ALCOVES. THE SLOPED SURFACES OF LARGE FOAM CUBES WERE AN INVITATION FOR RELAXATION.

CEMEX

RES. Ricard Galiana, Estel Ortega & Sergi Pons

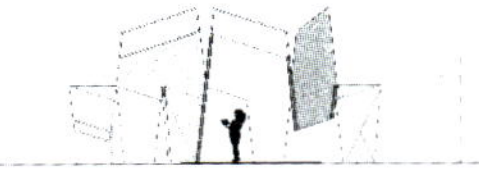

This stand was designed by students of the Cátedra Blanca 2000-2001, a graduate course organized by Barcelona's Técnica Superior de Arquitectura and taught by the architect Carlos Ferrater. During the course, various groups of students presented their programs for a competition sponsored by CEMEX that called for the construction of a 220m2 stand for the Construmat 2001 trade show.

The winning stand has been patterned on the idea of a large-scale game of strategy: a playing board covering an area of 12 x 16 meters, with a series of 1.5m2 meter "playing pieces". The object was to group the different units according to type, each unit having been formed from the "mother" piece and from the support pillar. The end goal of the "game" was to create a space that could be adapted to each round and to the three directions of the playing board.

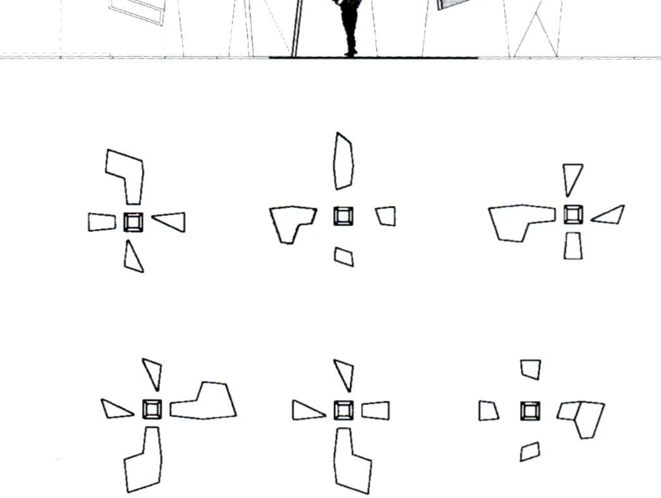

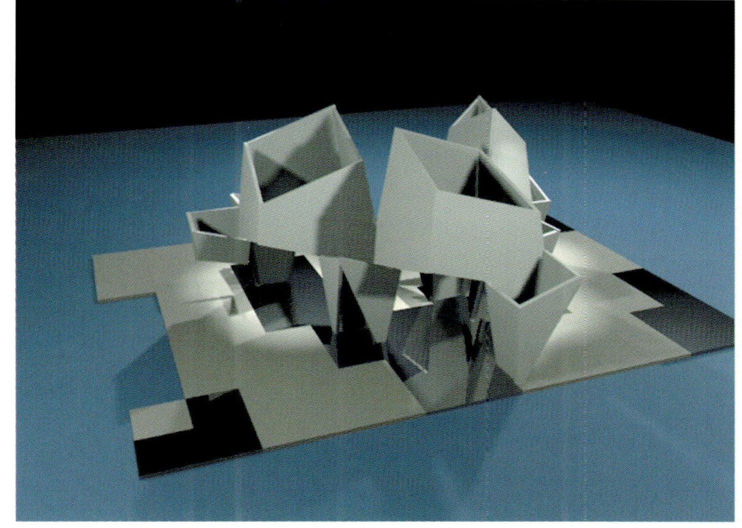

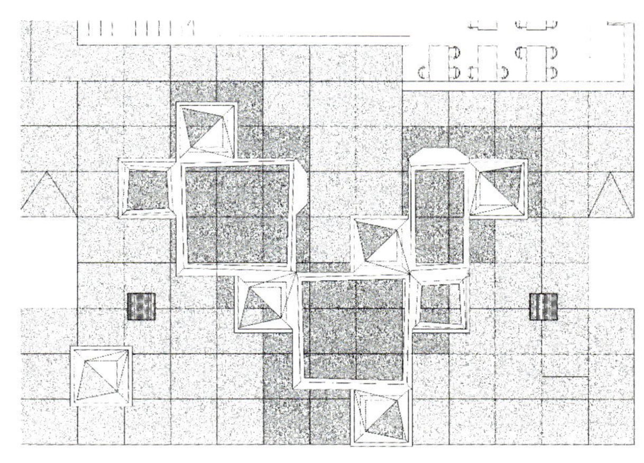

Photographs: RES

Automotive

Simone Micheli

A high, semitransparent curtain with silver and iridescent flecks is kept in perpetual motion by a computer-aided device that continuously changes it appearance; it opens and closes, like a screen, on the Automotive exhibition stand at 'Decosit 2001', an upholstery and textile trends fair in Brussels, emphasizing the present and future of the automobile world.

Inside a circular space of 12 meters in diameter, an intriguing 'Rover 25' (MG Rover Group) production model and the 'Bertone SKF Filo drive by wire car' prototype are on display, facing each other from two wide, inclined steel platforms.

The few totemic exhibition signs contribute to the characterization of this exceptionally evocative place: in the center of the exhibit, a long sculptural table shows the new fire-resistant textile samples, which have been used to dress the interior of the cars. Four large white and grey volumes, bearing fluorescent caption devices and alternating on a white and grey striped carpeting, frame the cars, which thereby take center stage of the installation.

A series of spot lights set along the circular perimeter of the hanging structure draw the focus of attention toward the center of the display, conferring a sense of strength and suggestiveness.

Photographs: Maurizio Marcato

Floor plan

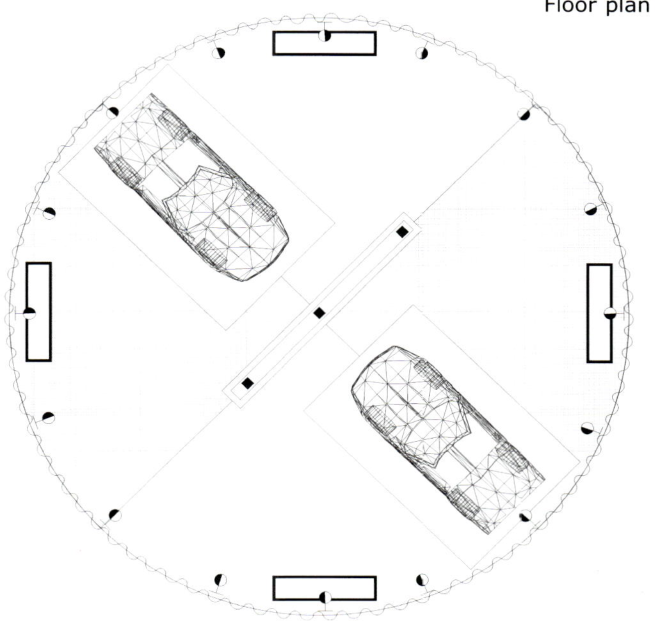

Casawell

Uniplan International GmbH

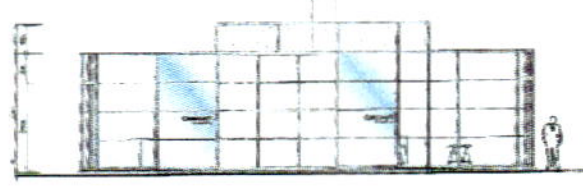

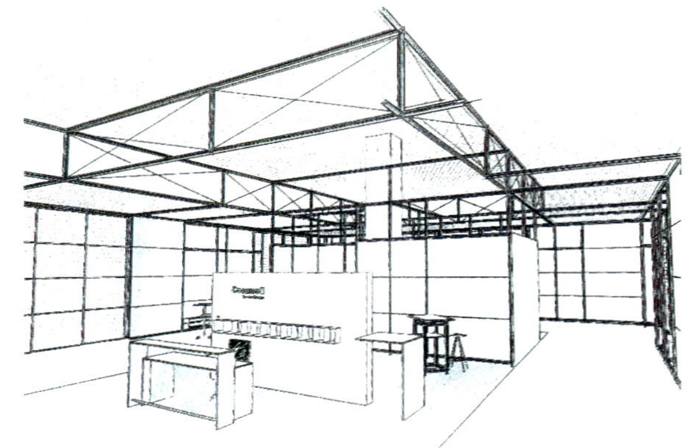

This stand, designed for one of the largest companies in the kitchen module manufacturing sector, aimed to show visitors the wide range of decorative and practical possibilities offered by the products to be displayed here.

The interior of the stand has been divided into different areas, each representing a different type of fixture, and each being characterized by a different color of flooring from the others, thus heightening the feeling of passing through distinct ambiences. Color photographs and illustrations line some of the spatial partitions. Overall, the stand has been given a somewhat less formal look than is customary in an attempt to create an approachable, inviting stand.

In addition to dividing the space, the partitions have also been used as a backdrop on which to display the furniture. A system of spotlighting covers the entire surface of the stand's ceiling.

Photographs: H.G. Esch, Chormann

Plan

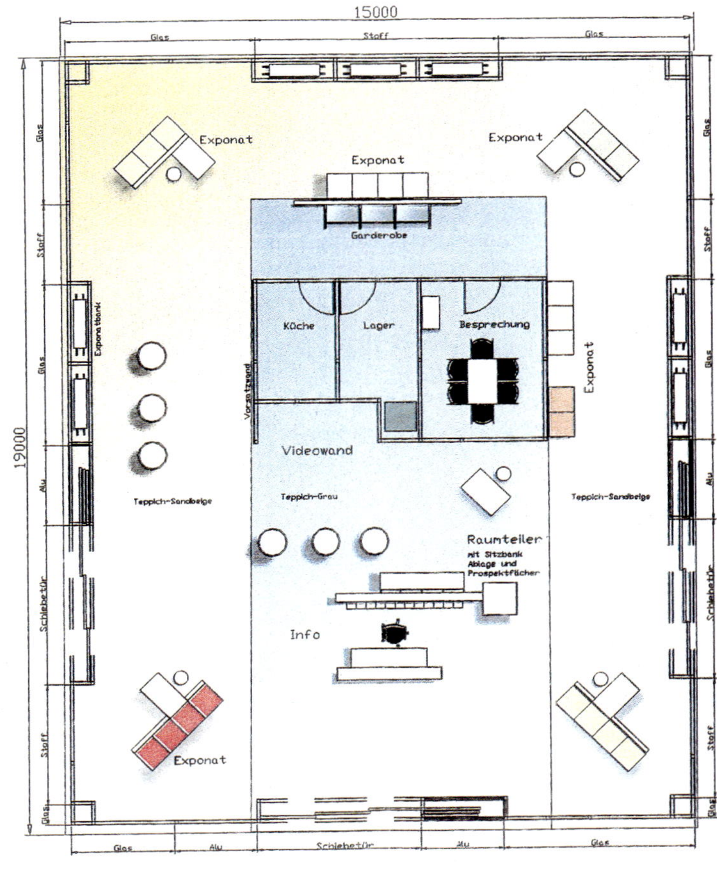
15000
Glas
Stoff
Glas
Exponat
Exponat
Exponat
Garderobe
Küche
Lager
Besprechung
Exponat
Videowand
19000
Teppich-Sandbeige
Teppich-Grau
Teppich-Sandbeige
Raumteiler
mit Sitzbank
Ablage und
Prospektfächer
Info
Exponat
Glas
Alu
Schiebetür
Alu
Glas

LG Electronics

Campos & Pradel

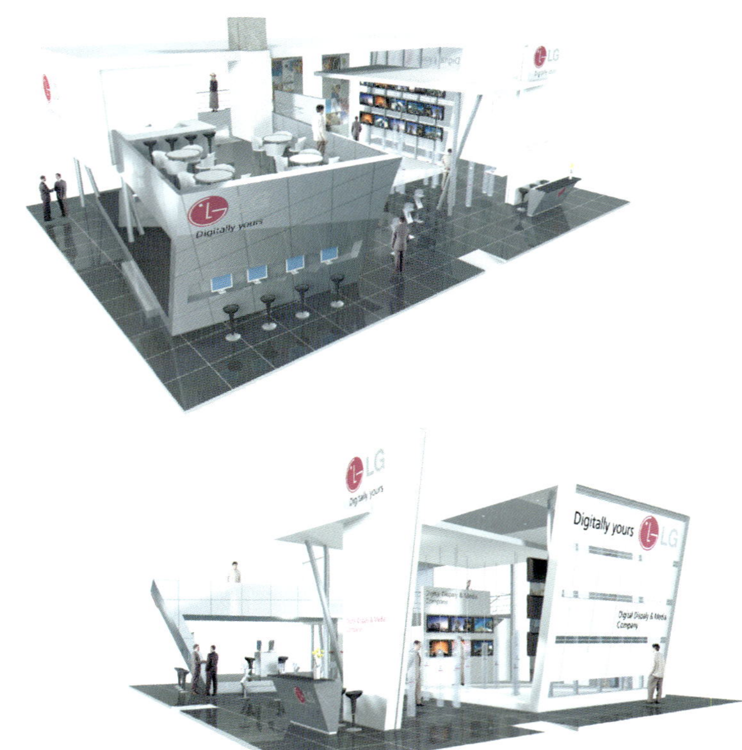

Consumers and minor distributors were the expected public for this stand, which was designed to be simple and functional, with clean lines, thereby placing greater emphasis on the product itself.
It has been designed with two, asymmetric levels, with the ground floor occupying 252m2 and an upper floor of 55m2. The forms were greatly simplified and broken down into their basic components -as seen particularly in the level changes- in order to make use of a modular structure which could be rented as needed.
Various interwoven volumes serve to organize the exhibition area and are supported by concealed metal structures and finished in melamine and polycarbonate paneling. The exhibit racks and fixtures are finished in stainless steel and methacrylate.

: Campos & Pradel

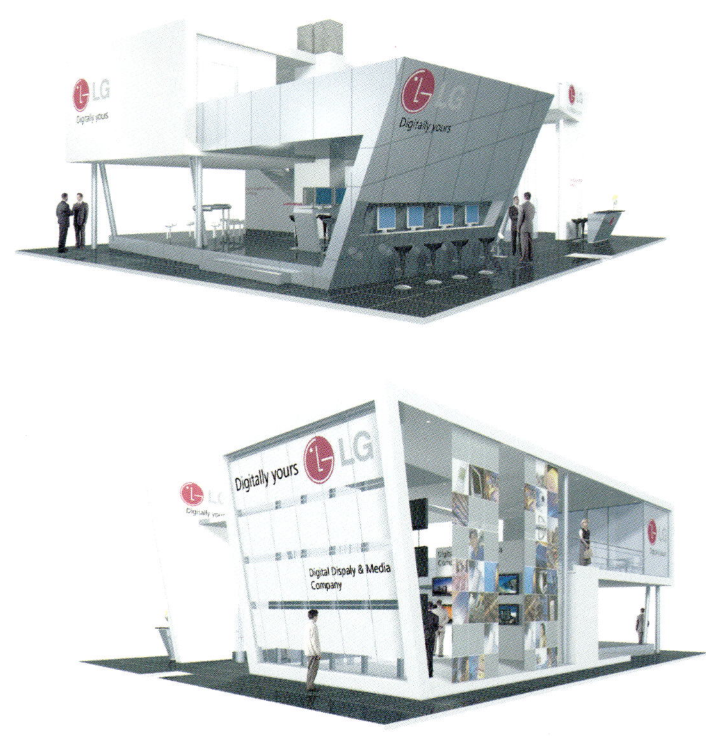

LG
Digitally yours

Digitally yours
LG
Digital Dispaly & Media
Company

LG
Digitally yours
Digital Display & Media
LG
Digitally yours

LG
Digitally yours
lider
n tecnologia digital
n mundo de conectividad
n sus manos

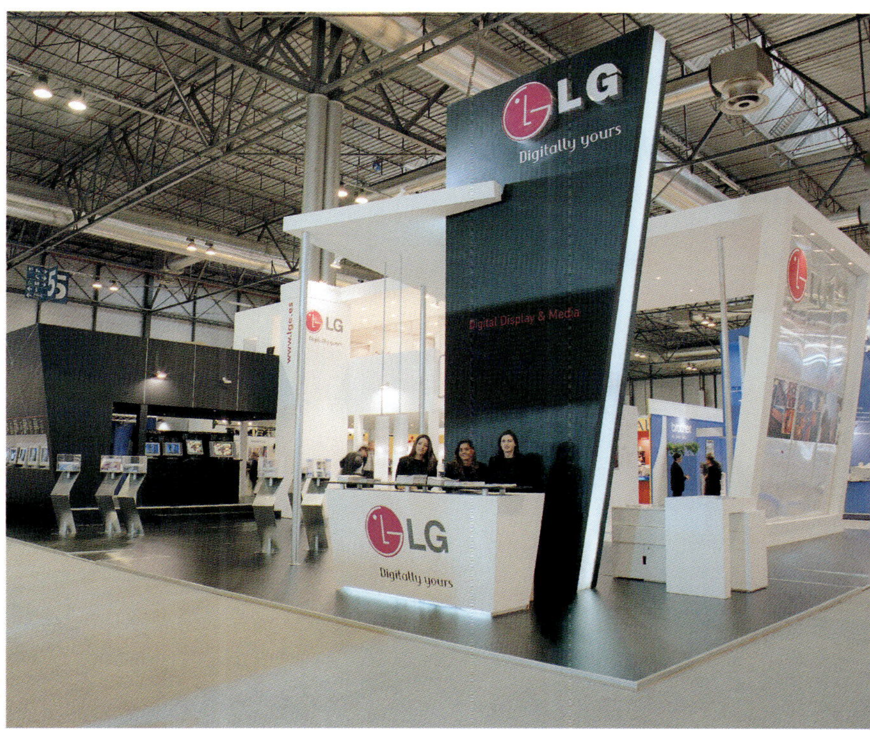

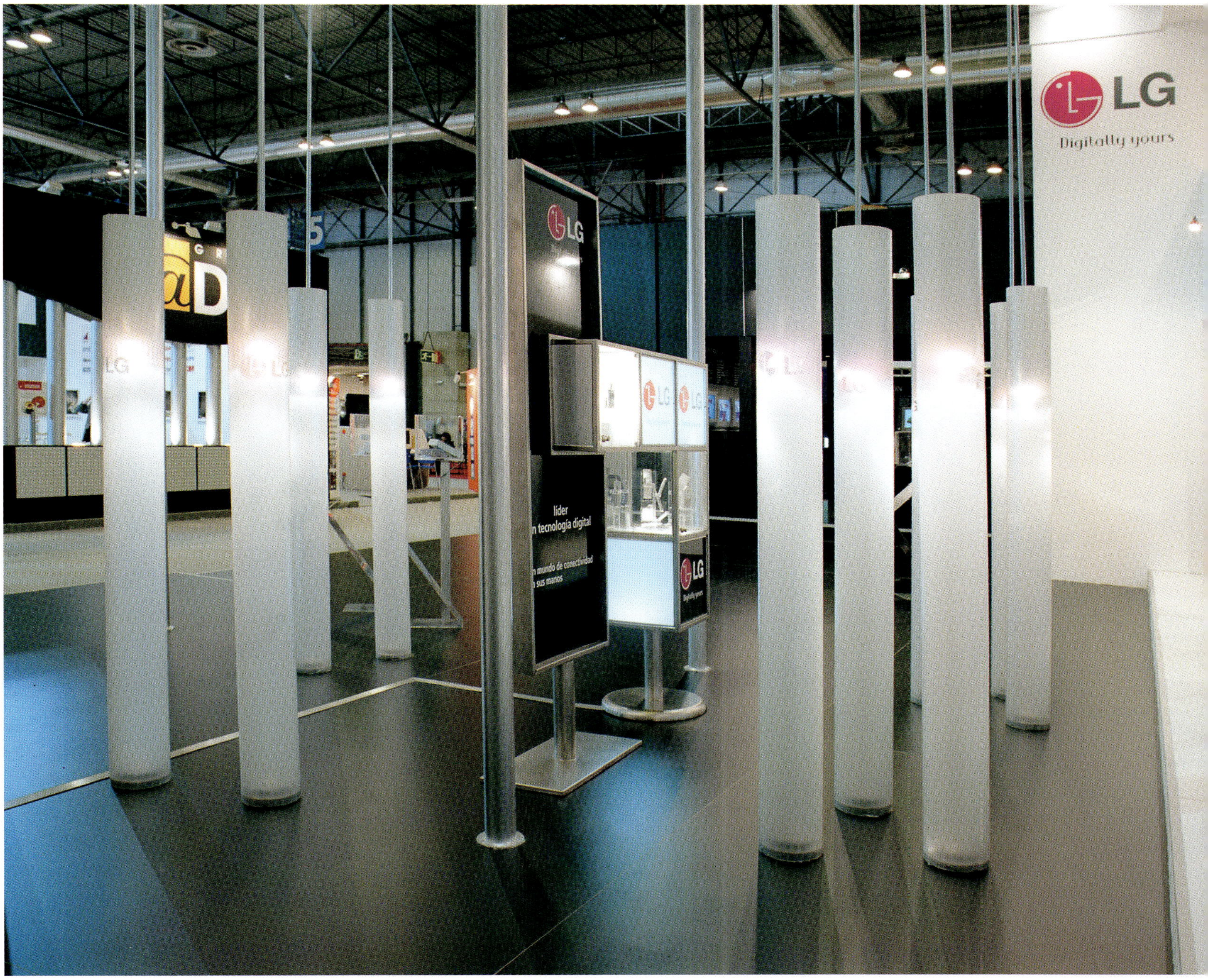

Welonda

Continuum

This stand was designed for Wella's division of professional hairdresser materials for the Cosmobelleza Fair of March 2002, which took place in Barcelona. The design took its inspiration from the sixties and seventies, the idea being to emulate a discotheque from the era by using a predominance of curved forms.
Circular wooden structures with back-lit images are placed at the entrance. The floor is grey rubber, while the ceiling consists of a stretch of fabric, behind which is concealed a discotheque-style lighting system with constantly changing colors. Music keeps the atmosphere lively, and the lighting scheme is topped off with assorted spotlights, creating the overall impression of a fun, youthful space.

Photographs: Continuum

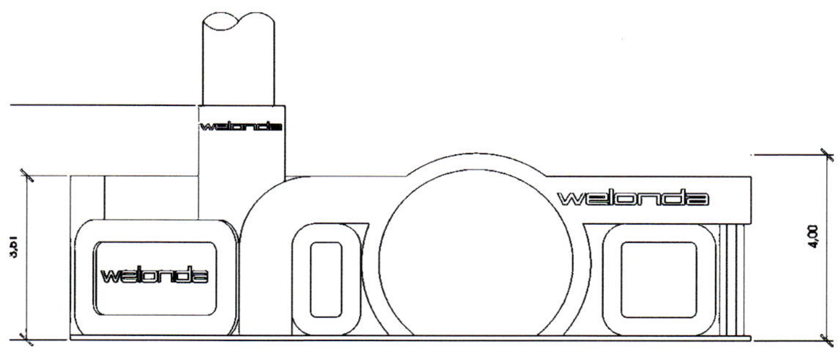

Elevation

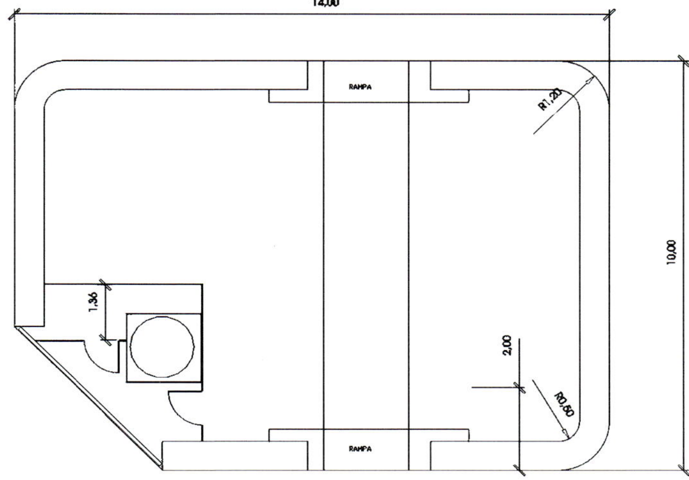

Floor plan

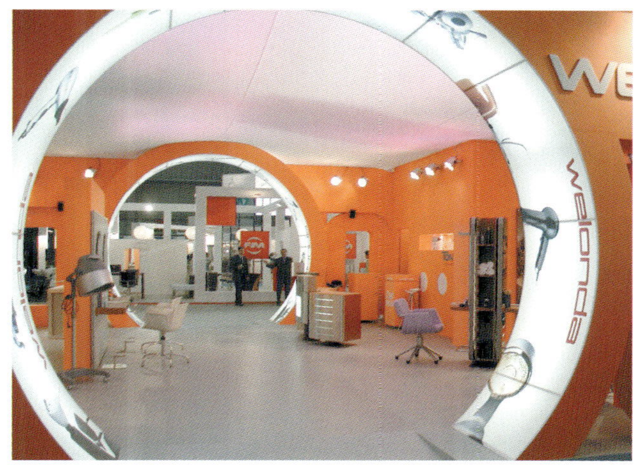

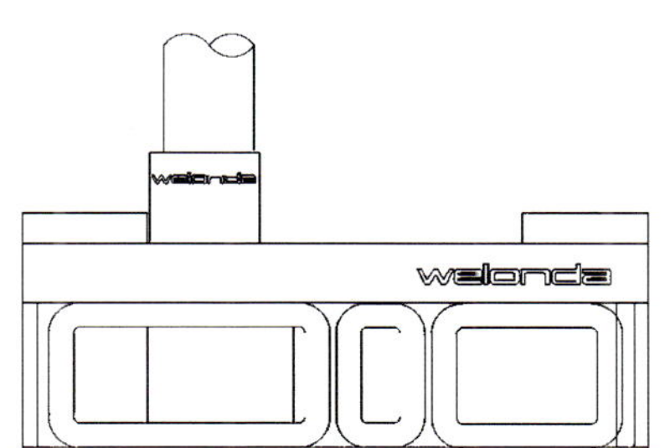

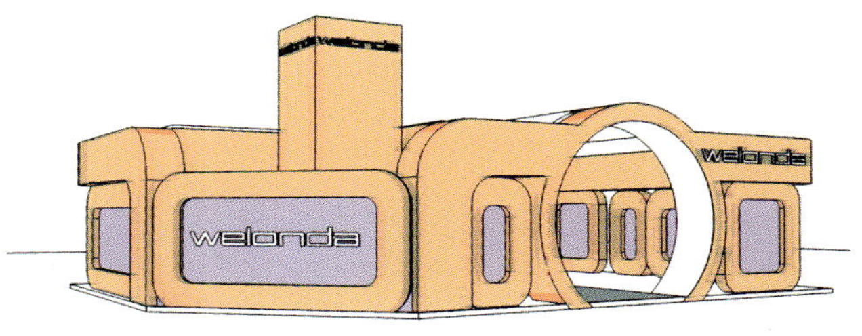

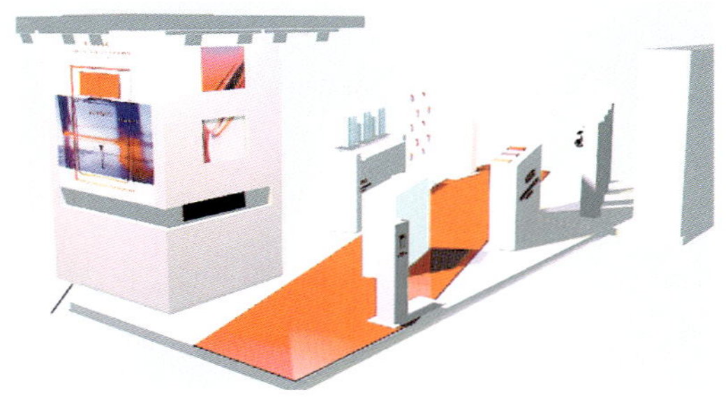

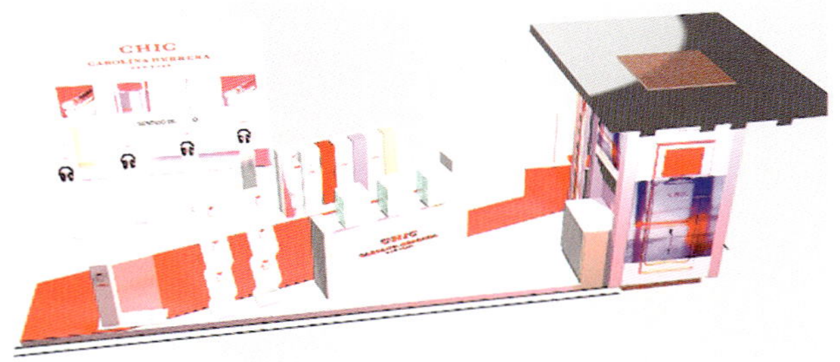

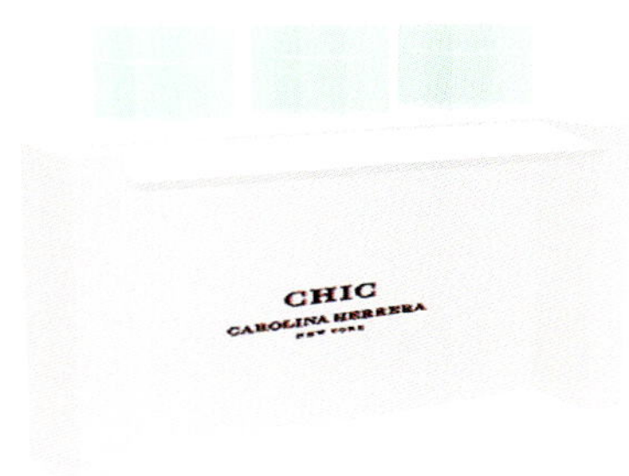

Chic

Carolina Herrera Internacional

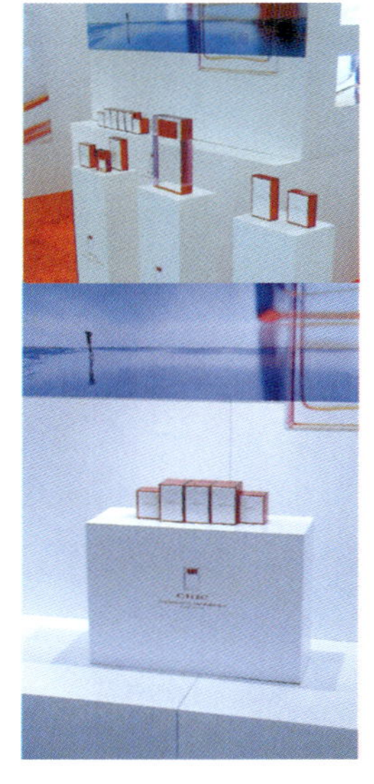

Featuring large expanses of white with red accents, this stand has been designed as a three-dimensional, life-sized representation of this cosmetics company's packaging and marketing strategies.

The general layout consists of a rectangular space divided successively into an entryway, a cocktail lounge, an art exhibit, the presentation room and, finally, a museum.

The art exhibit consists of five pieces, each in frames of 3x3m with a depth of 30cm. The so-called "liquid mural" is a chamber with a water machine projection featuring a smooth background of blue tones. Superimposed on this surface are images of a waterfall. The "color mural" has a background of MDF plates, on which is a grid of colors with 10mm thick methacrylate shelves holding small white candles. The "scent mural" is filled with a tapestry of white flowers. There is a row of five glass shelves containing transparent jelly with small fruits in red tones. Next, the "glass mural" features a fragmented, tear-drop mirror curtain and a bed of sea salt in the lower part. Finally, the "concept mural" is a scale reproduction of the new perfume pack with texts written by Herrerra in red metal.

All of the box-like display cases in the presentation area are in a clean, crisp white, with red carpeting guiding visitors through the stand.

Photographs: Carolina Herrera Internacional

look

taste

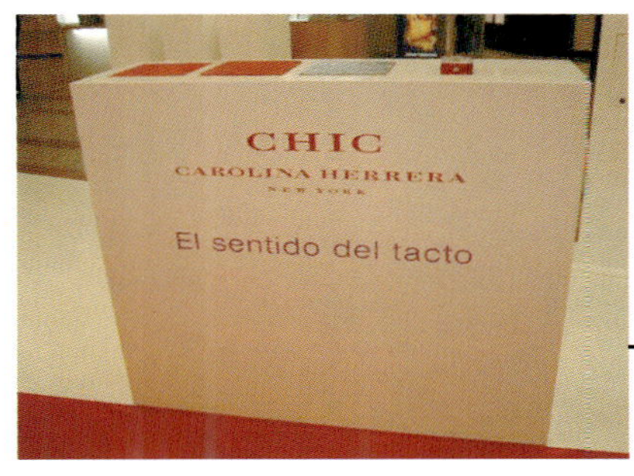

touch

smell

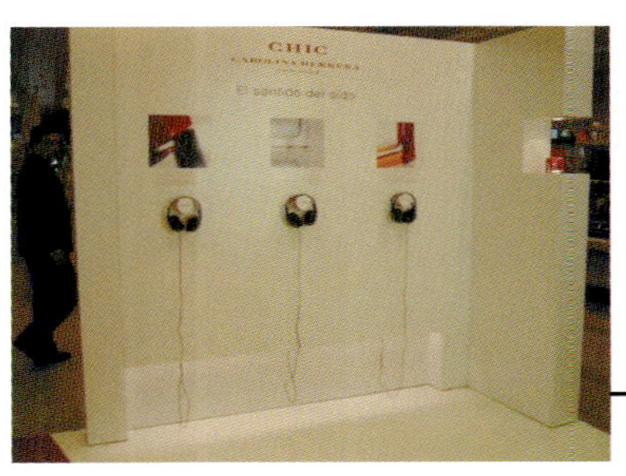

hear

Hispalyt

Vicente Sarrablo Moreno

Ceilings, walls and flooring are here fashioned from a single line, material and format. The continuous surface wrapping the stand shows the architectonic possibilities of new construction systems using reinforced ceramic: sheets of the minimum thickness, asymmetric domes, and roofing which is bent until turning downward to form walls and floors.

The design objective of this stand was two-fold. On the one hand was the desire to show how a new generation of architects is mastering techniques made possible by innovations in such traditional materials as, for example, baked clay and, on the other, to attract the interest of construction professionals in a system which enables the recuperation of ceramic domes in a competitive manner through the use of prefab sheets.

Fotografías: Vicente Sarrablo Moreno

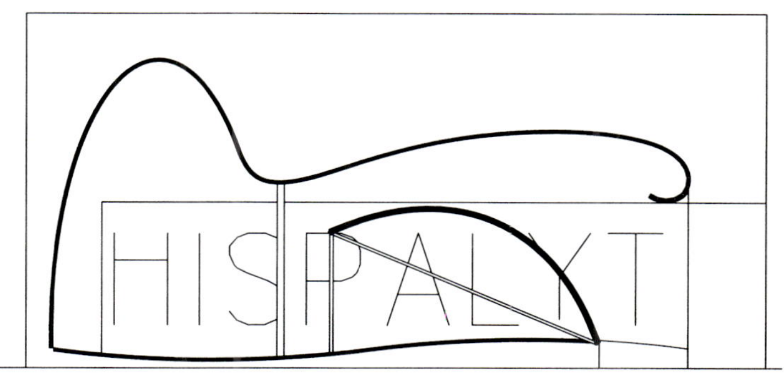

Elevation

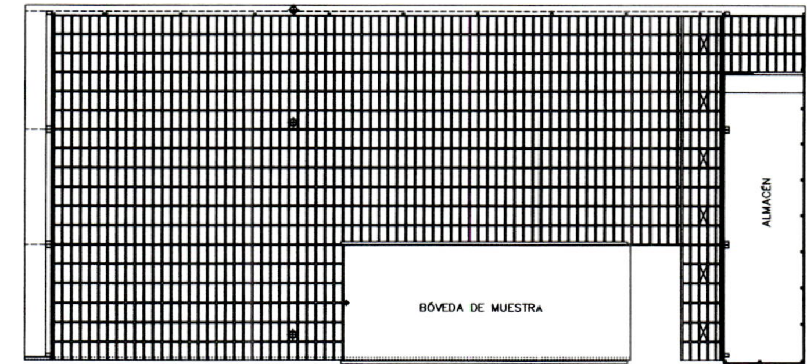

Plan of the canopy

Indian Motorcycle

Atelier Damböck Messebau

This stand was conceived and executed for the Intermot 2000 fair in Munich, Germany. The aim of the stand was to portray the legendary, pioneering name of the company and its products by showing the birth of Indian in Europe and officially launching two new motorcycle models.

The entire structure covers a surface of 132m², and has been designed to transmit a strong, unique corporate look, encapsulated through the spirit and lifestyle created with the motorcycles. The stand imitates a typical '50s-style motorcycle bar.

Photographs: Atelier Damböck Messebau

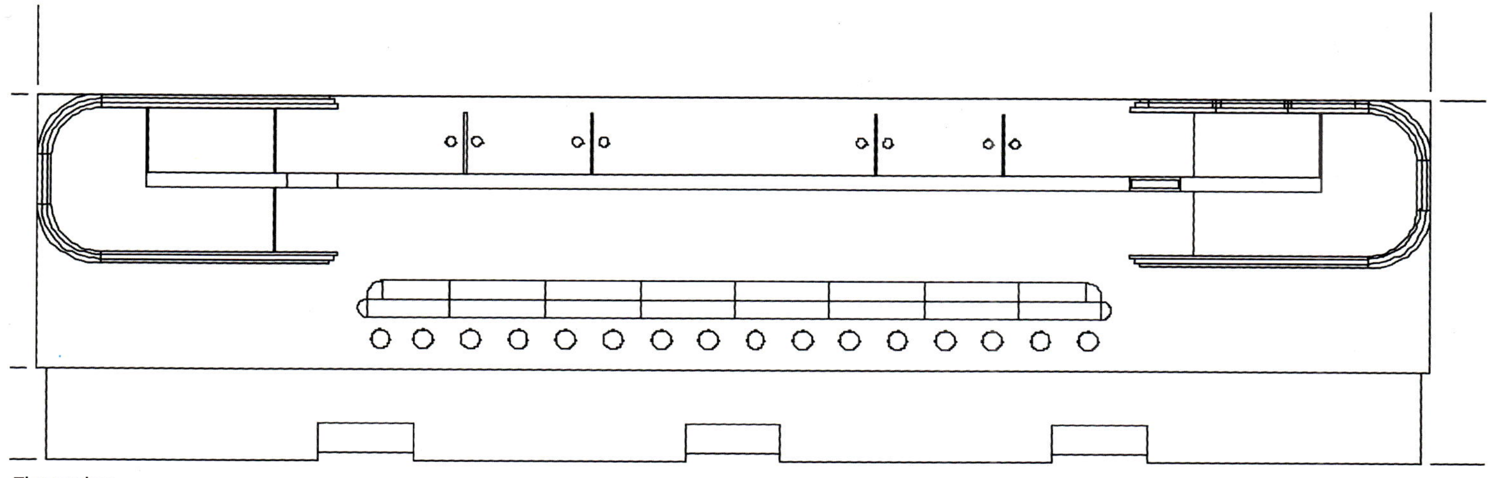

Floor plan

Indian
MOTORCYCLE

MOTORCY

Indian
MOTORCYCLE
Indian
MOTORCYCLE

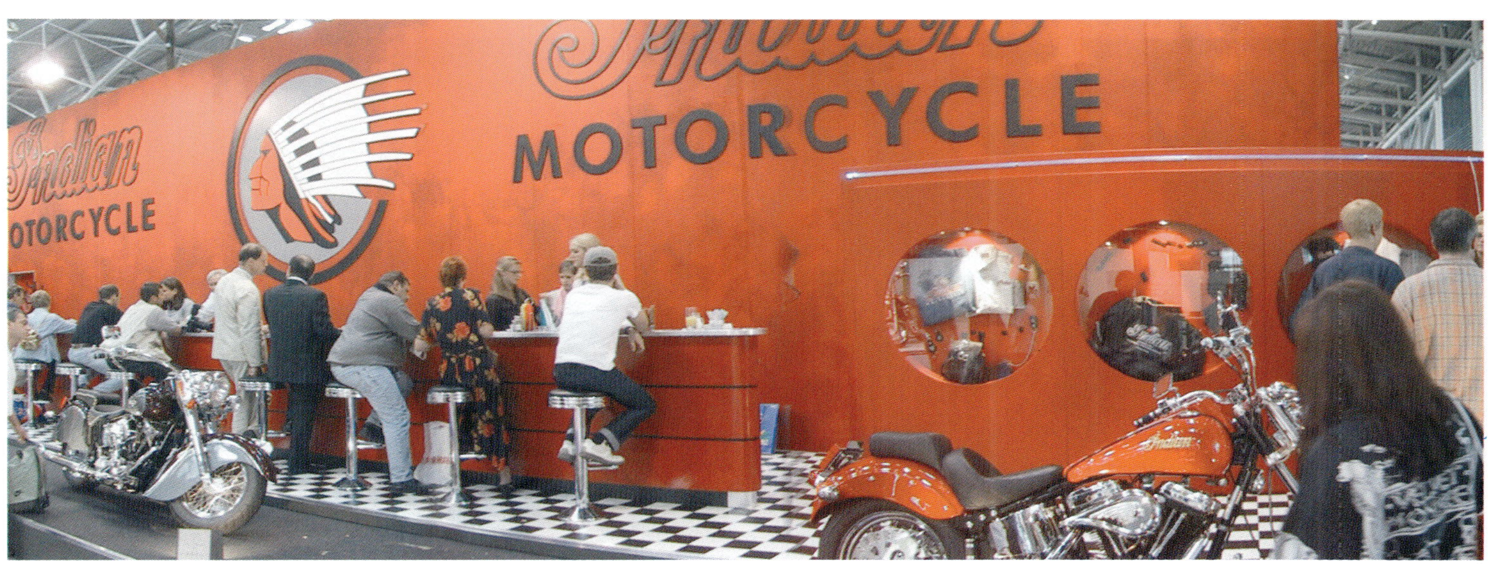
Indian
MOTORCYCLE
MOTORCYCLE

Info Pavillion Baden

Stefan Zwicky

The project to construct a series of bridges linking various areas of the German city of Badea was exhibited in this stand, which was set up in an industrial building near the work site. Aside from providing basic information for the public, it includes project layouts and models and is the place where visitors can arrange to have a guided tour of the site.

The concept behind the exhibit is to develop the exhibition space on the basis of the vocabulary of bridge building. A large wooden platform, which has been stained a grayish color, presides over the central space. On arrival, visitors are immediately greeted by a table with explanatory pamphlets. The center of the stand is occupied by a room built with thin, aged wood beams, which is a reference to an empty structure used in bridge building, allowing a partial view through the beams. At the end of the exhibition space is a meeting room furnished in folding wooden chairs.

The exhibition space is clad in a roof which begins at ground level and sweeps upward toward the four diagonal walls of the upper portion of the room. The weave is so thin that it filters the light so that the layouts on exhibit receive optimal lighting. Documentation is displayed on metal plaques hanging along the lower portion of the structure, while the names of the suburbs to be joined by the new bridge are shown on the upper portion.

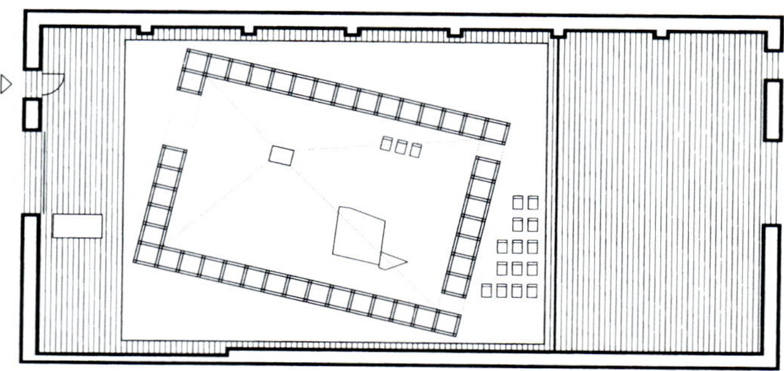

Floor plan

Photographs: Stefan Zwicky

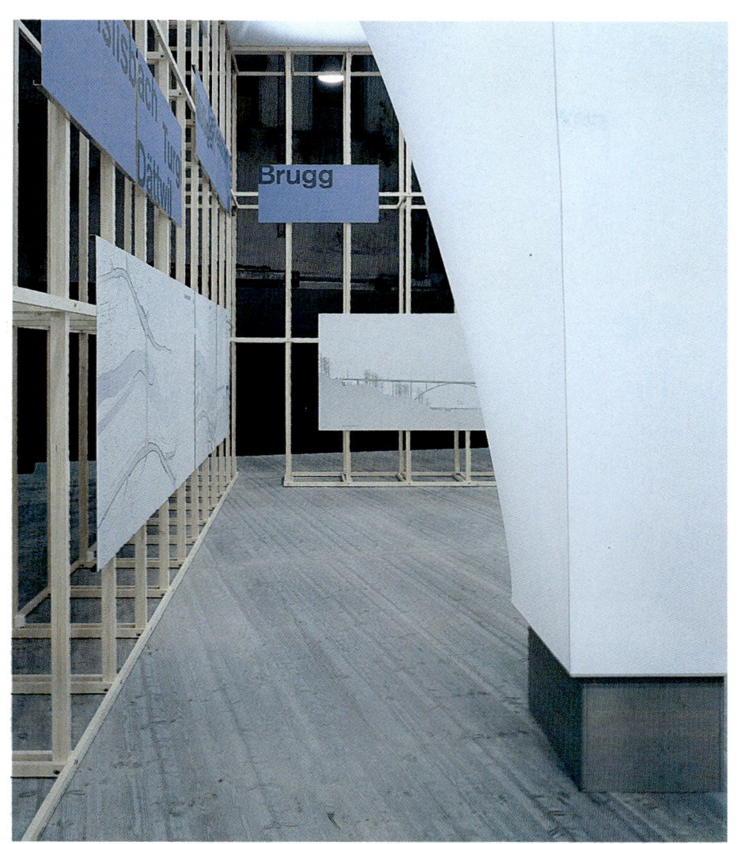

Brugg

Troms
Kirchdorf
Nussbaunen
Rieden
Siggen

Kirchdorf
Nussbaunen
Rieden
Enne
baden
Obersigg
lingen

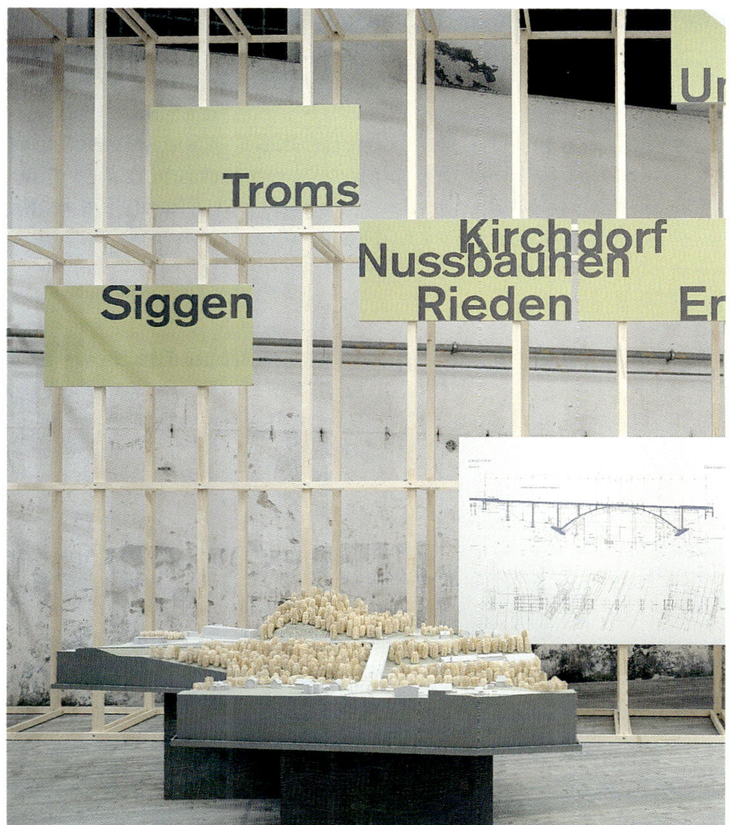

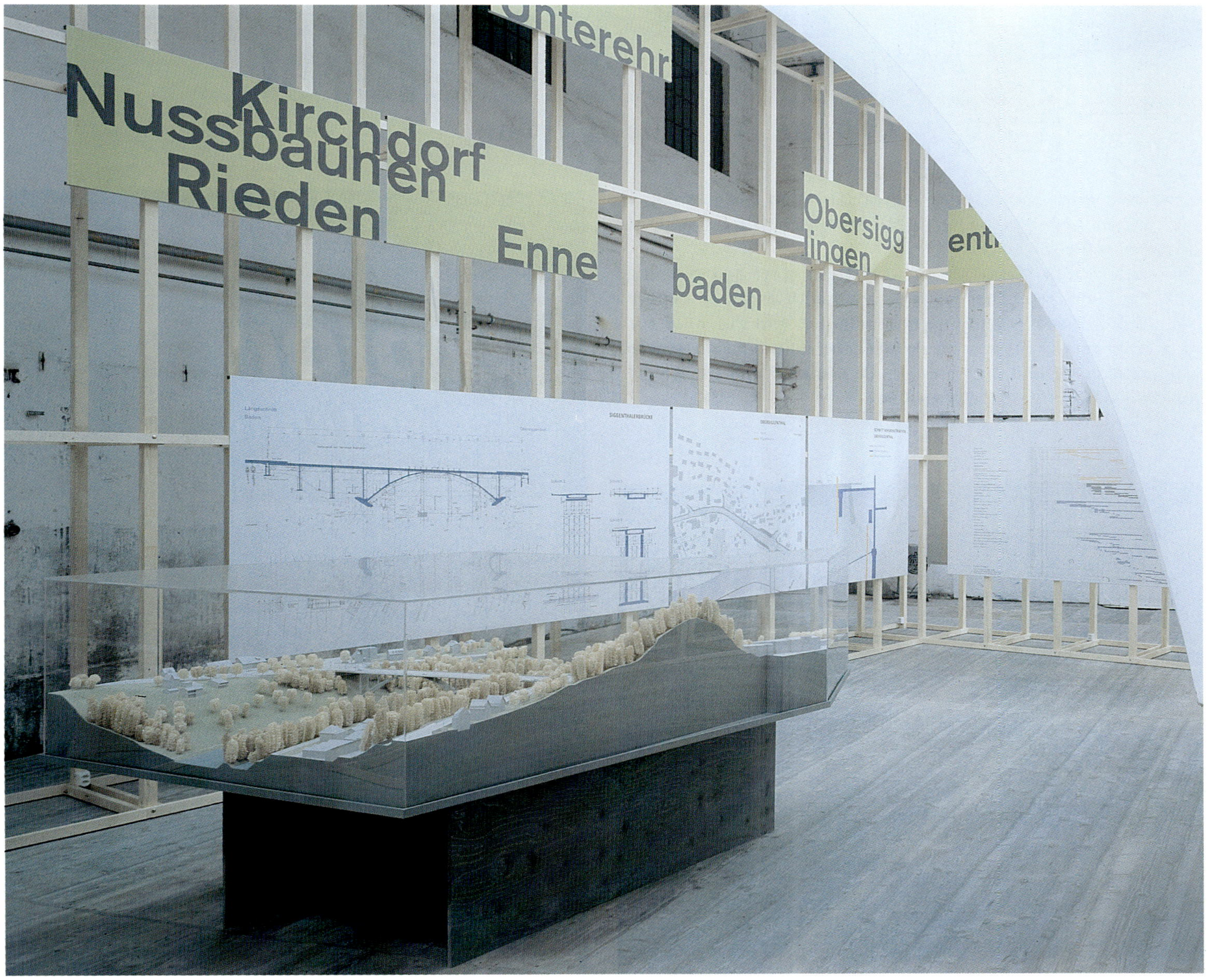

The concept and motto behind this stand at CeBIT 2001 was Explore!, inviting visitors to explore the core of things and discover the company. This aim was actively pursued in the design and concept of the exhibition stand. The closed architecture hides the interior from outside views, while the visitor is invited to get to know the company's product and philosophy. Deliberately reduced to an essential and basic form, the stand is of a simple cube design. The double-height entrance and stairway have been designed like a canyon splitting the side of this otherwise hermetic structure. The slogan, Explore!, heads the entrance and is meant as an invitation.

Passing through the canyon, visitors are treated to views of a bright interior or of the exhibition stand reflecting Systemfabrik's work.

Visitors then reach a brightly pulsing room: the core. The alternating white and yellow light represents the company's vitality. The room contains a number of fluorescent units, into which have been set monitors showing graphics and staff interviews which are meant to demonstrate the company's success and achievements. In addition to the monitor information, the interior design supports the central statements.

The first floor is a lounge, where one can again find the basic message literally written into the design. Surrounded by fluorescent walls, this is the area where communication between Systemfabrik and their customers takes place. A special atmosphere was created by the openly designed room to support communication processes. An individual sound design stresses the contrast between the hectic atmosphere of the fair and this enclosed refuge.

Systemfabrik explore!

GFG / Gruppe für Gestaltung

The construction of the stand consists of steel and plywood, with the outer and inner walls planked with a planar system. The outer surface is made up of AludiBond, and the inner surface is of acrylic glass. The fluorescent tube lighting system was installed behind the inner acrylic planking and can be dismantled without damage after use.

Photographs: Thomas Kleiner

explore!
systemfabrik.

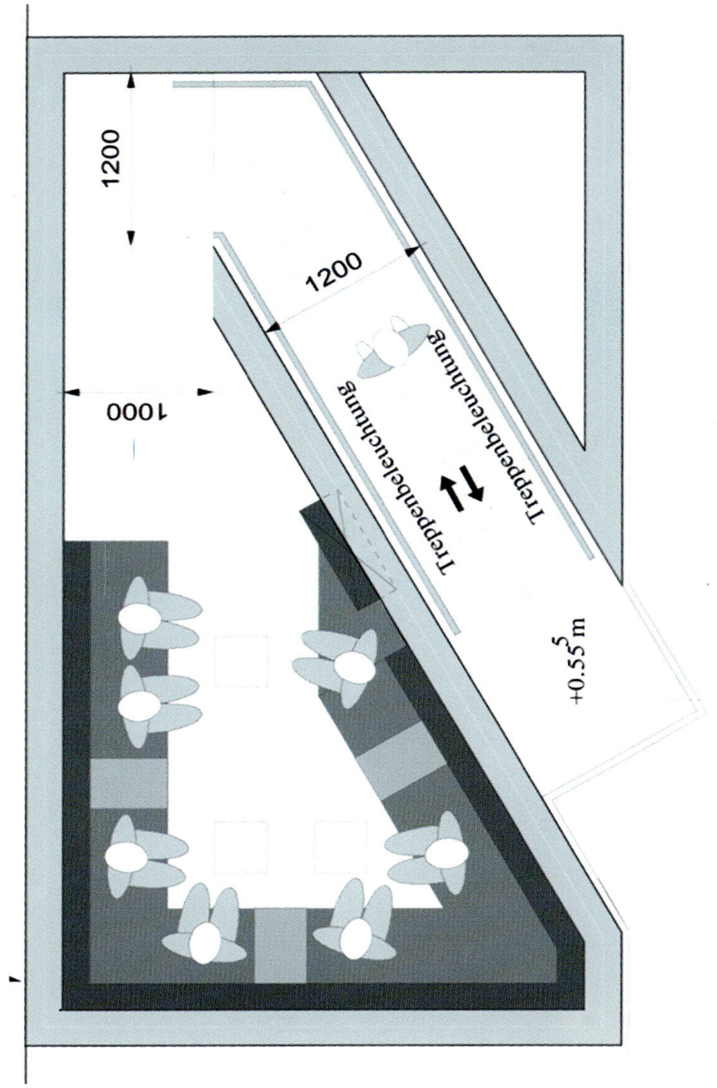

First floor

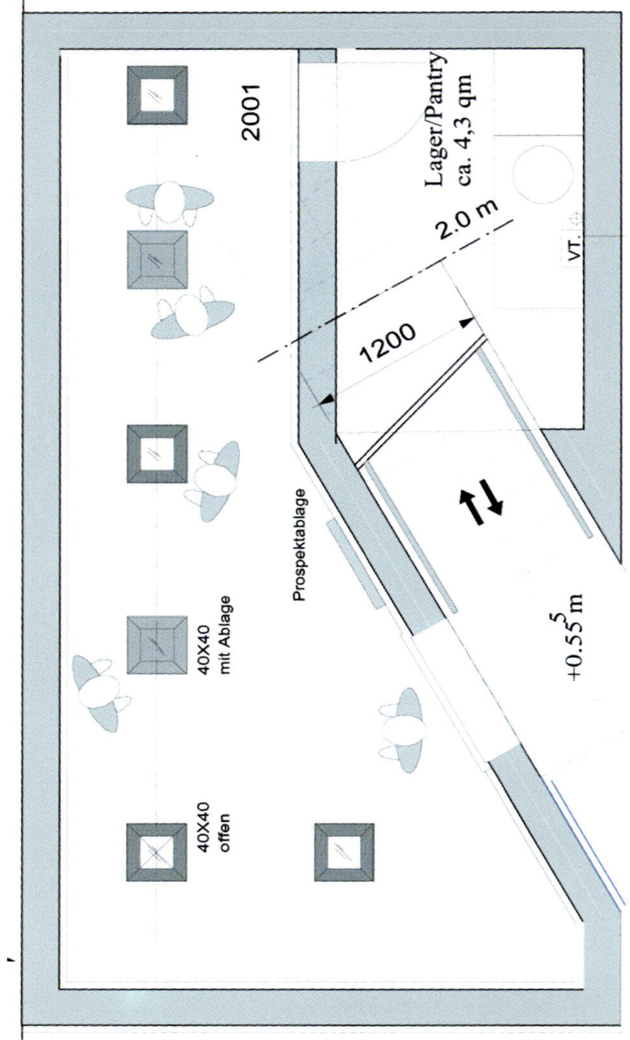

Ground floor

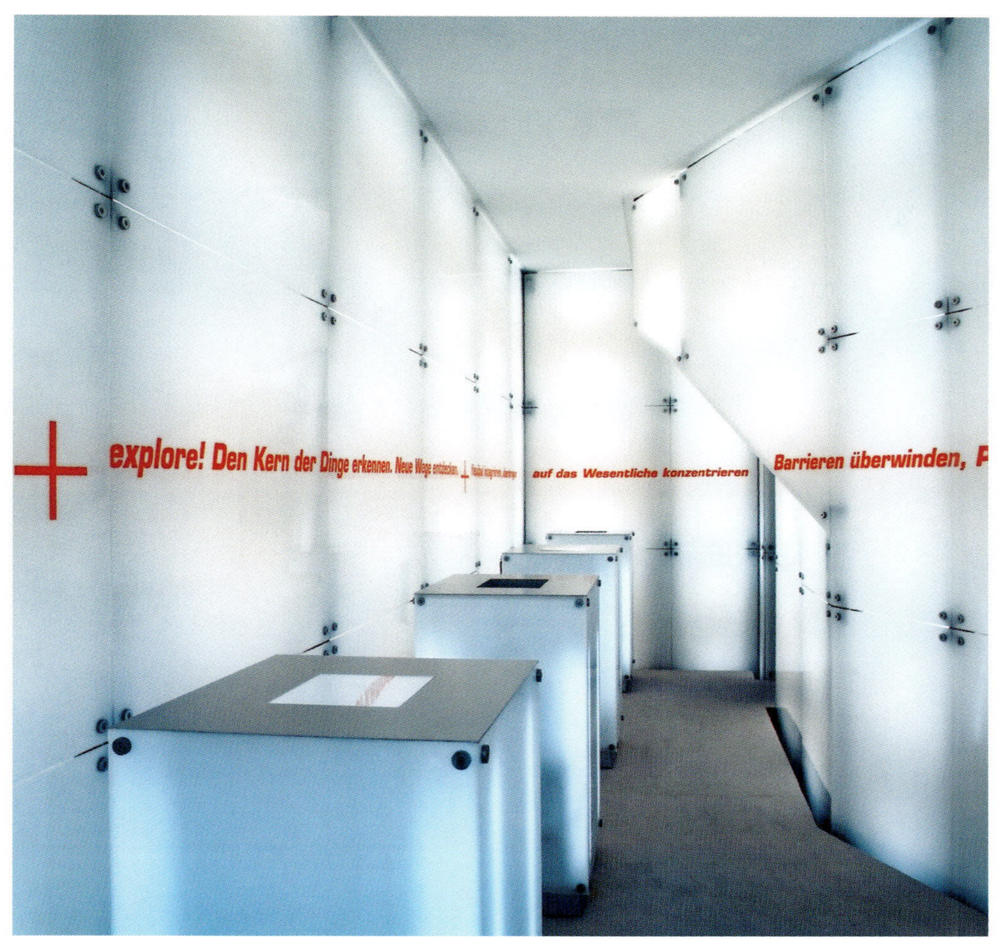

explore! Den Kern der Dinge erkennen.
auf das Wesentliche konzentrieren
Barrieren überwinden,

Komplexität reduzieren, erfassen,

übertragen, transformieren, verknüpfen, vernetzen
html
xml

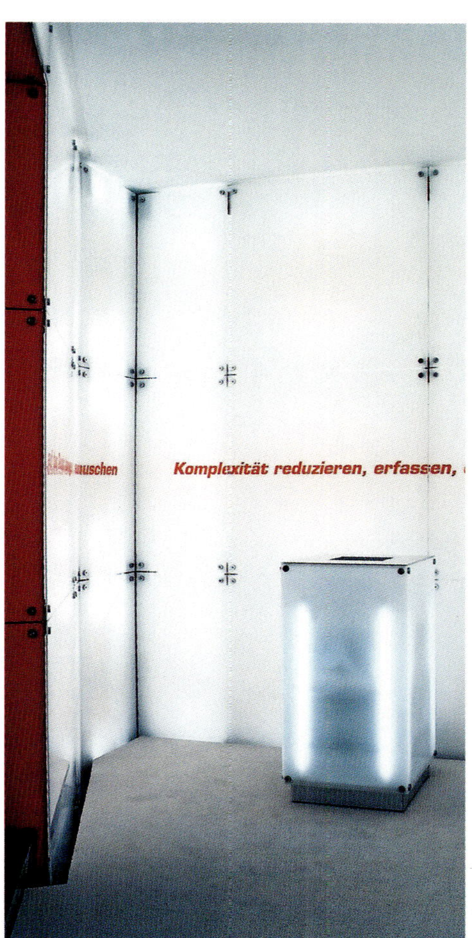

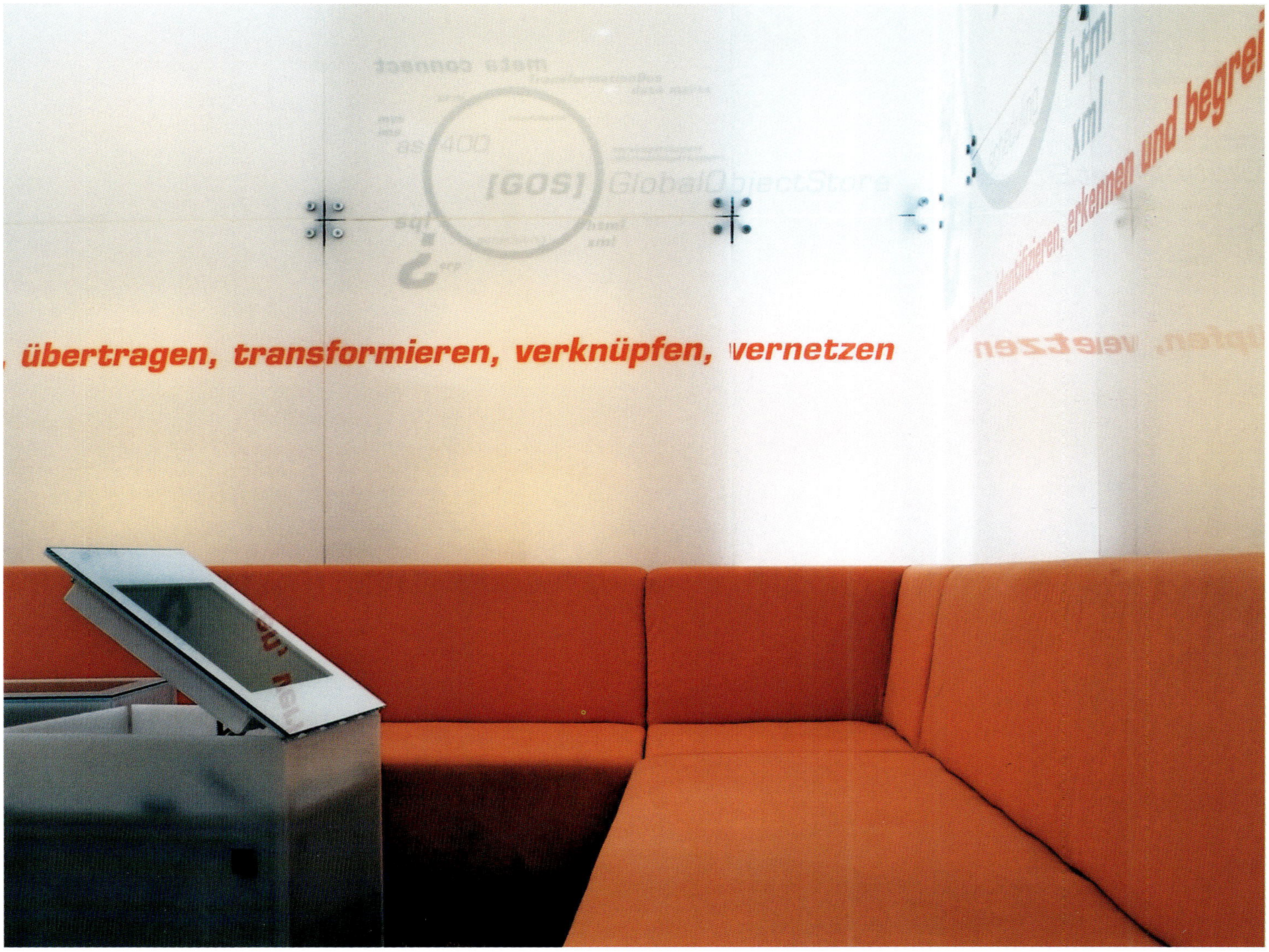

Damlier Chrysler AG

Kurz + Partner Architekten

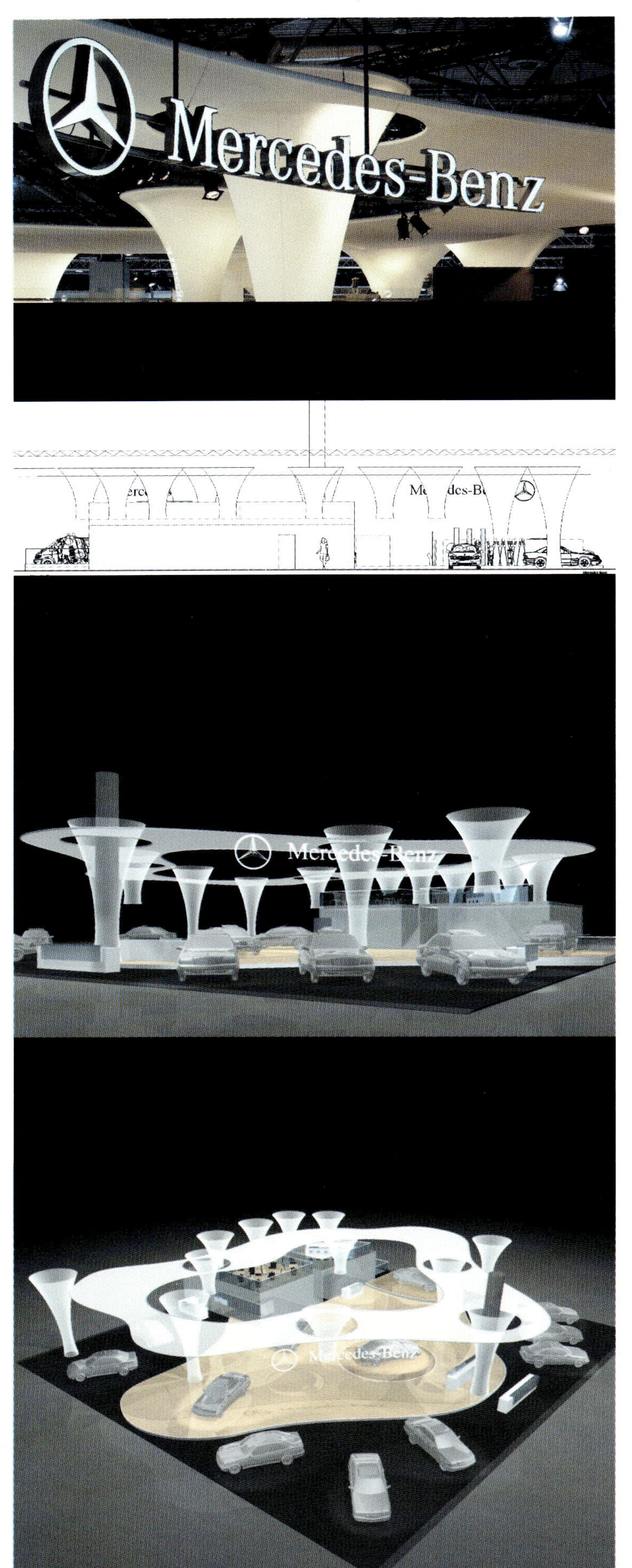

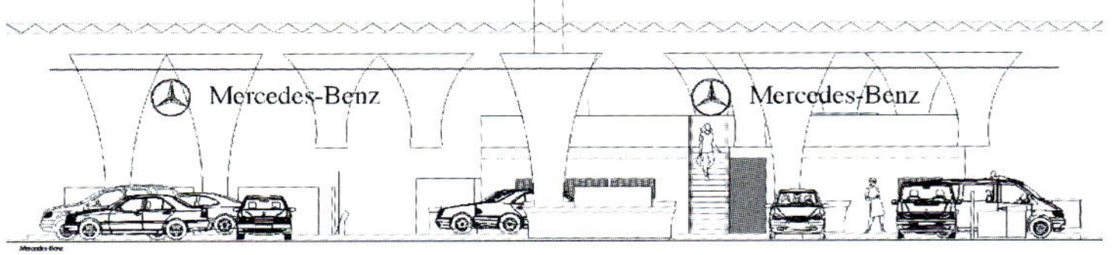

The conception and execution of this stand aimed to project Daimler Chrylser AG as a future-oriented, global brand; thus, a unified space was defined for the presentation of the individual passanger car model.

On display at the Auto Mobil International 2002 trade fair in Leipzig, Germany, its central design element was a sculptural ceiling with illuminated cylinders containing graphics and sound, which had a tremendous impact from a distance and attracted the attention of visitors to the fair. The cylinders also divide the stand into various areas and give it greater visual volume. An introverted interior space has been created by the illuminated columns without excluding the surrounding environment.

The color blue has been adopted from the corporate logo to act as a central unifying element in combination with the highlighting effect of white.

Photographs: Andreas Keller, Altdorf

Jeep

Premiere

Felgen
AMG

Exquisit
Die neue E-Klasse.
Faszinierend.
E
E 320

DTM
Komfortabel
Komfortabel
WARSTEINER
Fahrprog

Mercedes-Benz Collection
Exquisit.

DTM
Innovativ.
Souverän.
Elegant.
Die neue E-Klasse.
komfortabler...
Innovativ.
Souverän.
Elegant.
Die neue E-Klasse.
1995
Bernd Schneider gewinnt mit der AMG-C-Klasse die DTM und die Internationale Tourenwagen-Meisterschaft ITC.
1996
Bernd Schneider wird mit sieben Siegen in der AMG C-Klasse Vizemeister der ITC.
1997-1999
Zweimal Markensieger. Fahrertitel für Bernd Schneider, Klaus Ludwig und Ricardo Zonta in der Internationalen FIA GT-Meisterschaft. Bestleistung: zehn Siege in zehn Rennen.
2000
Deutsche Tourenwagen-Masters: mit acht Siegen gewinnt Mercedes-Benz die Herstellerwertung. Bernd Schneider den Fahrertitel.
2001
Bernd Schneider verteidigt mit dem D2 AMG Mercedes als erster Fahrer erfolgreich seinen DTM-Titel.

Edra

Morozzi & partners

This stand was designed by the company's own art director, the same man who orchestrated the Edra 2002 project, which is a presentation of various expressive styles of designers from all over the world. Being especially familiar with the product, he had a clear idea of the modern and youthful, yet sophisticated, look that was necessary in the exhibition area.

The end result is a partially enclosed stand with five entrances along two sides and eight different loosely divided sections where these highly eclectic pieces of furniture have been put on display. The partitions, which are primarily aluminum with acrylic finishes and rounded edges, have been placed so as to only partially conceal the space behind it, leaving just enough visible to lure visitors from other sections and thereby guarantee constant movement throughout the stand.

Photographs: Emilio Tremolada

Floor plan

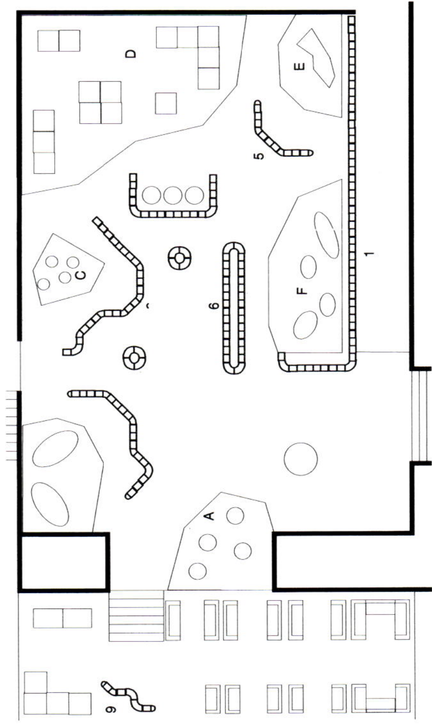

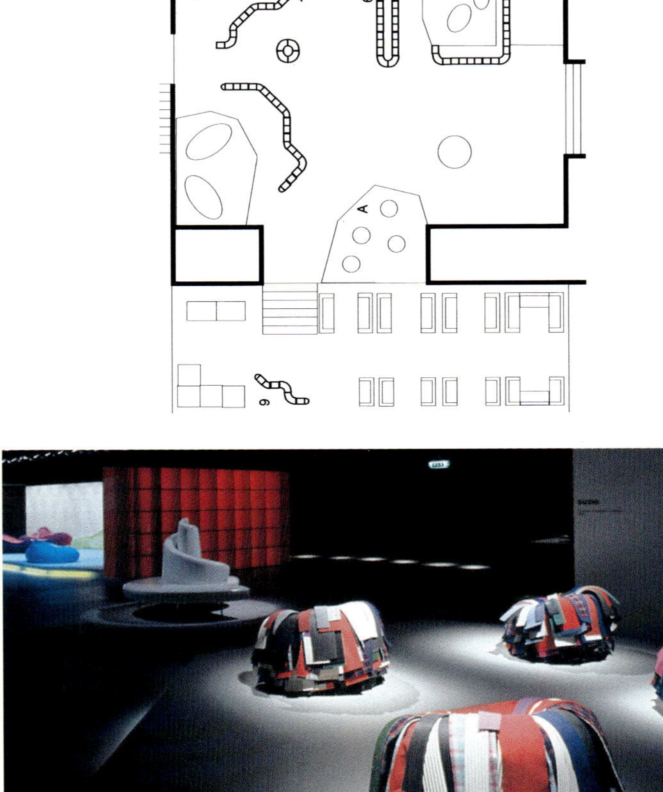

Fluid forms and rounded edges were chosen for the dividing screens in emulation of the organic shapes of the pieces on display. Likewise, colored lighting in red, blue, green and yellow emanating from below the platforms and occasional splashes of color along the walls (for example, a neon yellow acrylic band as accent or an entire wall in deep red) have been inspired by the wide range of tones used in the product. On the whole, though, clean white and elegant silver surfaces predominate throughout the stand's design in order to let the furniture speak for itself.

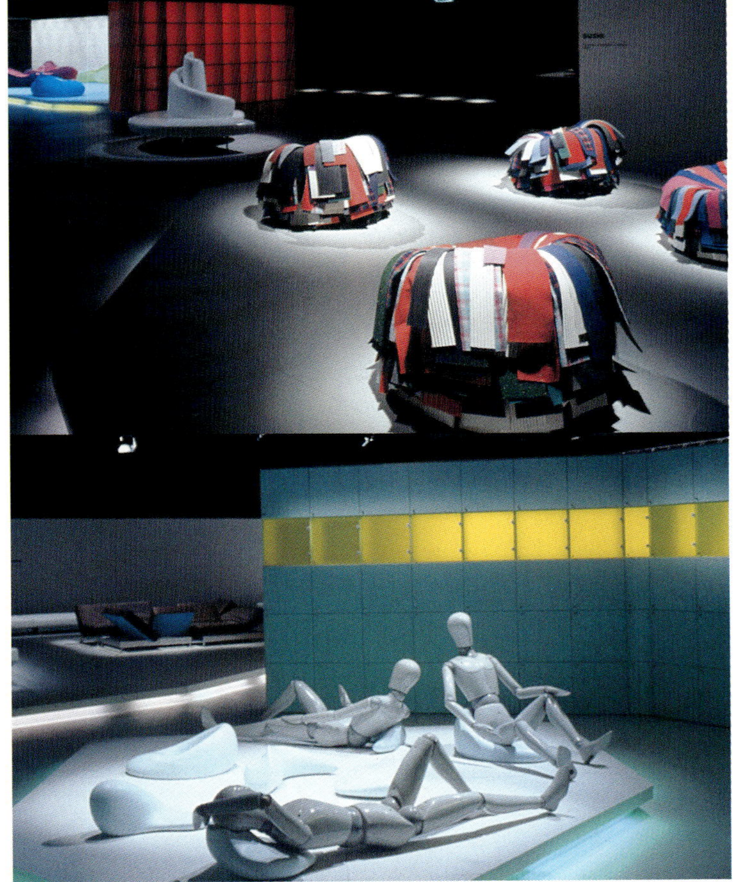

Wella

Totems

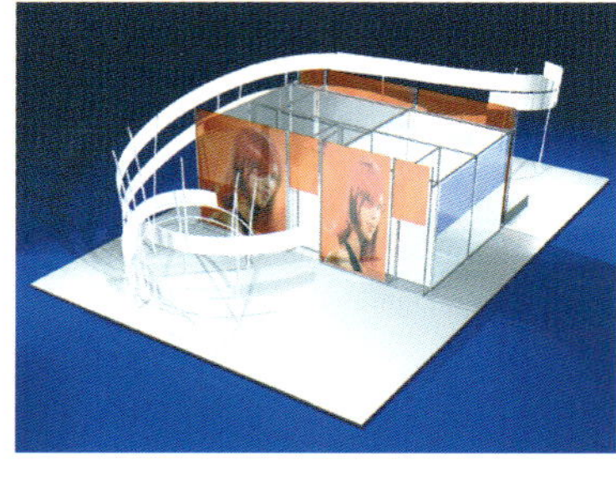

The design group for this stand started with a study of Wella's identity as depicted on its logo. They then focussed their findings on the more specific situation of fairs, exhibitions and events.

The ideas and sensations that Wella wished to transmit were inspiration, dynamism and energy, followed by qualities of rationale (competence, quality and trust) and emotion (extravagance, beauty and femininity).

As the company's logo, the Wella wave connects all the different areas of the exhibition space, curling around specific parts of the stand, such as the information desk or even creating a space of its own, such as a hospitality area. The wave is made of semi-translucent opalescent plastic and is supported by a metal construction that is anchored to the floor. It can also be suspended from the ceiling by using a rigging construction.

The high-quality "Pila Petit" system by Berkhardt Leitner is used for the functional spaces and the back walls of the stand. Like the floor, which has a solid, high-quality feel, the system has a highly functional character.

The screens have a very important visual function: to create an energetic, warm and intense background. Moreover they can display specific product information or create a product atmosphere. These large fabric screens are directly connected to the Pila system. They are basically red, but they can also be reproduced in a range of colors. Backlighting lends extra warmth and care to the themes.

Photographs: Markus Mahler

WELLA

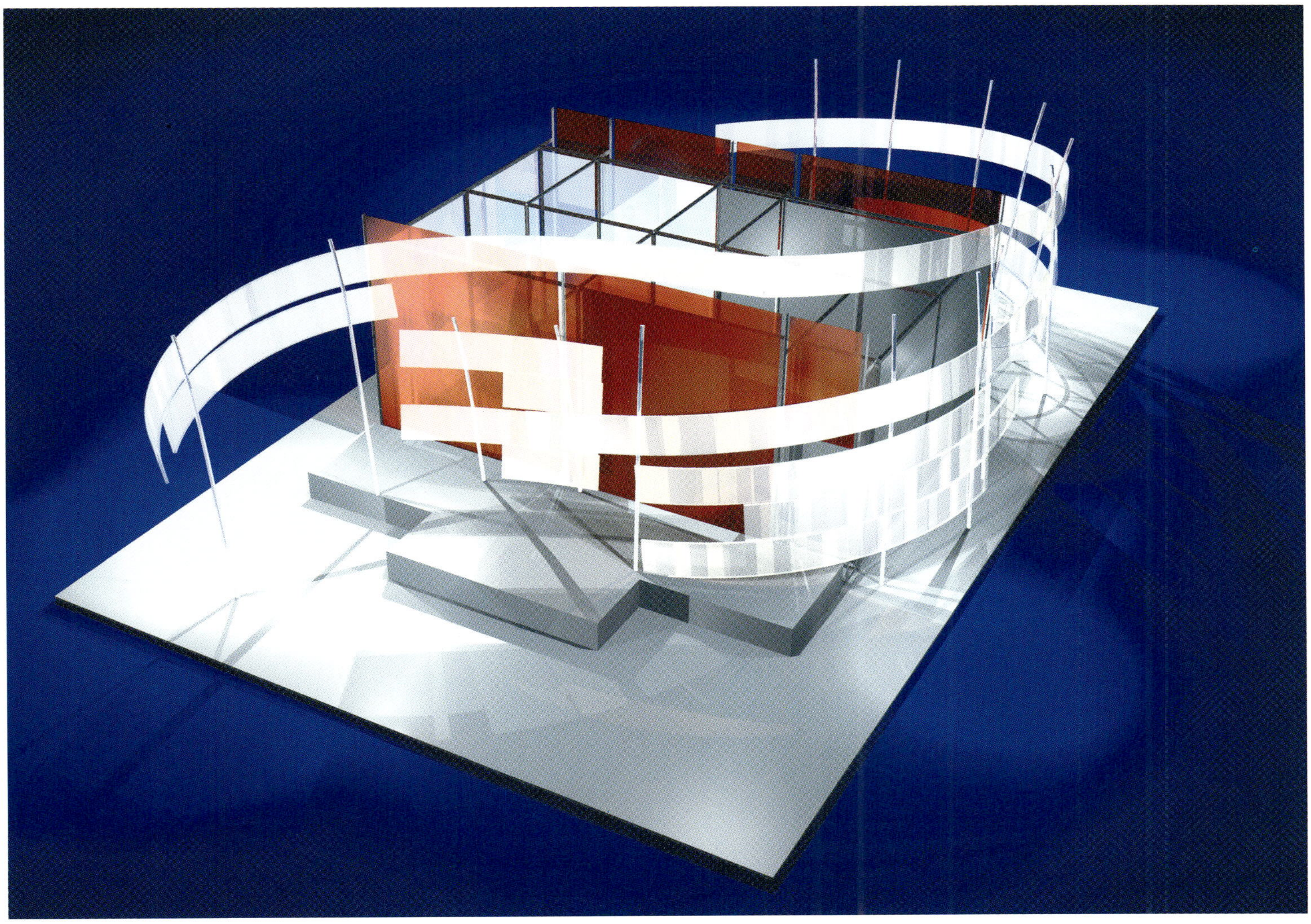

Prospa

EMBT arquitectes associats

Architects Enric Miralles and Benedetta Tagliabue designed this stand for a pharmaceuticals trade show in Paris. A precise and sophisticated look was the goal; an image which would represent the pharmaceutical technology produced by their client, while at the same time one which would be sufficiently spectacular and attractive so as to entice people to stop and take a look. Furthermore, the components had to be economical, easy to transport and easily adaptable to a limited exhibition space (only $24m^2$).

With these determining factors, a stage of movable, wood-framed partitions over which are stretched a titanium mesh bearing a screen print of the company's logo were designed. These screens rest on metal tripods, creating an interplay of transparency and reflection as a symbol of water in the pharmaceutical industry.

The stand, which can be adapted to other fairs, had to have at least one side wall, internal modular divisions, flooring, furnishing (tables and cushioned armchairs) and support structures for the modular walls and for the lights.

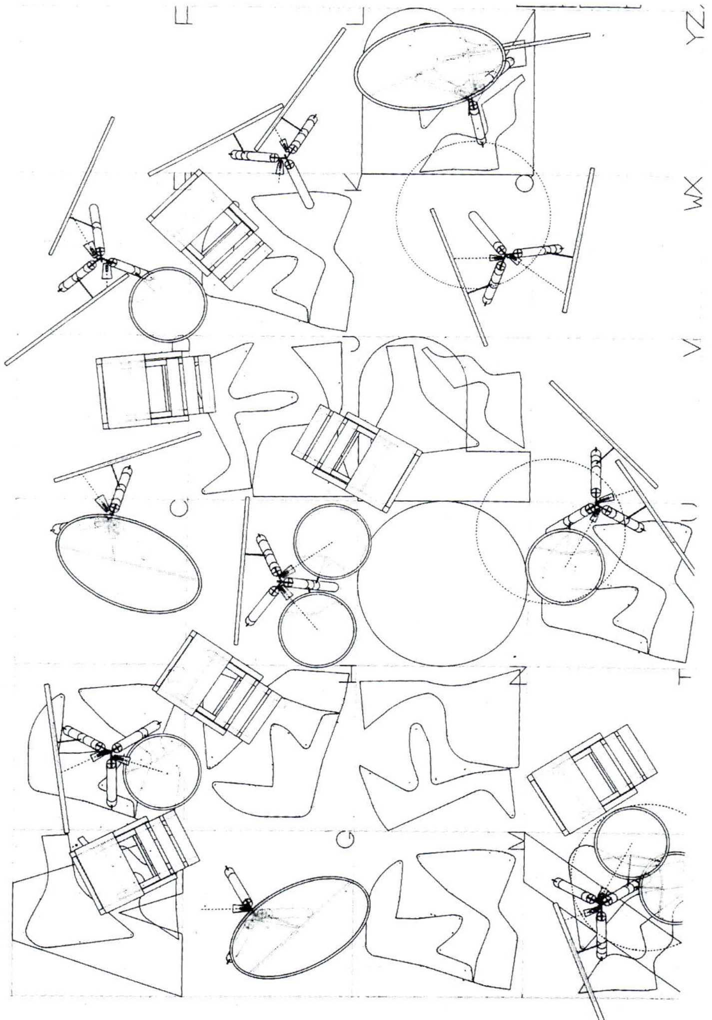

Photographs: Gery Hulton

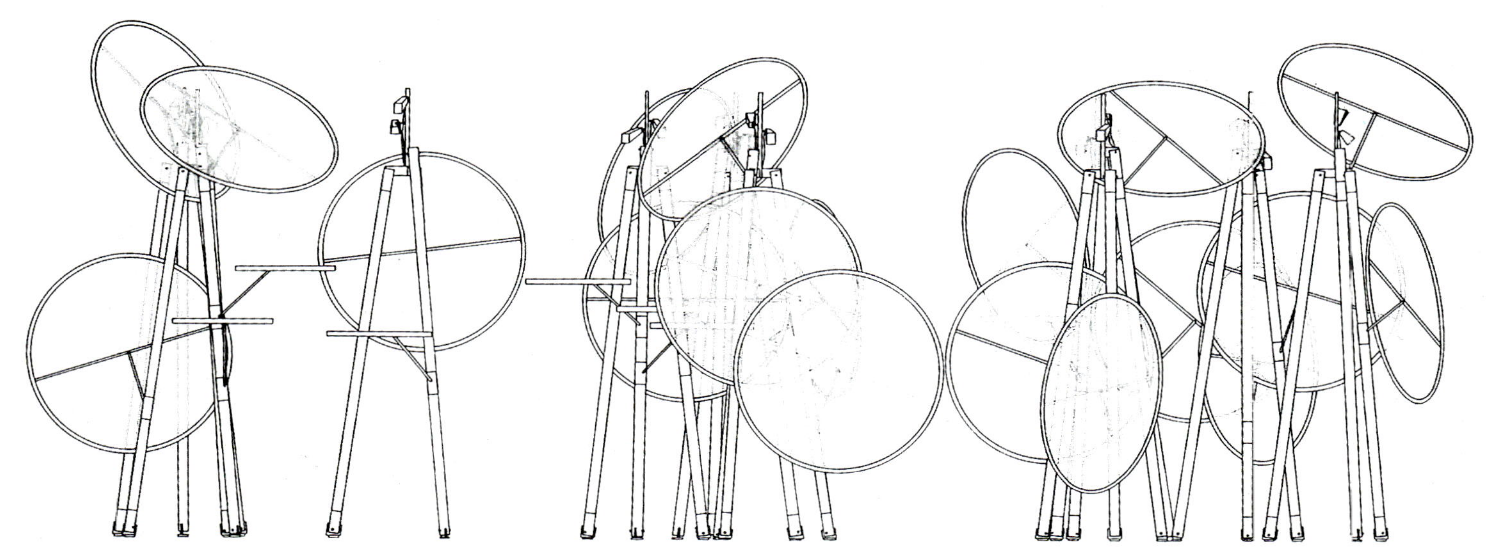

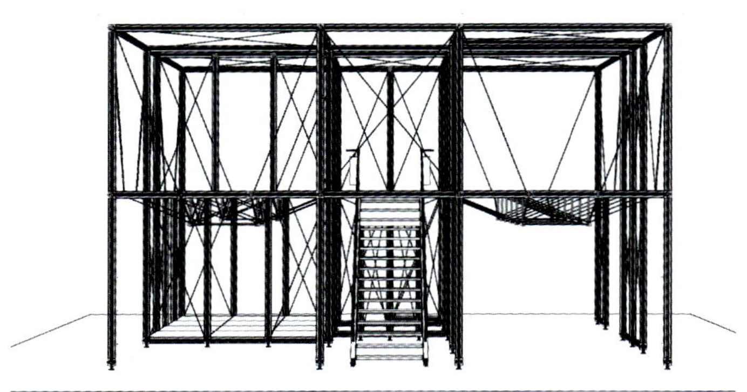

Burkhardt Leitner constructiv

Burkhardt Leitner constructiv

This stand, created for the EuroShop 2002 trade show, is based on a modular system which is easy to transport and assemble and takes up a minimum of space.

A translucent and elastic outer skin encloses the stand, creating sequences of organic curves which resemble a pulsating and living mebrane. Business is conducted on the ground floor, while visitors relax in the bar and lounge areas, where blue and green tones predominate.

The cloth walls and ceiling panels provide visitors with the sensation of being protected and, at the same time, visually and atmospherically connected with what is happening at the event via the double translucency of the inner and outer skin.

The modular design -economical, reduced to its essentials- is the sensible component of the stand, while pleasant lighting and color schemes create an aesthetically pleasing dimension.

Photographs: Lothar Bertrans

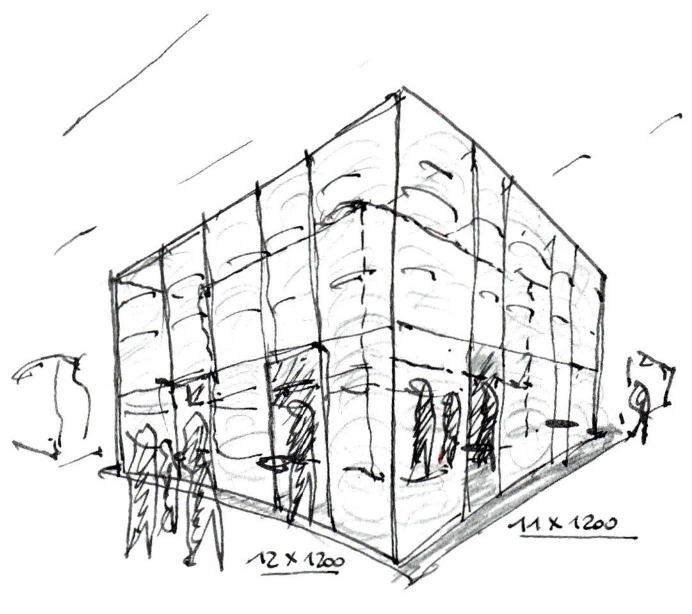
12 x 1200
11 x 1200

Construction details

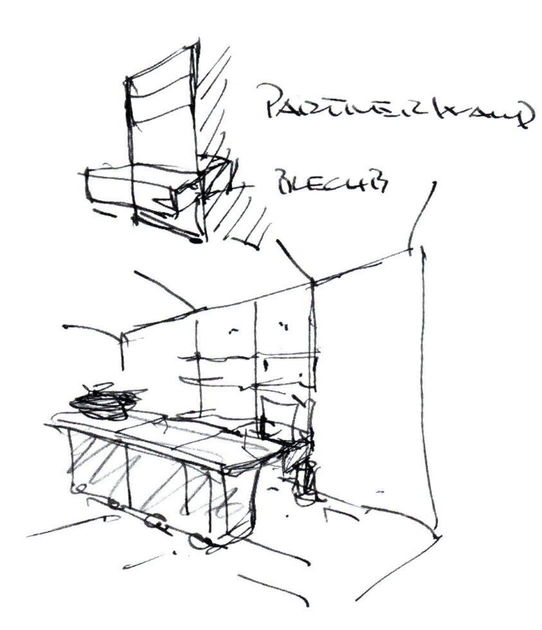

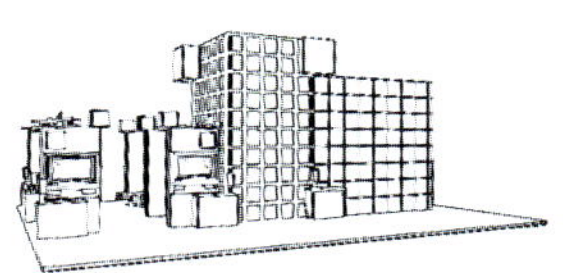

Live in Spain

Continuum

The Live in Spain stand for the trade fair Viva España 2002 in London was designed combining different modules that confer dynamism onto the whole.
These modules, built with metal structures and a backlit methacrylate skin, are display cubes for enlarged photographs of Spain.
Live in Spain is a group of Spanish real estate firms and, as they habitually attend international fairs in London, Paris, and Berlin, it was crucial to the design concept that the final assembly of the stand should be simple, adaptable and easy to transport.

Photographs: Continuum

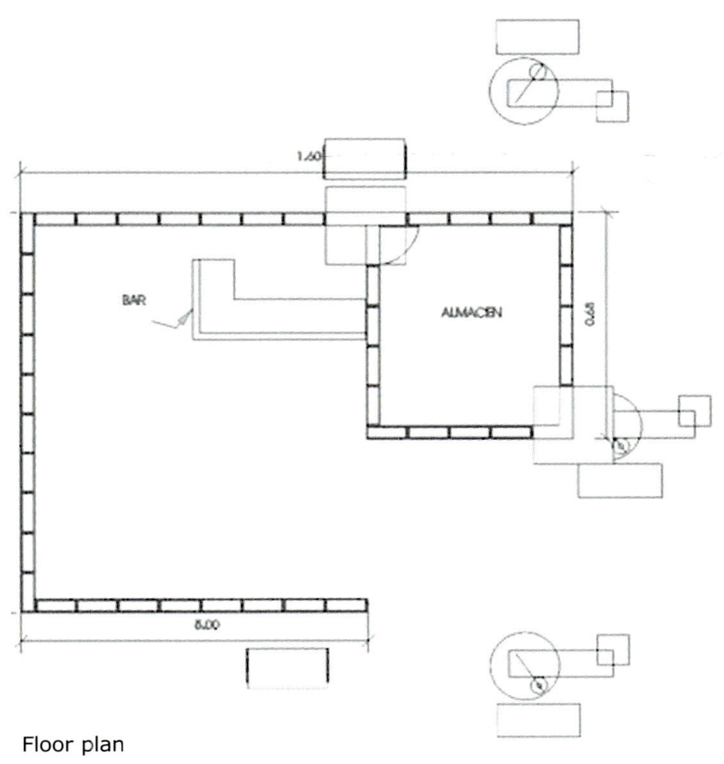

Floor plan

Looky

Marva S.A.

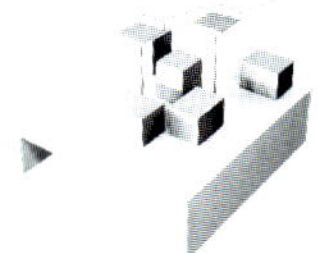

This stand was designed with a view to exchanging the display window concept for that of urban entertainment; an attempt was made to achieve a shop facade which could conceivably be found on any street.

It is a 56m2 space which is almost entirely closed off to exterior views and which features tidy rows of display cases. The interior is "camouflaged", altering the properties of transparency and opacity via the use of small, light-filled display windows. The overall design, the choice of materials and lighting, the route and the selection of the pieces to be put on display has all been carried out in adherence to the clients needs and requirements. This involved the translation of a clean and dynamic contemporary image into a more visually attractive, minimalist, functional and didactic style.

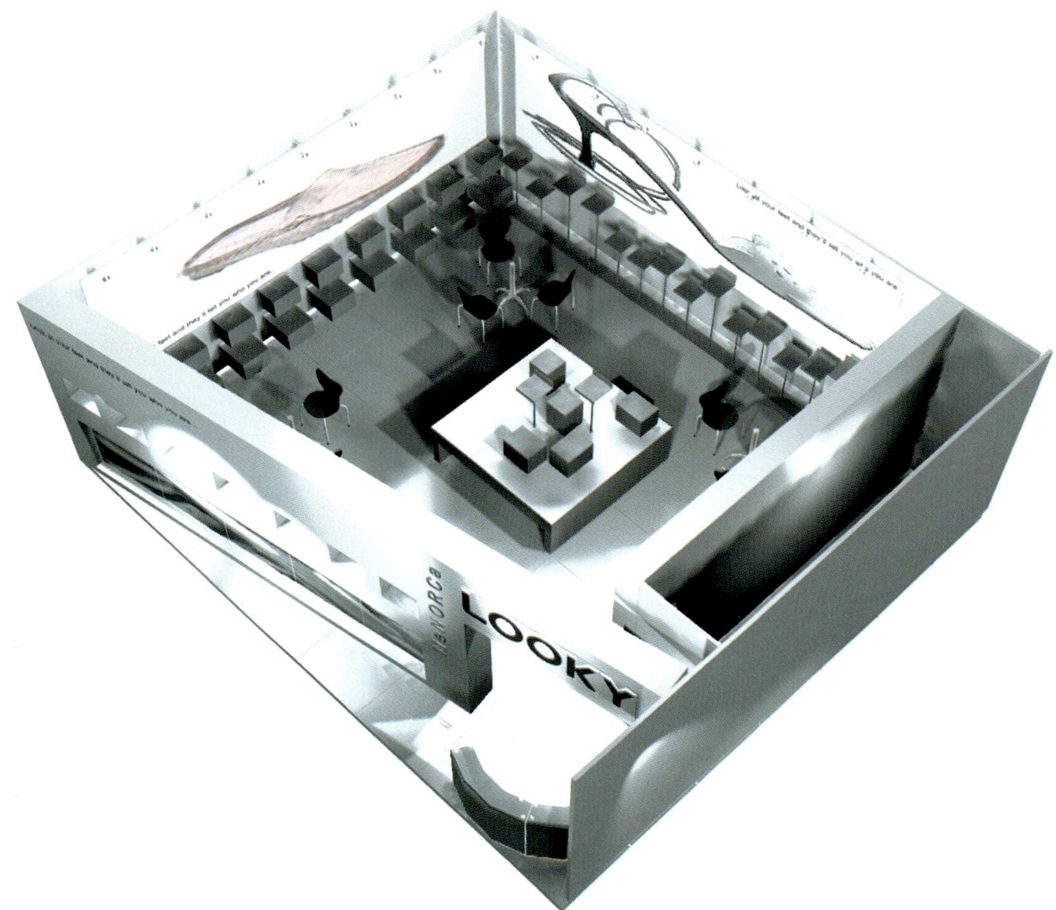

The design of the construction was based on a series of modules which would ease the setting up process in subsequent editions of the same trade show. A changing graphic presentation would personalize the stand for future shows.

A raised, melamine-treated platform was used, its vertical faces (also in melamine) acquiring the look of polished steel. Cubes projecting outward from the wall plane, glass cases along the facade and a centerpiece of rusted iron platforms in varying heights were all used as supports for displaying the company's footwear.

The brand lettering on the facade was done on lacquered metal, thereby successfully combining melamine, metal and glass in the same design scheme.

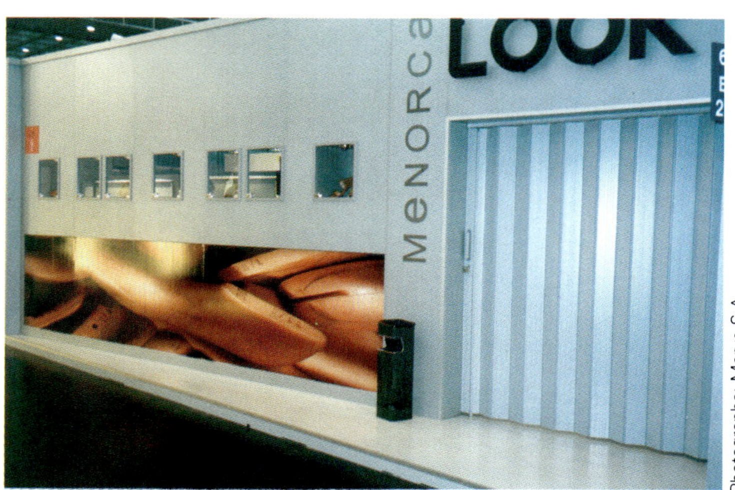

Photographs: Marva S.A.

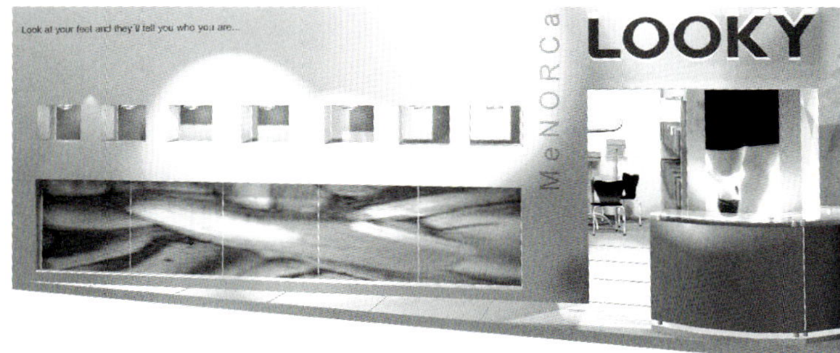

Main elevation

Perspective

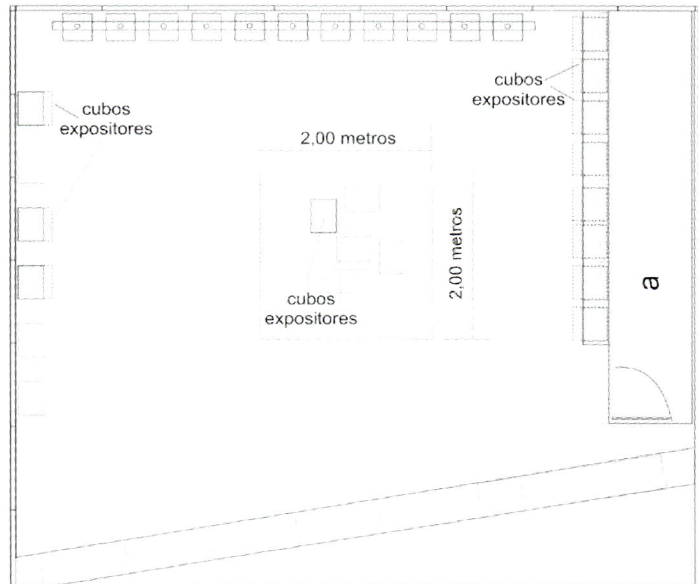

Floor plan

Knauf

Rudolf Schricker

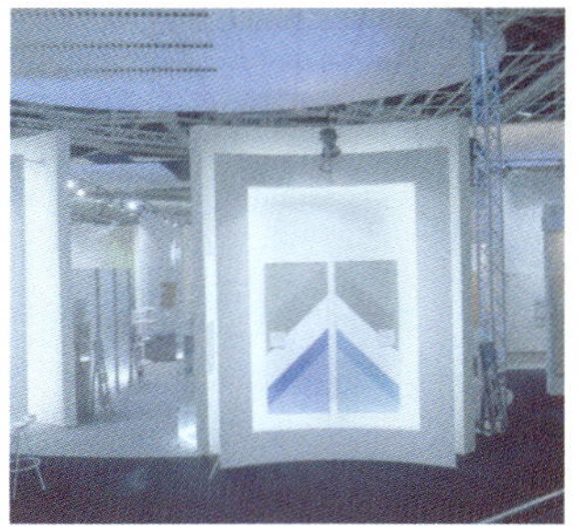

A modern, high-tech design displaying particular artistry of composition characterized this German company's stand at the Bau 2001 trade fair in Munich.

With a juxtaposition of slats and smooth surfaces as the dominant theme, the stand appears almost disordered at first glance. Irregularly arranged vertical lines and overarching ceiling bars are respectively illuminated by spotlighting and fluorescent tubes. A grid of beams designed specifically for this type of event is supported by unevenly placed supports or suspended from the ceiling of the main building in some sections. The load-bearing supports are fitted at their highest point with the company's logo, which is lit by blue fluorescent tubes along the entire length, making it visible from a distance. As the main color in the company's logo design, blue is likewise the determining element here.

Fabric-clad panels for acoustic absorption conceal views of the hall ceiling and finish off the stand at the top, along with aluminum slats and oval-shaped lighting supports.

A modular structure was designed in conjunction with sculptural forms made from gypsum that blend with the lighting and acoustics, creating a heterogenous composition of curves, concave and convex tension, slats, perforations and folded planes.

Countless models and spatial computer animation were essential components in the process of designing this divergent and playful basic concept. This blending of elements and the stand's spatial diversity link together the overall composition, piece by piece, like a puzzle.

Photographs: Mark Hindley

KNAUF
MARMORIT
KNAUF
Perlite
Info

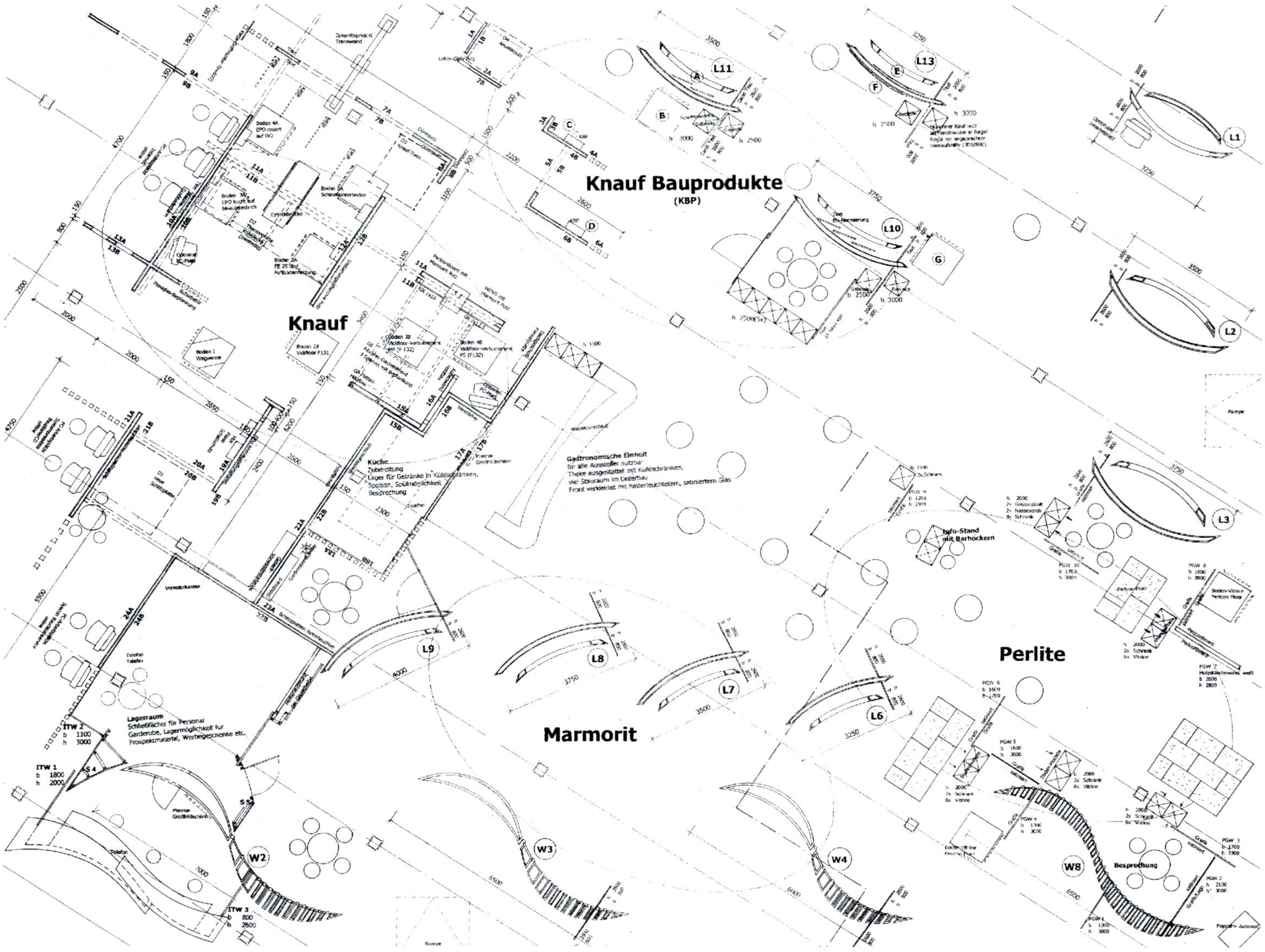

Knauf Bauprodukte
(KBP)
Knauf
Marmorit
Perlite
L11
L13
L1
L10
L2
L3
L9
L8
L7
L6
W2
W3
W4
W8

General floor plan

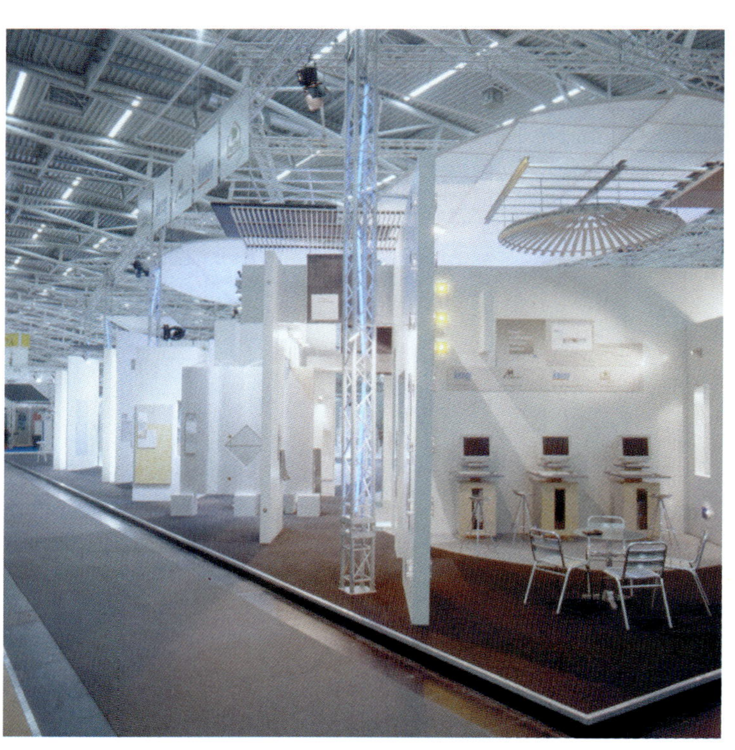

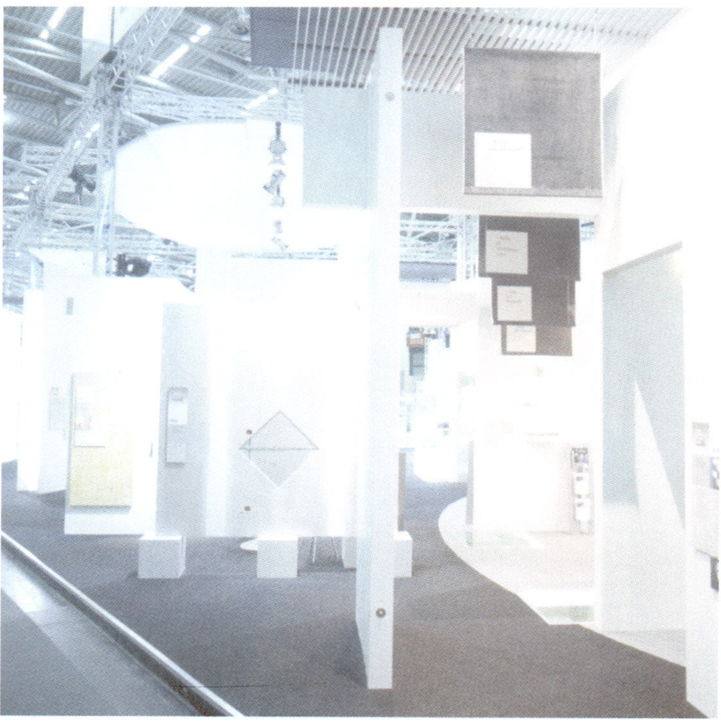

Knauf

Schweizer Textilverband

Thut und Knup

The Swiss Textile Association's pavilion, at the 2000 Heimtextil textile industry trade fair in Frankfurt, invited visitors to take a walk through the textile valleys of its country –the Alpine panorama of Switzerland– as seen from Frankfurt.

Directly at the main entrance the visitor is confronted with a massive topographical panorama, giving visitors the impression of standing more than 3000 meters above Switzerland's mountain ranges. The uniting elements behind this associated presentation were 350 real-size trekking path signs and a 3-meter-high yellow arrow pointing to 60 Swiss textile manufacturers who were exhibiting in various locations at the trade fair. In order to be able to find these exhibitors, an invitation designed as a trekking map was developed as an accompaniment for visitors.

A conscious decision was made not to show actual products, but rather to suggest ideas. Thus, 23 different "mountain tops" surround the Trend Area in Hall 7: virtual mountains, sensual mountains, light and shadow mountains, erupting Etnas, climbable mountains, and textile mountains, all of which gives an impressive interpretation of the various textile companies taking part.

One mountain allows the visitor to ascend and descend by separate stairways, with landings filled with diverse natural fibers, such as wood shavings, pine needles and pebbles, for example, each giving a sense of exploring while creating an awareness of the diverse materials that come from the mountain areas.

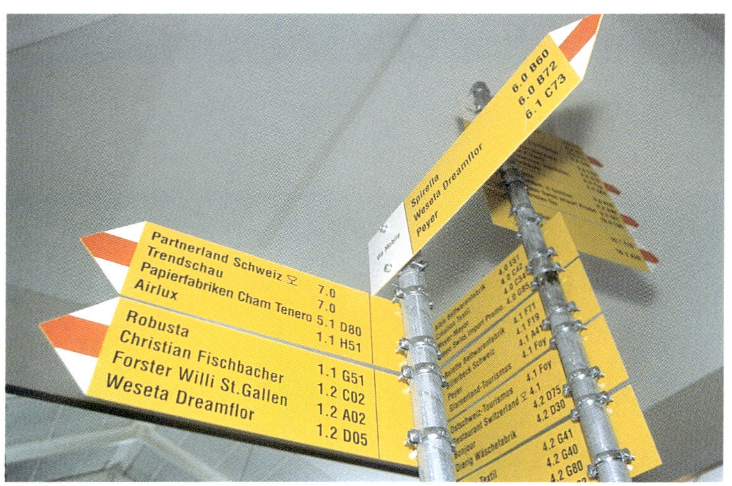

Photographs: Peter Knup

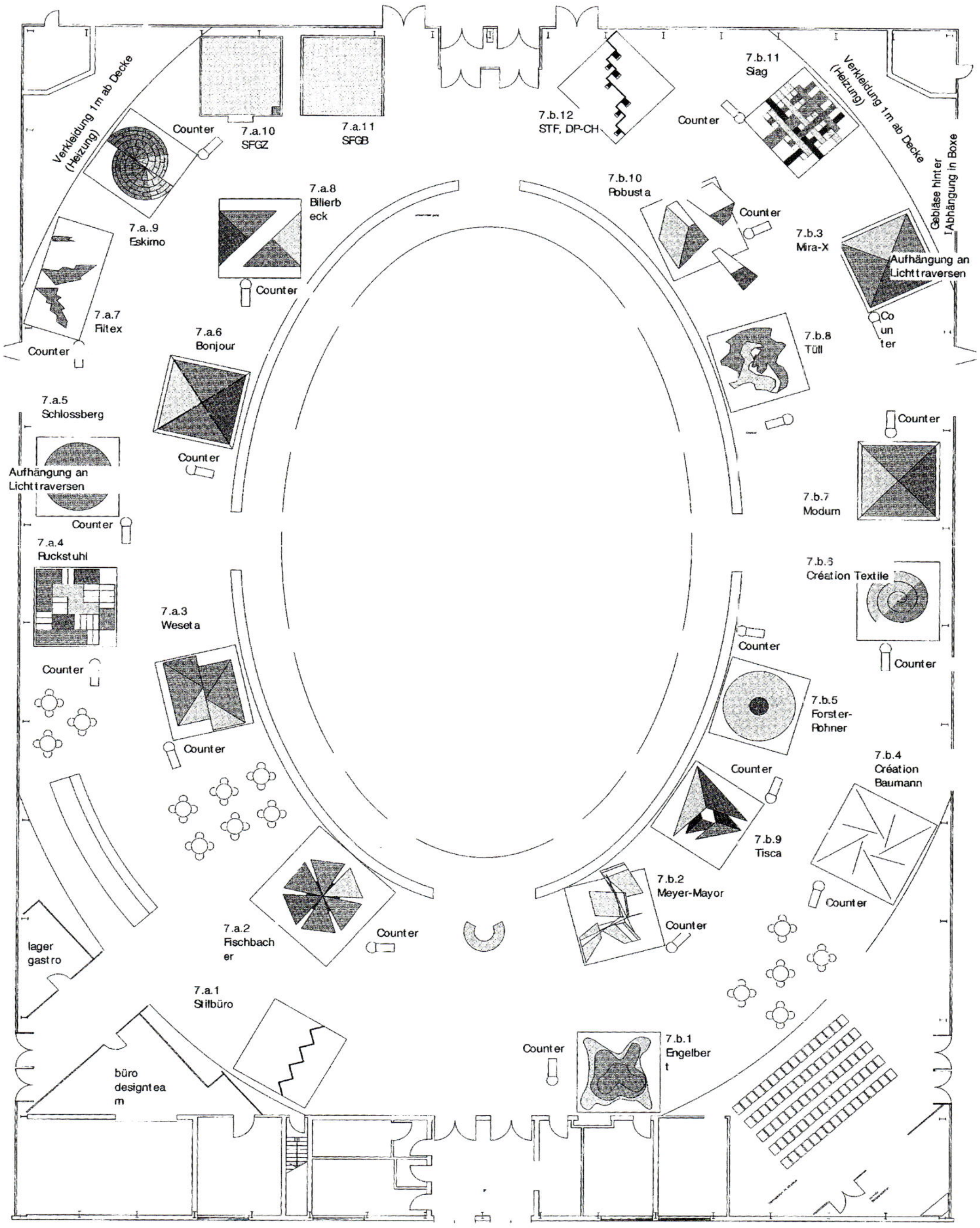

Verkleidung 1m ab Decke (Heizung)
Counter
7.a.10 SFGZ
7.a.11 SFGB
7.b.12 STF, DP-CH
Counter
7.b.11 Siag
Verkleidung 1m ab Decke (Heizung)
Gebläse hinter Abhängung in Boxe
7.a.9 Eskimo
7.a.8 Billierbeck
Counter
7.b.10 Robusta
Counter
7.b.3 Mira-X
Aufhängung an Lichttraversen
Counter
7.a.7 Ritex
Counter
7.a.6 Bonjour
7.b.8 Tüll
7.a.5 Schlossberg
Aufhängung an Lichttraversen
Counter
Counter
Counter
7.b.7 Modum
7.a.4 Ruckstuhl
7.b.6 Création Textile
7.a.3 Weseta
Counter
Counter
Counter
7.b.5 Forster-Rohner
Counter
Counter
7.b.4 Création Baumann
7.b.9 Tisca
7.b.2 Meyer-Mayor
Counter
Counter
lager gastro
7.a.2 Fischbacher
Counter
7.a.1 Stilbüro
büro designteam
Counter
7.b.1 Engelbert

Plan

Mercedes-Benz

Schindler architekten

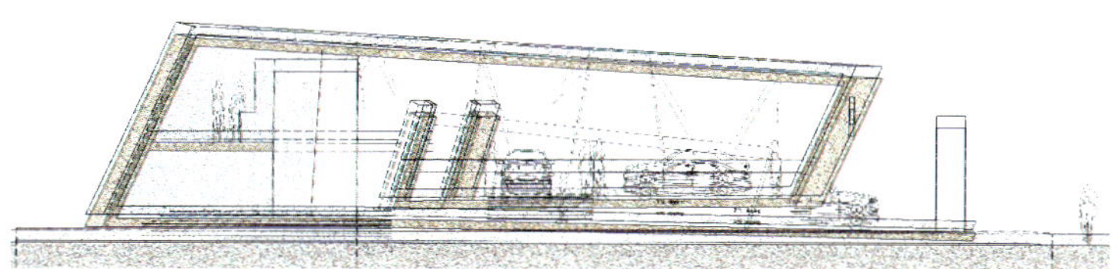

The plot for this stand is surrounded on three sides by open space, with the remaining side delimited by the stand of another exhibitor. The Mercedes-Benz stand consists of a walk-in sculpture with various exhibit floors, each of which is easily accessed from the center.

The primary element is composed of wood surfaces clad in bamboo parquet, emitting a warm, tactile feel.

The cube housing the restricted entryways is comprised of sheets of aluminum, which transmits the idea of precision. Black carpeting, suggesting elegance, covers most of the ground floor. The "magnetic field" generated by these materials –their tangibility, precision and elegance– conveys the uniqueness of the ambience of this stand.

The ground floor has an extensive surface area in order to comfortably and unobtrusively accommodate a high number of visitors. The restricted access to areas such as offices, coat check and storage is located at the back. More offices and a café with views of the stand are located on the upper floors.

Photographs: Andreas Keller

Mercedes-Benz

Mercedes-Benz
Vision Grand Sports Tourer

Vision
Grand Sports Tourer

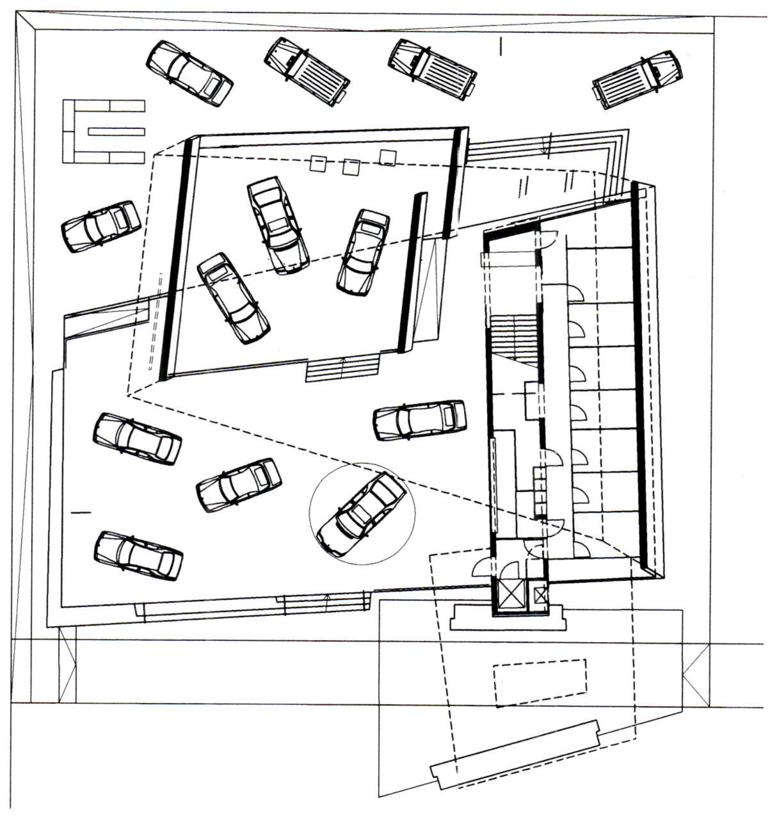

Thirst for Exce lence.

LOADING AID
SL-Class
Sensotronic Brake Control
SL-Class
High Quality Interior
SL-Class

VIAG Interkom

Schmidhuber + Partner

The motto 'Creating Contact' is the theme behind the VIAG stand, which is a social point of contact and an attractive backdrop for displaying products. With a surface of almost 1700m^2, it takes on a U shape. The central part is used to display the new features and constitutes an open transit zone.

Gauze layers separate the square laterals, where the different information booths and sales floors create transparency and depth. The initial visual contact is created through this semi transparency without losing a sense of a clear boundary and internal direction. The urban analogy helps visitors easily find their way around. The stand's depth responds to the spatial gradation: a general view on the outside, information and advising inside.

Color is one of most powerful modes of communication. Color identifies and defines, creates and influences emotions and, here, creates a diaphanous atmosphere that the visitor cordially receives.

The products are displayed in specific thematic areas and have a clear and defined position. One of the most outstanding parts is the Vision Center conformed by a gigantic blue cube, with 5-meter-high panels, located in the center of the stand. Small cracks are opened on three sides, offering views of the interior. Written words and texts appear on the inner face, while a video projected on LED screens displays the advantages of new technology on the exterior. Thus, the visitor feels virtually integrated into the world of communication.

Photographs: Stefan Müler Nauman

Interkom
vision
center
Interkom

creating contact

Interkom
vision center 0179-2000-000
directaccess

This stand at the Euroshop 2002 trade fair expresses the company's forward-looking philosophy.
In accordance with the clients' wishes, the designers of the stand sought an elegant, streamlined look which would epitomize their line of office lighting. However, at the same time, they avoided excessive seriousness and managed to incorporate a distinctly original and modern air in order to characterize the company's domestic lighting products.
Several modules, on varying levels, have been placed unevenly throughout the stand's allocated space. These modules have been planned just as sections of a home or office might be laid out (one of the "homes" even has a simulated garden), so that visitors can wander freely through them and see how the products look and feel when in use in "real" situations.
Groupings of seating arrangements have been scattered throughout the exhibit, not only to further enhance the true-to-life ambience pervading the stand, but also to encourage visitors to linger.

Euroshop 2002

Ansorg

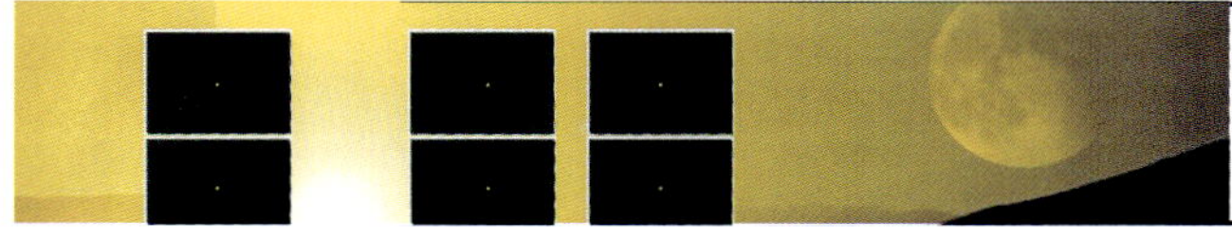

Photographs: Hans Georg Esch

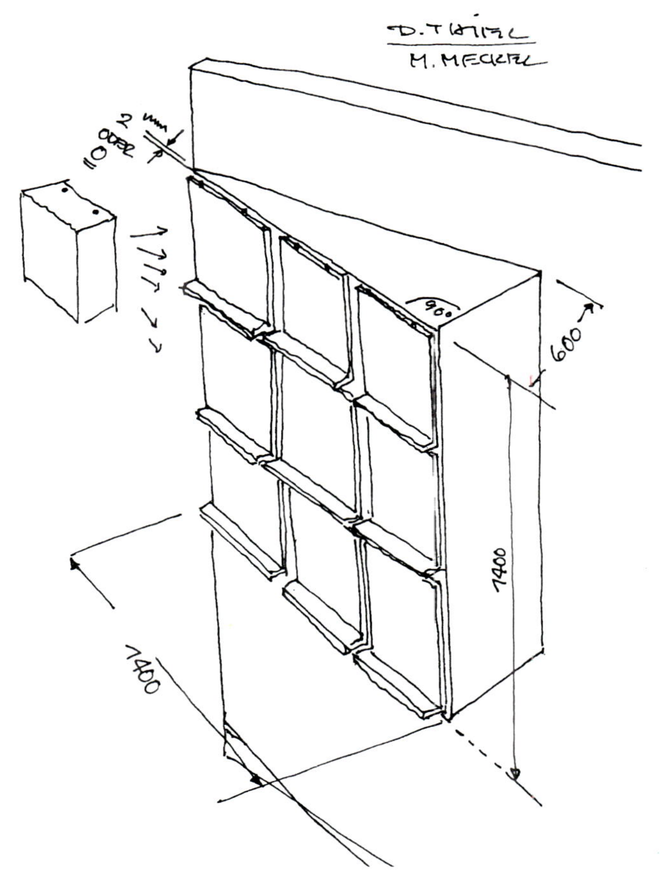

D. THIEL
M. MECKEL
90°
600
1400
1400

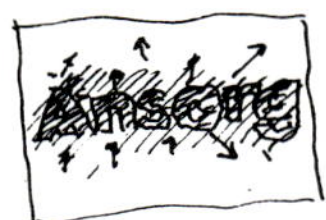

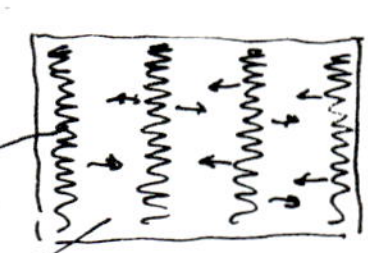

Ansorg

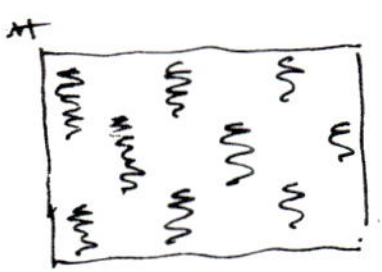

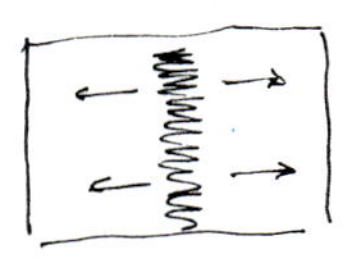

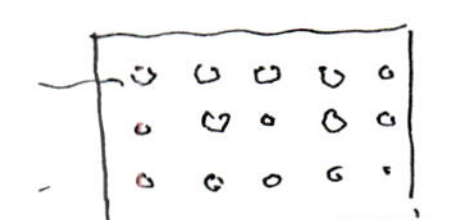

Plan

Cube

Esprit jewel

Burkhardt Leitner constructiv

The design of this stand for Munich's Inhorgenta 2001 trade fair is based on a single ceiling module measuring 100m² and resting on a framework of beams. The faces of this module bear an assemblage of plastic awnings printed with images from this clothing manufacturer's advertising campaign.

A rectangular customer service desk is located just opposite the entrance, which is also rectangular. On approaching the stand, visitors perceive the elegant composition of superimposed rectangular forms that has been created by this desk/entrance relation. A bright blue neon light casts a certain mood here, as well as in the interior of the stand.

Once inside, the season's collection is exhibited in a modern atmosphere that evokes a feeling of nightlife. The Esprit stand manages to give the product an air of daring modernity.

Photographs: Lothar Bertrans

Renault

Patrick Norguet

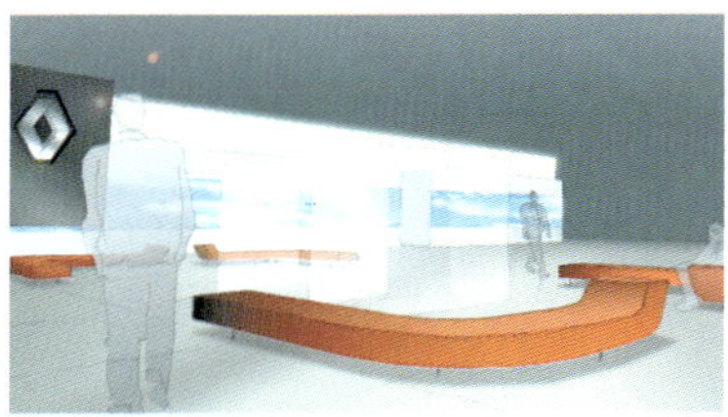

Patrick Norguet's program for this stand for the Brussels Automobile trade fair was, above all, a "design" concept patterned after the idea of temporary display case arrangements. Designer of furniture, objects, stage sets and boutiques, this young French creator has come up with a graphic and spatial concept in keeping with the Renault image.

The 3150m2 stand is divided into two groupings of spaces by a 36-meter-long sign, made with the use of car headlights affixed to two interconnected panels.

Behind this screen of suspended Plexiglas, the more private spaces -above and below the mezzanine- are visually isolated from the activity of the main floor. Offices and technical installations are located on the ground floor, with more offices, the marketing department and a restaurant above.

The 550m2 mezzanine, conceived as a large piece in white wood with rounded angles, turns in on itself and merges into the stand with a thick wall concealing a kitchen and diverse offices. In order to attract visitors and professionals in the sector, Renault decided once again on the comfort and sociability of a restaurant.

The graphics behind the signage have been done with particular care and were inspired by the yellow in the company's logo, as well as by photographs of their upscale line of vehicles.

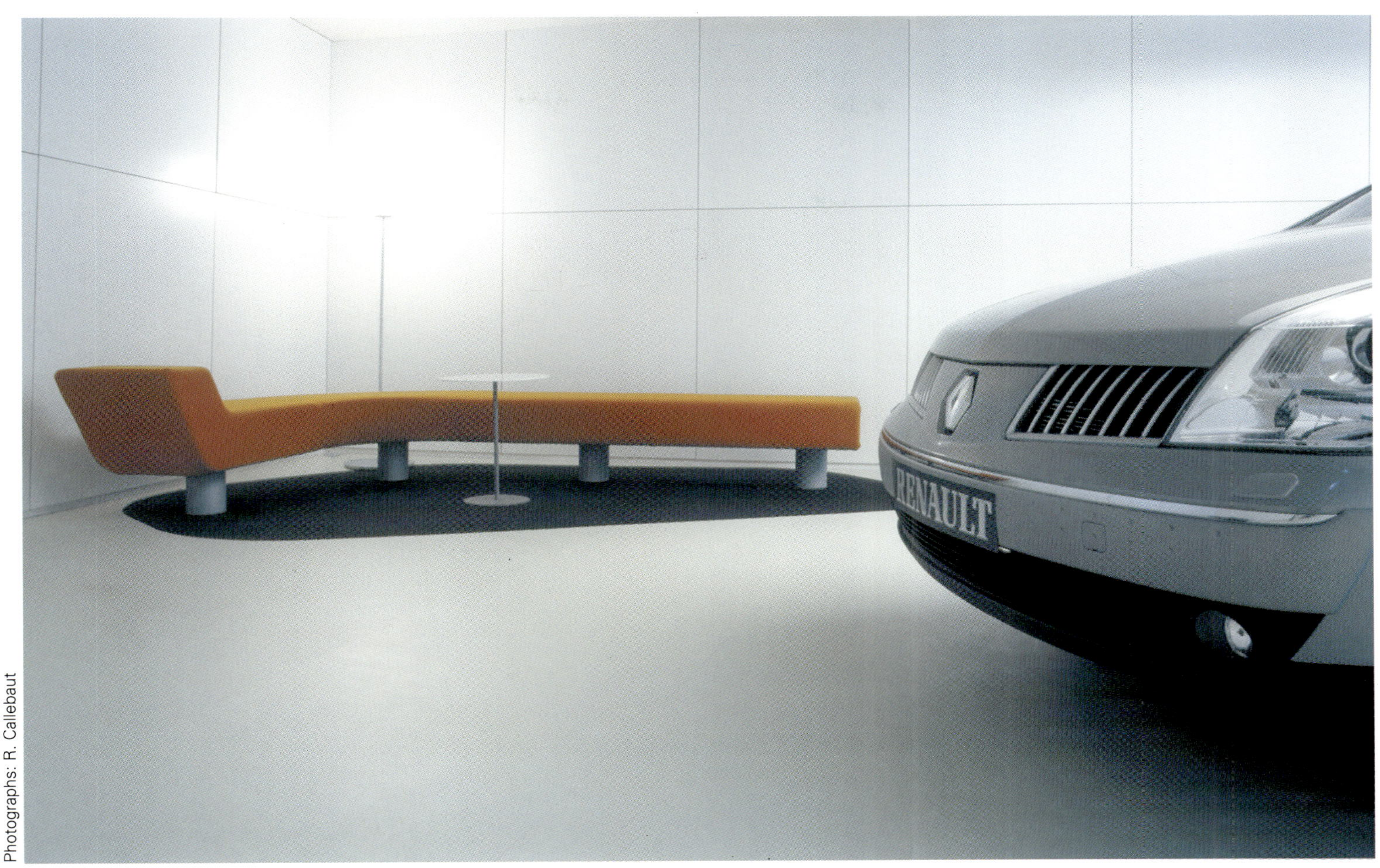

Photographs: R. Callebaut

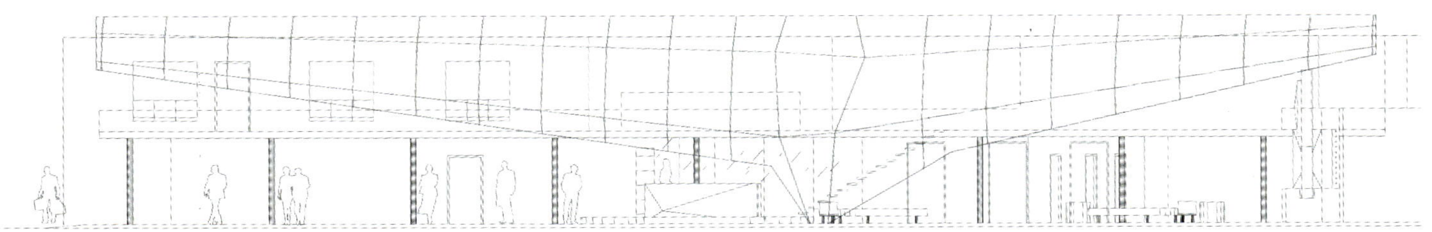

Elevation